AF600475

ALL WONDERS IN ONE SIGHT

The Christ Child among the Elizabethan and Stuart Poets

All Wonders in One Sight

The Christ Child among the Elizabethan and Stuart Poets

THERESA M. KENNEY

UNIVERSITY OF TORONTO PRESS
Toronto Buffalo London

Toronto Buffalo London
utorontopress.com

ISBN 978-1-4875-0906-4 (cloth) ISBN 978-1-4875-3962-7 (EPUB)
ISBN 978-1-4875-3961-0 (PDF)

Library and Archives Canada Cataloguing in Publication

Title: All wonders in one sight : the Christ Child among the Elizabethan and Stuart poets / Theresa M. Kenney.
Names: Kenney, Theresa M., author.
Description: Includes bibliographical references and index.
Identifiers: Canadiana (print) 20200409891 | Canadiana (ebook) 20200410091 | ISBN 9781487509064 (cloth) | ISBN 9781487539627 (EPUB) | ISBN 9781487539610 (PDF)
Subjects: LCSH: Christian poetry, English – Early modern, 1500–1700 – History and criticism. | LCSH: Religious poetry, English – History and criticism. | LCSH: English poetry – Early modern, 1500–1700 – History and criticism. | LCSH: Jesus Christ – In literature.
Classification: LCC PR545.R4 K46 2021 | DDC 821/.40938232 – dc23

University of Toronto Press acknowledges the financial assistance to its publishing program of the Canada Council for the Arts and the Ontario Arts Council, an agency of the Government of Ontario.

Conseil des Arts
du Canada

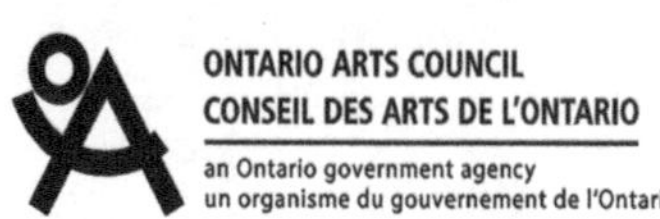

Funded by the Government of Canada | Financé par le gouvernement du Canada | Canada

Contents

Acknowledgments

My deepest gratitude is due to two friends: Dr. Mary Dzon, who co-edited with me our earlier volume on the Christ Child for the University of Toronto Press and who was an unfailing help in my research for and development of this book; and Dr. Cheryl Kinney, MD, who made sure I had "a room of one's own" to write in many a Saturday when research and maternal duties did not mix. Our lunch break discussions will always be a dear memory. I also thank other good friends, Dr. Bernadette Waterman Ward, Ashley Harbers, and Wendy Briones Reimann, for their time and care in reading portions of this book and giving advice and guidance. My sister Anne and my husband Mark also devoted many hours to reading, re-reading, and critiquing text and notes. In addition, I am grateful for the comments of my anonymous readers and above all for the support and sage advice of my editor, Suzanne Rancourt. I am also deeply thankful for the immense care with which my copyeditor, Carolyn Zapf, has laboured over this book. My home institution, the University of Dallas, has supported this endeavour financially and with a recent sabbatical leave. *English Literary Renaissance* has permitted the reprinting (with some changes) of my essay on Robert Southwell.

My own little baby Stella has gotten a lot bigger and learned to read in the course of this book's composition; she and her big sister Annamaria have definitely kept real childhood before my eyes as I wrote. To them and to my patient husband Mark, to my always-supportive parents, Edward and Roberta, sisters Anne and Maria, and brothers Steve, Tom, John, and Robert, this book is affectionately dedicated.

ALL WONDERS IN ONE SIGHT

The Christ Child among the Elizabethan and Stuart Poets

Chapter One

Sacrament, Time, and Space in the Tudor and Stuart English Nativity Lyric

What the Virgin Mary sang over Jesus's cradle we will probably never know. But the tradition of the Nativity lyric starts there, at his Nativity itself, and we know something of the first words sung to or about baby Jesus: the second chapter of the Gospel of Luke records them as the angels' Gloria. By the early second century, according to tradition, the martyr Pope Telesphorus had added this song to the Midnight Mass celebrating Christ's birth.

It is not saying too much to claim that, together with Ambrose, Sedulius thereafter becomes the father of the Nativity hymn in the Western portion of the Church. Seven verses of Sedulius's twenty-three–verse abecedarian hymn recounting Christ's life, "A solis ortus cardine," or "From the Pivot of the Sun's Rising," fixed themselves in the Christian imagination of the Incarnation and the Nativity by their inclusion in the breviary for Christmas matins and later in the Protestant hymnaries after their translation into the vernacular by Martin Luther and others.[1] These verses, contrasting Christ's glory as the second person of the Trinity to his vulnerability and humility as a small child in the hay-filled manger, contain the germ of many a Nativity lyric written in the millennium and a half after their creation. In fact, one could say that Sedulius unwittingly penned one of the most popular songs the world has ever known, in constant use for over 1500 years and translated into almost every language one could imagine. One of the few facts we know about Sedulius is that he wrote in the first half of the fifth century; his poem was already old, much revered, and enshrined in the Christmas liturgy when Bede cited his hymns in *De arte metrica*, c. 710. Other Anglo-Saxon translations survive, demonstrating the early influence of "A solis ortus cardine" on English hymnody. Alcuin quoted the entire hymn in *Officia per Ferias* between 609 and 611. It is even enshrined in the Mozarabic Rite by the sixth and seventh centuries (though oddly, not in the

Ambrosian Rite) and thus remained an expression of the mysteries of Christ's life through the period of the Muslim conquest of Spain.

In addition to the hymn tradition stemming from Ambrose and Sedulius, during the Middle Ages a multitude of anonymous lyrics celebrated Christ's birth. We know from Bede that the father of English poetry, the cowherd Caedmon, also composed a Nativity hymn, though his is lost to us. The flowering of the Franciscan lyric under Friars James Ryman and William Herebert in England in the fourteenth century left us with a large number of Nativity carols or hymns. In a time before Christmas trees, the medieval poet still offers a child dreaming in his mother's arms, and the dramatist a baby who might reach out to a ball or a "bob of cherries," as in the *Second Shepherds' Play*. In these texts, most of them meant to be sung, doctrine and devotion merge. The greater number of Nativity lyrics from the English Middle Ages are recorded in fourteenth- and fifteenth-century manuscripts, but then their production as a popular form, meant for educating the laity in doctrine and arousing their love for the Christ Child and his mother Mary, seems to have ceased with the advent of the Reformation. At this point the Nativity is no longer hymned by angels or friars, but by learned Catholic and Protestant university men, most of them priests.

In the seventeenth century, though many leading poets wrote poems about Christ's infancy, charm and sweetness were not the leading notes. Because the poets were university-educated classicists, and many of them were also priests, Catholic or Anglican, they wrote in an elevated style, with elevated language, and their concerns were deeply theological as well as poetic. It being an age of religious controversy, their poems also have controversial elements, and because these poems were mostly intended for private use and limited circulation, they are not generally singable hymns of public celebration of Christ's birth. They are far from dry academic pieces, however, and they offer a wide variety of approaches to both their subject, the infant Jesus, and the means of presenting it.

At the end of the sixteenth century, the English Jesuit poet Robert Southwell wrote a number of poems on the Christ Child. He would die on Tyburn Hill as a martyr in 1595, but his epistolary appeal to other poets to write on religious subjects in preference to secular ones would nonetheless give him an influential voice in the poetic developments of the ensuing century.[2] His choice to write on the Christ Child also seems to have had an impact on the oeuvres of almost all the major English poets of the seventeenth century. When his influence wanes with the waning of that century, the poem on the Christ Child also seems to die out as a subgenre. My purpose in this study is to trace the similarities and differences among the Nativity poems of the greatest names in seventeenth-century English lyric, starting with the sole poet who would not survive into that century, Southwell himself. Theological differences among these poets, especially regarding the issues of Christ's ability to be present on earth after the Ascension, prove to affect the portrayal of the Nativity and of the Christ Child himself.

Whether the Christ Child is in a poem celebrating his birth is the initial test question to which I subjected all the poems investigated here: I ask, "Where is the baby?" The Christ Child's fleshly presence in a Nativity poem may seem to be a given, but as the reader will see, it is not, and I argue that his presence or absence is meaningful. From the outset I should clarify that the beauty or technical quality of the poems studied here does not depend on the answer to this question. And it is a simple question, one readers can immediately determine for themselves, so some of my conclusions may seem to be so painfully obvious they need no elaboration. However, the question is a starting point and not a terminus, and it leads the willing and interested reader to a host of issues regarding the Incarnation, sacraments, the liturgical cycle, and even a concern outside my scope, the way babies and children are imagined in the period. This study, I hope, will open the door to more investigations of these issues. There are also other writers to consider. I begin with these five poets, however, as writers to whom we can also pose the more difficult question, "What kind of sign is the infant wrapped in swaddling clothes and laid in a manger?"

Many forces converged to make the seventeenth century the century of the Nativity lyric in England, not least of which was the example of Southwell cited earlier. Many forces combined to extinguish the trend during the Interregnum, the Restoration, and the Enlightenment. Paul Cefalu's recent work on the rebirth of Johannine Christology in the early modern period in England demonstrates a counter-influence to the focus on the material aspects of Christ's Incarnation, the conviction that "the flesh profiteth nothing," leading to an erasure of fleshly presence in English religious poetry and theology.[3] Citing Ernst Käsemann, Cefalu remarks that "eschewing the Synoptic narrative of Jesus' humble origins and the way in which Jesus is abased during the Passion, John's Christ is more privileged than any other prophet, including Moses, because he has directly 'seen God.'"[4] Cefalu's book observes in multiple works by Herbert, Vaughan, and others a striking reticence about Jesus's body and its ability to be present on earth. The reformed poets accept the resurrected Christ's "Noli me tangere" ("Touch me not") as a guideline to interactions with Christ, Cefalu argues convincingly.

Richard Crashaw, however, opposed the trend when he wrote in his introductory poem to his poetic works before his death in the middle of the century: "Here you will be near [his] cradle and [his] body scented for burial: hence the passions of a witness arise and thence my passions."[5] Crashaw promises his reader proximity. The audience of the poem will not just be remembering the historical event along with the poet; they will be watching the poet witness the events. Crashaw may represent the last attempt in the century to draw his reader close to Christ's cradle and to represent the Christ Child in the flesh. He is very aware of what he is doing. As Walter Davis once argued, the final arrangement of the poems in *Carmen Deo Nostro* foregrounds the Nativity sequence, placing it first, and creates a liturgical framework for the whole.[6]

As the seventeenth century continues, however, we can see that the poets' treatment of the material aspects of the Incarnation does indeed diminish. The celebration of Christmas was specifically targeted by the Puritans, who legally banned both liturgical and domestic observations. During the Interregnum, churches were even locked up on Christmas day to prevent religious observation, and ordinary homes were policed so Cromwell's men could confiscate meat pies, roast fowl, Yule logs, sweets, and Christmas puddings. Thomas Lewis, in his sarcastic 1720 work *English Presbyterian Eloquence,* remarks: "Under the censure of lewd customs they include all sorts of public sports, exercises, and recreations, how innocent soever. Nay, the poor rosemary and bays, and Christmas pie is made an abomination."[7]

Henry Vaughan would decry the banishing of Christmas and Passiontide from the English calendar: "Alas, My God! Thy birth now here / Must not be numbred in the year."[8] As Cefalu points out, these are the two events that require remembrance of the divine Son's humiliation, and we might note that they are the two events most celebrated and meditated upon in medieval devotionals and poetry, particular favourites of the Franciscans. Rather than seeing these pivotal moments in Christ's work of salvation as moving proofs of his love, worthy of continual remembrance, many reformers saw them as singular necessary but transient moments in Christ's mission that would result in his glorification; it was indecorous, even faithless, to dwell on the Son's degradation. The stark contrast in attitudes is still visible today in the Catholic crucifix and the Protestant cross without a corpus. The manger is less controversial today because it has been stripped of its power to convey hardship and humiliation, but it too was a tinderbox that could burst into flame in the seventeenth century.

This literary historical study investigates a small number of the many poems written in the wake of the publication of Robert Southwell's oeuvre, an event that stands as the pivotal moment in the transition of the Nativity lyric from instrument of religious education and celebration – in England mostly the work of priests for the people – to a learned subgenre of the newly elevated poetic craft. These poems are significant in the main because of the people who wrote them: Southwell of course to begin with, but then John Donne, George Herbert, John Milton, and Richard Crashaw. The Nativity lyrics of the Tribe of Ben must wait for separate treatment, and they have for the most part very different qualities. Gary Bouchard has argued that Southwell is the father of the metaphysical poets in England, and my research presented here tends to underscore his thesis.[9] All these poems share intertexts – biblical, liturgical, theological, and poetic – and I would add that Southwell himself seems to have exercised a far great influence than heretofore imagined in ways we have yet to examine fully. In this particular case, it seems far from coincidental that, after Southwell, every major poet of the seventeenth century writes at least one Nativity lyric. All of the poets in this study, including Milton, could be classed as Metaphysicals for the very reason Samuel Johnson invented the name by which they have come to be classed. They write on metaphysical subjects, not just mundane ones, and they craft their language and imagery to answer to the challenges presented by topics that involve the spiritual and unseen world. In the eighteenth century, however, we must begin to do some detective work to discover even one such lyric, at least by a major writer.

Southwell's special devotion to the Christ Child at first seems unremarkable. Frank Brownlow[10] has called Southwell's series of Nativity lyrics "the Nativity group," but they have evoked no particular study *as* a group. Again, when Nativity lyrics crop up among the works of the major poets of the period, no one is surprised; it is a traditionally hymn-worthy event, and thus the existence of the poems provokes no comment. But the learned Nativity lyric of this century differs widely from the didactic works of the thirteenth, fourteenth, and even fifteenth centuries, collected in the scholarly editions of R.L. Greene and Carleton Brown years ago.[11] They also differ from the hymns of the Methodists and other low church groups in the following century. As far as we know, none of the poems in this study was written to be sung. As a side note, no Nativity lyric would have been sung in a liturgy in England until after 1815 or so because of liturgical restrictions, both Catholic and Anglican. These poems are learned, artistic works, though in some cases they also seem to be meant for private devotion. Poets of any note in this period wrote at least one Nativity lyric, sometimes more, and they often plunged into intellectual and theological problems when treating the subject without worrying about the accessibility of the poem to a large public or even, at times, the creation of devout sentiments in the hearts of the laity. In Donne's and Herbert's cases, their poems were probably never meant to be published for a larger audience than an original circle of friends or patrons.

Taken as a group, the seventeenth-century Nativity lyrics are also aesthetically and formally quite different from one another and exhibit different theological emphases. It was discovering those differences that led me to analyse them, at first individually and then side by side, in a chronological progress. Presenting them this way in the book allows the reader to line up the evidence in similar fashion.

Whether their poems concerned the child wrapped in swaddling clothes and lying in a manger of Luke's gospel narrative or the primal Word and Light entering into the world of darkness of John's account, these writers are describing, or pondering, or praising the Incarnation of the Son of God. The incarnate child himself is not always present in these poems because differing theological emphases affect the artistic selection of details, and differing understandings of the immediacy of the event and the accessibility of the babe of Bethlehem to the speaker lie behind the poets' presentation of him.

All the poets, nonetheless, strive for some sense of immediacy in these lyrics. As Gary Kuchar has said of Crashaw's Epiphany Hymn, it "aspires to be more performative than constative; it seeks to make an encounter with God happen rather than to describe God in se."[12] That desire to make the poem an encounter with God – which reaches a kind of apex in Crashaw, to be sure – makes us think of the implications for the long-running debate over whether the metaphysical poets in this study may be counted as mystics or simply meditative poets. Southwell, Donne, Herbert, Milton, and Crashaw do not merely describe a Nativity scene in their poems, but wish to be present at the event itself. A solution to that debate may be found in the unitive desire these lyrics express: as Andrew Louth argues in *The Origins of the Christian Mystical Tradition*, the division in the patristic age between mystical and doctrinal theology did not exist.[13] Inspired by their study of the Fathers of the Church in particular, but also by more contemporary devotional works, the Tudor and Stuart poets enact a mystical ascent to union with the divine or imitate the incarnational descent while also explicating doctrinal points. However, the means to union they describe are markedly different. A sure indication that the poem is imitating union is the use of the present tense for the past event of the Incarnation or Nativity. A focus on the speaker's ascent to God indicates a neo-Platonic, Dionysian theology at work; a focus on the physical body of the Christ Child, conversely, indicates a more sacramental approach.[14] Above all, if the baby is actually present in the poem, there is a desire to make contact with him and, by virtue of that contact, to participate in the eternity of the incarnate Christ.

I argue in the ensuing pages that the understanding of the potential for the temporal collapse between the poet's own time and the Nativity, which allows this immediacy, hinges on the way in which the poet understands the sacrament of the Eucharist. More precisely, the poet's espousal of a sacramentology and use of representational modes arise from a conviction about where and when Christ *is*. I propose that, in this endeavour to speak of Christ's Incarnation and birth, viewing the event from the aspect of God's eternity is often privileged over the linear succession of events in human time. When a writer thinks in this way, it is because of a kind of temporal collapse familiar to the poet's imagination that had more force than simple recreation of a past event. I call this mode sacramental time because it is the sacrament of the Eucharist in particular that provides the believer with direct contact with the living God and with the timelessness of eternity. Imitating a real immediacy that the poet experiences is different from referring to a past event as present merely to increase its impact. In all the cases this book treats, from Southwell the Jesuit to Milton the Calvinistic freethinker, the poet de-historicizes the past event of Christ's Incarnation and birth to make it a truly effective agent in the poet's own Christian story – and, as Caroline Walker Bynum has reminded us, a self is a story, "not just a performance, as some contemporary theory would have it."[15]

Yet none of these poets is usually described as a visionary, though their poems on Christ's Incarnation and birth might seem to participate in aspects of the Christian visionary tradition. What they create is not a description of an event they have ever beheld, as far as we know. A Nativity poet of any stripe is not remembering the scene in Bethlehem but Luke's description of it, and often verbal and painted or sculpted representations of that narrative that we can never know. Memory is not exactly the intellectual power at work in the Nativity poems of Robert Southwell, who seems to have launched the trend, nor in the poems of the metaphysical poets who follow in his literary footsteps. Although the investment of memory in objects is a concern of recent critics, that literary critical approach does not assist the reader in understanding the views of time and space the Tudor and Stuart poets relied on when depicting the Christ Child.

However, we can still be arrested today by the seemingly simple question of *where* and *when* is Jesus in these poems. In the sixteenth and seventeenth centuries, that question of Christ's location and his relationship with earthly time arose most often in the context of disputes over the sacrament of his body and blood, the Eucharist. It likewise arises in the English Nativity lyrics in the author's choice to represent Christ's body or not. In a poem on Christ, such a choice can touch on the presumptions at the heart of Roman Catholic and reformed sacramental theologies. Whereas Roman Catholics and Lutherans saw the real body of the historical Christ as present in the host, whether by transubstantiation or consubstantiation, and therefore believed they made real contact with his flesh as well as his spirit, once again on earth, Calvinists, and the Anglicans convinced by Calvin's arguments, believed that the Holy Spirit raised the communicant to a spiritual union with Christ where he sits reigning in heaven. The mystical notion of the "Sursum corda" (which was borrowed from the Roman Catholic liturgy) was the best description of the way contact with him is made – by lifting up the heart heavenward.

A poem might have a hope of performing the latter sort of union but cannot do anything but produce a mimesis of the former. Interestingly, none of the poets considered in this study, whatever their faith, chose to memorialize the Nativity in Bethlehem as Luke represents it, either by reproducing the narrative or the few details of the physical setting.

Recent studies of the religious poetry of Donne, Herbert, and Crashaw in particular have suggested that the poets invent a kind of sacramental or incarnational language, often without reference to what the poets themselves thought about the Incarnation, the enfleshment of the second person of the Trinity, and his Nativity in Bethlehem.[16] Because the actual Incarnation of Christ is a unique historical event, I suggest we look at poems that all the most famous poets of the period wrote to examine exactly this issue: how did Southwell, Donne, Herbert, Crashaw, and Milton represent God's taking on flesh?

The Incarnation in the Seventeenth Century in England

That the Son of God descended from his glory at the right hand of the Father and became incarnate, true man and true God, in the womb of the Virgin Mary was an uncontested fact for almost all Christians in England during the Reformation and Counter-Reformation, whether Catholic or Protestant. Among the poets in this study, only John Milton will go on, after writing his major Nativity lyric, to cast any doubt on the divinity of the Son, but both *Paradise Lost* and *Paradise Regained* dwell on the Incarnation as a central event of human history. The dogma of the Incarnation of the Son is thus a perfect locus to unite the poets of different cults whom we normally understand as deeply divided over religious issues. However, other forces come into play, causing the poets to approach representing the Christ Child in different ways.

None of these poets witnessed the Nativity, not even in a mystical vision, and therefore they are all aiming to represent an unremembered event 1600 years in the past. This obstacle does not seem to pose a pressing problem to Southwell, Donne, Herbert, Milton, or Crashaw. The following problems, in fact, seem more important for them: How can the writer, who is existing on the line of time that is racing past and through him, represent the eternal God? Even more problematic, how can the writer represent the eternal God who is subject to time in the flesh but remains always in possession of his divine attributes? Nativity poets consistently wish to overpass the temporal gap that separates them from the event of the Incarnation. They also wish to represent both the eternal and temporal aspects of the incarnate Christ. In the seventeenth century, they begin to have a parting of the ways over how this task is to be accomplished.

Current Thought on Incarnational or Sacramental Poetics

Recent work by Paul Cefalu, Kimberly Johnson, Gary Kuchar, and Ryan Netzley has revisited the question of how the metaphysical poets' incarnational mindset allowed them to flex language's power to represent the divine and also the material world. Cefalu discusses the growing preference among the reformed poets of the period for John the Evangelist's view that the "flesh profiteth nothing," a view that married well with the reaction against Aristotelianism in English higher education.[17] Cefalu's erudite study helps explain the diminution of the sense of Christ's fleshly presence in the sacrament and in literature. Johnson conversely concentrates on the reification of word as sign, arguing that Donne in particular makes metaphor a conduit for God's presence, whereas Crashaw has an ambivalence about "corporal expressivity" that manifests itself in hyperbolic sensuality.[18] Netzley defines the similarity between conceptions of the Eucharist and the poets' expressions of religious desire as affirming God's presence in an affective bond – even when, for instance in Donne's Holy Sonnets, the poet seems to complain of Christ's absence. For Netzley, seventeenth-century poems "mean" nothing; they do not actually "say anything." They act out a gulf, which is really a Deleuzian gap, and the gap is love and desire: immanence, not lack.[19]

Whether one accepts Johnson's view of metaphor as a means of making God present or not, or Netzley's understanding of this poetry as enacted desire, for both Catholic and Protestant poets in the period, sacrament never means a representation of the mere physical world as good or holy but rather something from the physical world signifying or conveying divine grace through direct divine intervention. The different faiths divide over the question of whether or not it is the physical thing that conveys the grace, but God is always the source and the goal. Sacraments are not materialized language for either a Southwell or a Herbert. If, as Patricia Phillippy says, the "bread and wine of the Protestant Communion did not confer grace but were 'signe[s] of remembrance' to confirm salvation,"[20] they were nonetheless meant to lift the recipient's heart to where Christ dwells in heaven and thus to enact a spiritual union.

In his work on Crashaw, Gary Kuchar has spoken of the ambition of approaching God, arguing that Crashaw "aspires towards the status of liturgy" by "verifying" his poetry's rootedness in "scriptural revelation" by means of the "Eucharistic-event."[21] This idea I take to mean that Crashaw does not write poetry as a substitute for but a demonstration of and engagement in the power of the co-dependence of scriptural revelation and sacramental reception of the body of Christ. Thus, although Kuchar would not put it this way, even a poem that aspires to being liturgical is not sacramental language unless God himself is participating in the transformation of meaning or sound into grace as the poem is received by the reader. Also, union with God must be the goal. It cannot happen automatically, and it cannot happen because of the sound of any word or combination of words. It is not a human power. This understanding is true for Catholics as much as it is for Calvin, for Southwell as much as for Herbert. Although John Donne in particular might court a broader meaning of sacramentality (and Netzley argues that Milton means by it a sign of a union that has already occurred), for most Protestant poets, expanding rather than contracting the definition of what was truly a sacrament would go against the grain.

The Christ Child in Time

> Christmas is not an event within history but is rather the invasion of time by eternity.[22]

Christ being contemporary to the poet, he is not distant in time. Because early modern studies are currently focused on memory and objects as carriers of memory, it is also important to point out that Christ is not "remembered" like an object or event lost in the past or washed up on the shores of today from yesterday. He is not a relic of an age gone by preserved in amber. For both the Catholic and Protestant poets of the age, he is not a memory but a living person. However, he is a living person who as God exists outside of time and whose human nature is not abandoned at the Ascension. Thus, the use of the present tense to speak of the Nativity is mimetic. As a result, the use of the past tense is also meaningful where it occurs, but, in general, the poets imagine themselves at a point in the line of time identical with Christ's gestation or birth and thus describe him in the present tense.

The crumpling or folding of time in the objects referred to in drama, discussed in such works as Harris's *Untimely Matter*, perhaps evokes a similar temporal effect, though the cause is quite different: "Untimely matter ... challenges the fantasy of the self-identical moment or period, of the sovereign moment-state divided from its temporal neighbors. It materializes instead a temporality which is not one."[23] In such a view, time can always be seen as multifold, not an Augustinian point. However, among seventeenth-century academic poets, a postmodern sense of always being uprooted from any temporal order in the way Harris describes would have been highly unusual. Tudor and Stuart poets, thinking of the "polychronic," would have been – like most of us – inclined to imagine many times over the extent of history, as in Ranulf Higden's fourteenth-century *Polychronicon*, rather than many times present at once. In any case, they would not have imagined the Christ Child as a thing, and things do not appear as material objects with polychronic identities in Nativity poetry, though in Southwell's "New Heaven, New Warre" one could say the identity of things in the stable at Bethlehem is radically destabilized.[24] To study the material culture of Nativity poems would severely reduce our selection of examples, since the early modern English poets were more interested in the Incarnation itself than in representing Bethlehem.[25]

Apostrophe is another poetic way of "making present." Yet, in her important study on this poetic figure, Helen Vendler understands the invocation of or address to God in George Herbert's lyrics as apostrophe to something that is not there.[26] There could be no more characteristically modern approach to the religious poets of the century we are considering than to style their God a fiction. Given this understanding, Christ would be no different from the moon, say, in Sidney's "With how sad steps, O moon, thou climb'st the sky." The ridiculousness of making an inanimate object an interlocutor would always be present in any poems addressed to God, were we to read the works through this lens. Sidney's self-mockery would be present in the voice of every beguiled devotee. In fact, for every poet in this study, whether Southwell or Milton, Christ is a person who exists in the poet's lifetime and beyond. Nor is he distant, like Poseidon off among the Ethiopians when the gods decide it is high time they should allow Odysseus to have his homecoming. Whether the poem is a prayer or a meditation, no Christian poet, it is safe to say, imagines that Christ cannot hear him or her. The opposite is true: even if the poet imagines no other audience for his or her poem, the one audience who cannot be deaf and who cannot be deceived is God. He is definitely listening.

For making the past present, the writer of course always has the historical present to use: it is a mode found in the writers of classical Greece and Rome. To make a scene vivid a writer simply transposes it out of the past into the present tense. We still commonly use this mode to write about historical objects and texts. Past events are also seen as present by virtue of their yearly repetition: liturgical commemoration of a feast day, and to a lesser degree national celebration of a political holiday, can provoke the imagination of past events as occurring in the present. However, at this point we are already starting to blur into yet another reason for speaking of a past event in the present: the eternity of God in Judaism and Christianity who lives outside of time. In an Easter liturgy or even a daily Mass, God may be spoken of as present because he does not slip into the past or arrive from the past, unlike any other person or object. The liturgical and prayerful recognition of the aspect of eternity is a common mode for Christians of all types in the seventeenth century.

In addition, considerations of Christian concepts of time should include a concept of sacramental time, or time affected by the presence of the eternal God in the sacrament of the Eucharist. When a human being consumes the Eucharist, according to Roman Catholic belief, he or she is in physical contact with and strengthened to eternal life by Jesus himself, present body and blood, soul and divinity. The identification of eternity with the Eucharist originates with Christ himself: "And I say to you, I wil not drinke from henceforth of this fruite of the vine, vntil that day when I shal drinke it with you new in the kingdom of my father" (Matthew 26:29).[27] Matthew reports these as the last words of the Last Supper, immediately following the institution of the Eucharist. In these words, Christ informs the apostles that any subsequent sacramental union with him occurs in "the kingdom of [his] father." All celebrations of the Eucharist occur in the context of eternity.

If we were to talk of a reformed concept of sacramental time, on the other hand, it would be understood as union with Christ via the raising of the speaker through the power of the Holy Spirit and not through fleshly sight or contact. In general, reformed thinkers do not attempt to imagine contact with Christ as he was in history because the time of his degradation in human flesh is past, and he exists now only in his glorified body.

The Christ Child in Space

When Elizabeth I forbade the elevation of the host in her presence as one of her first acts determining the religion of England, she was declaring her discarding of the Catholic belief that Christ is present in the physical host on earth. If Jesus was not present, the host should not be elevated for the viewing and worship of the congregation because he was not literally there. Jesus was not where the worshipper was. Elizabethan and, later, Stuart English men and women clearly saw the "where" of Jesus and the "when" of Jesus as intertwined.

The poets of the Tudor and Stuart period all agree that Christ is alive at the same time they are alive. Where they differ is on the question of where Jesus is. Is he in the poem they write about or to him? No. Has he ever been on earth? Yes. Is he on earth now, ever? Yes, or no, depending on the individual's conviction about the powers of Christ's physical body. Surprisingly, sixteenth- and seventeenth-century English authors wrote quite a lot on this question, but in one particular context.

Christ's Physical Body and the Eucharist

In the Roman Catholic faith, which Southwell died for, Donne abandoned, and Crashaw adopted, the reception of the Eucharist is the making present of Christ. As described in both the decrees on the Eucharist of the Council of Trent and also in the British Eucharistic prayers, all elements of his life are there, but particularly the Incarnation, which the confecting of the sacrament also makes present. The priestly prayers of the Sarum Rite, used in many parts of England throughout the almost five hundred years between its institution by the eleventh-century St. Osmund, bishop of Salisbury, and its abolition by Elizabeth I in 1559, underscored the belief in the corporeal presence of Christ on the altar and its identity with the fleshly Christ Child born in Bethlehem. Although the Sarum Rite influenced Cranmer's composition of the liturgy in the *Book of Common Prayer*, he edited out these prayers. (They also do not appear in the Roman Rite.) The Sarum Use was the Mass the English recusants knew (since Henry VIII had mandated its extension through all the dioceses of England, suppressing the uses of York, Bangor, and Hereford) and the one that many of the seminary priests in exile celebrated in the seventeenth century.

> O God the Father, Fount and Source of all goodness, Who, moved by Thy loving-kindness didst will Thine Only Begotten to descend for us to this lower world and to take Flesh, which I unworthy here hold here in my

> hands, *Here let the priest incline himself to the Host,* I worship Thee, I glorify Thee, I praise Thee with the whole purpose of my mind and heart, and beseech Thee not to forsake us Thy servants, but forgive us our sins: that so we may be enabled to serve Thee, the only Living and True God, with a pure heart and chaste body. Through the same Christ our Lord. Amen.[28]

When the priest himself received communion, he was to say these words: "Hail for evermore, most holy Flesh of Christ, to me before all and above the highest source of joy. The Body of our Lord Jesus Christ be unto me a sinner the Way and the Life." The priest bows to the host because it is the same body of Christ, which descended to "this lower world."[29]

This rite was the way in which Roman Catholics understood their physical proximity to the Incarnation. However, England had already had an important voice disputing the idea of such presence, which favoured rather the idea that the sacrament of the Lord's Supper made Christ present through memory alone. The strict memorialist position of Tyndale (also held by Zwingli) has an important place in the sacramentology of England in the sixteenth and seventeenth centuries, although most of the poets treated in this study rejected it. Tyndale viewed the sacrament of the altar as a memorial only; he taught against the doctrine of the Real Presence, even as it would be articulated by later Anglicans. As Glen Bowman has argued, "the elements, to Tyndale, had to be merely physical: since Christ was in heaven, he could not also be physically present in the sacrament."[30] As far as Tyndale could see, the adoration of the sacrament was nothing more or less than idolatry, since the bread and wine always remain bread and wine. All the poets in this study were familiar with the memorialist position, and in their sermons Donne and Herbert even refuted it explicitly.

Between the two positions lay John Calvin's understanding of the presence of Christ in the Eucharist, one which influenced the convictions of those forming the belief of the English Church. Calvin is not a memorialist, but he never conjoins the cross and the manger in the manner of a John Chrysostom or a Bernard of Clairvaux, Church Fathers whose influence on Donne, Herbert, and the other Metaphysicals is well known. Though Calvin does indeed talk about the Eucharist in his second Christmas sermon, his comments lead the reader to envision the manger and swaddling clothes as allegories of the difficulty of perceiving Christ:

> Let us not cease to draw near to our Lord Jesus Christ and to be assured that it is He in Whom we shall find all good, all rejoicing, and all glory,

> although it seems that He is still, as it were, in the stable and in the manger, wrapped with swaddling clothes. That is to say, there might be many things which could debauch us and dazzle the eyes of a few that they might not perceive the heavenly glory which was given to Him by God His Father, I say, even in the human nature He took from us.[31]

Calvin adds, to impress upon the listener not Christ's bodily presence in the Eucharist but his bodily absence:

> And therefore, though He be absent from us in body, and is not conversant with us here on earth, it is not that He hath withdrawn Himself, as though we could not find Him; for the sun that shineth doth no more enlighten the world, than Jesus Christ showeth Himself openly to those that have the eyes of faith to look upon Him, when the gospel is preached.[32]

Christ is present through preaching. Calvin does not understand a physical presence of Jesus Christ to be available to, or desired by, the speaker or his audience. The two sacraments of Baptism and the Lord's Supper, for Calvin, are signs of a spiritual union between the soul and God, but the material elements of the sacraments neither convey nor cause it. Calvin quotes John Chrysostom about the need to have "spiritual things under things visible." But Calvin emphasizes that "Chrysostom is quick to add that the spiritual thing is not 'inherent in the nature of the [material] things.'"[33]

Both Baptism and the Lord's Supper are empty signs that God's gift of salvation and life make full. Calvin quotes Augustine:

> He is not here, for he sits there, at the right hand of the Father. And yet he is here: for the presence of his majesty is not withdrawn. Otherwise, as regards the presence of his majesty, we have Christ always; while, in regards to his bodily presence, it was rightly said, "Me ye have not always." In respect of bodily presence, the Church had him for a few days: now she holds him by faith, but sees him not with the eye.[34]

What Calvin says here is what the English Church would in essence teach in the seventeenth century. The rationale behind this interpretation of Jesus's words lay in an intertextual interpretation of Peter's words in Acts 3:21, referring to Christ as him "whom the heaven must receive until the times of restitution of all things, which God hath spoken by the mouth of all his holy prophets since the world began." A full discussion of the problem presented by this biblical passage is beyond the scope of this book, but the Lutheran and Calvinist disagreement over it devolves upon the Greek verb δέχεσθαι, which can be translated in passive or middle voice. The question is whether the passage means that the heavens must contain Christ or whether he must contain them. Calvin's commentary maintained that Jesus must remain in heaven until the Second Coming. The Lutheran argument would be that the scriptures also speak of the Father inhabiting the heavens without implying that he is restricted from being omnipresent.[35] Roman Catholics would agree with the Lutherans on this score. This verse was central to the Calvinist rejection of Catholic sacramentology; Lutherans explicitly denied the accuracy of the Geneva translation.[36] The argument, as Calvin expounds it in the *Institutes*, is as follows:

> For as we do not doubt that Christ's body is limited by the general characteristics common to all human bodies, and is contained in heaven (where it was once for all received) until Christ return in judgment [Acts 3:21], so we deem it utterly unlawful to draw it back under these corruptible elements or to imagine it to be present everywhere.[37]

This conviction of Christ's bodily absence from the world motivated many an English Protestant to reject transubstantiation, as we see, for instance, in the arguments Protestant martyr John Lambert made against Archbishop Cranmer before King Henry VIII in Foxe's *Acts and Monuments of the Church*:

> Seeing then that this natural body of our Saviour, which was born of his mother the Virgin Mary, is wholly taken up to heaven, and departed out of this world, and so saith St. Peter, he must remain in heaven until the end of the world, which he calleth the time when all things must be restored; this I say, seen and believed according to our creed and the scriptures, I cannot perceive how his natural body can be in the world, and in the sacrament. And yet notwithstanding is this true, that the holy sacrament is Christ's body, and blood, as after shall be declared.[38]

Cranmer had been more or less Lutheran in his views of Acts 3:21 and of the Eucharist until he befriended Martin Bucer and Peter Martyr in the mid-1540s. Calvin had already convinced Bucer of his view of the "whereness" of Christ's body using this particular text, which then became key in Cranmer and Ridley's rejection of the Catholic view.[39]

Inevitably, Catholics and Protestants alike brought up the Incarnation itself in these discussions. The incarnate Christ in particular could not be present, as Calvin observes, since Christ's body observes the laws governing all natural bodies, a premise the Council of Trent's declaration on the sacrament explicitly denies.[40] It is also true that, for many Protestants, the age of miracles was past, an idea the Catholic Church still does not accept.[41]

These observations lead to the question, Did Christ's body always obey the laws of physics? Although, after Calvin, there was increasing insistence in reformed countries on the physical body of the Son remaining in heaven after his ascension, and on the impossibility of natural bodies being in multiple places at once, Thomas Aquinas had argued in his questions on the Eucharist that, even in his mortal life, Christ's body adopted qualities of his post-resurrection body, including subtlety and, by inference, bilocation (Christ gives his body with his own hands to his disciples in the Last Supper).[42] Aquinas says:

> I answer that, Hugh of St. Victor … maintained, that before the Passion, Christ assumed at various times the four properties of a glorified body – namely, subtlety in His birth, when He came forth from the closed womb of the Virgin; agility, when He walked dryshod upon the sea; clarity, in the Transfiguration; and impassibility at the Last Supper, when He gave His body to the disciples to be eaten. And according to this He gave His body in an impassible and immortal condition to His disciples.[43]

In other words, for Roman Catholics, without ever accepting Docetism, it would have been impossible to assume that Christ's natural body had to obey at all times and even in eternity the rules governing our mortal bodies.

Anglican Sacramentology

Understanding Anglican sacramentology of the seventeenth century is challenging because over the century it changed, depending on what government held power, and because there was some latitude already in Calvin's definition. Moreover, Martin Luther and Philip Melanchthon still wielded a great, yet underexplored, influence on the Reformation in England.[44] Anglican divines disparaged scholastic philosophizing and eschewed the very tendency to search for fine theological definitions they thought detracted from true devotion to God. Anglicans also deliberately avoided defining the mode of Christ's presence because it would show disunity. Nonetheless, tracing the outlines of an Anglican sacramentology is vital to this book's argument since Donne converted to the Church of England; Herbert was raised in it and, like Donne, served as an Anglican priest; and Crashaw too was raised and ordained in it, though he left it for the Roman Catholic faith. The main texts to which historians of religion can turn are the Thirty-Nine Articles and the *Book of Common Prayer*, both bearing the imprint of Thomas Cranmer. However, if we look at Richard Hooker's *Laws of Ecclesiastical Polity* and sermons by Lancelot Andrewes, Donne, Herbert, Bishop Laud, and others, we see that those two sources did not completely confine the Anglican priest's range of options in defining the sacrament.

First, like Calvin, the English Church elevated the two dominical sacraments of Baptism and the Lord's Supper over other usages it considered extra-biblical. Articles 25 and 28 of the Thirty-Nine Articles insist that the elevation of the host and adoration of the sacrament were idolatrous. Revisions to the liturgy had expurgated these acts.[45]

Article 28 states in part:

> The Body of Christ is given, taken, and eaten in the Supper only after an heavenly and spiritual manner. And the mean whereby the Body of Christ is received and eaten in the Supper, is Faith.
>
> The Sacrament of the Lords Supper was not by Christs ordinance reserved, carried about, lifted up, or worshipped.[46]

Calvin would desire the worship of latria to be given to the body of Christ were it physically present. However, for him, even in the moment of communicating, the human body does not consume the body of Christ. He is eaten by means of faith in only a spiritual manner. Article 29 re-emphasizes that it is the disposition of the recipient that determines whether or not there is any contact with Christ in receiving the Eucharist:

> **29. Of the wicked which eat not the Body of Christ in the use of the Lords Supper.**
>
> The wicked and such as be void of a lively faith, although they do carnally and visibly press with their teeth (as Saint *Augustine* saith) the Sacrament of the Body and Blood of Christ; yet in no wise are they partakers of Christ, but rather to their condemnation do eat and drink the Sign or Sacrament of so great a thing.[47]

Sacrament and Christ are here clearly spoken of as separate and distinct things.

Article 31 brings up the issue of the location of the Eucharist on the line of time:

> The offering of Christ once made is the perfect redemption, propitiation, and satisfaction for all the sins of the whole world, both original and

actual, and there is none other satisfaction for sin, but that alone. Wherefore the Sacrifices of the Masses, in the which it was commonly said that the priests did offer Christ for the quick and the dead, to have remission of pain and guilt, were blasphemous fables, and dangerous deceits.[48]

The Anglican argument is against multiple sacrifices of Christ; however, the Catholic Church did not maintain any such multiplicity. At the heart of the difference between the two faiths is the conception of time. For the Protestant English man or woman, a Mass occurs on the line of time separate from the moment of Christ's sacrifice. It has to be a repetition or a memorial and cannot be a "making present."

The famous and controversial black rubric of the 1552 *Book of Common Prayer* had stated that the body and blood of Christ were not present in the bread and wine:

> Lest yet the same kneeling might be thought or taken otherwise, we do declare that it is not meant thereby, that any adoration is done, or ought to be done, either unto the sacramental bread and wine thereby bodily received, or to any real and essential presence, there being of Christ's natural flesh and blood.[49]

In 1562, the words "real and essential" were changed to "corporal," possibly to avoid any potential misinterpretation of the regulation.[50] The meaning is clear: the natural flesh and blood of Christ are not present in any way that would demand adoration of his divine majesty. Cranmer argued in his 1555 *A Defence of the True and Catholic Doctrine of the Sacrament of the Body and Blood of Our Saviour Christ* that "although Christ in his human nature substantially, really, corporally, naturally and sensibly, be present with his Father in heaven yet sacramentally and spiritually he is here present. For in water, bread, and wine, he is present as in signs and sacraments, but he is indeed spiritually in the faithful Christian people, which according to Christ's ordinance be baptized, or receive the holy communion, or unfeignedly believe in him."[51] Cranmer deliberately used language similar to that in the Tridentine definitions to locate Christ's body definitively in heaven rather than on earth.

Cranmer also argued that the Mass was sacrificial only in its being a sacrifice of laud and praise rather than one of propitiation. In the *Defence*, he stated:

> And in like manner Christ ordained the sacrament of his body and blood in bread and wine, to preach unto us, that as our bodies be fed, nourished,

> and preserved with meat and drink, so as touching our spiritual life towards God we be fed, nourished, and preserved by the body and blood of our Saviour Christ ... And no less ought we to doubt, that our souls be fed and live by Christ, than that our bodies be fed and live by meat and drink. Thus our Saviour Christ, knowing us to be in this world, as it were, but babes and weaklings in faith, hath ordained sensible signs and tokens whereby to allure and to draw us to more strength and more constant faith in him. So that the eating and drinking of this sacramental bread and wine is, as it were, shewing of Christ before our eyes, a smelling of him with our noses, feeling and groping of him with our hands, and an eating, chewing, digesting, and feeding upon him to our spiritual strength and perfection.[52]

For all the language of sensation in the end of this passage, Cranmer insists on "as it were."

Following Calvin, Hooker and Cranmer understand the communicant's union with Christ's divinity and humanity as taking place through the power of the Holy Spirit. In *Ecclesiastical Polity*, Hooker explains that it is through this power that the communicant is united to Christ's humanity, which is not on earth in any way. For Hooker, the change that takes place in the Eucharist is not in the elements themselves but, rather, in the believer who receives the elements. "The real presence of Christ's most blessed body and blood is not therefore to be sought for in the sacrament, but in the worthy receiver of the sacrament."[53] Roger Beckwith puts it thus: "It could therefore, perhaps, be said that, whereas in Aquinas's eucharistic theology we are united with Christ's divinity through his humanity, in Hooker's we are united with Christ's humanity through his divinity ... As Calvin said, 'He does not descend to us, but we, through the Spirit, ascend to him' (*Institutes* 4:17:31, 36f)."[54]

Hooker made a serious effort to tread a middle ground between the Catholic and Calvinist senses of real presence. His *Laws of Ecclesiastical Polity* state that "it is on all sides plainly confessed, first that this sacrament is a true and a real participation of Christ, who thereby imparteth himself even his whole Person as a mystical Head unto every soul that receiveth him, and that every such receiver doth thereby incorporate or unite himself unto Christ as a mystical member of him, yea of them also whom he acknowledgeth to be his own."[55] The person of the Trinity who effects this participation is the Holy Spirit, "to whom the person of Christ is thus communicated, to them he giveth by the same sacrament his Holy Spirit to sanctify them as it sanctifieth him which is their head."[56]

Hooker argues that all the virtues of Christ's body and blood are fully conveyed to the recipient and that it really changes the communicants' "souls and bodies from sin to righteousness, from death and corruption to immortality and life." However, "because the sacrament being of itself but a corruptible and earthly creature must needs be thought an unlikely instrument to work so admirable effects in man, we are therefore to rest ourselves altogether upon the strength of his glorious power who is able and will bring to pass that the bread and cup which he giveth us" will truly be the thing Jesus says it is.[57]

Hooker searches for the ways in which Roman Catholic, Lutheran, and Calvinist doctrines cohere – what God does in the Eucharist – while not demonstrating any concern with the manner in which God effects the end. The physical presence of Christ is a thing "indifferent" if the grace is channeled to the recipient of the sacrament just the same.[58] Like many other Anglicans, Hooker rejects transubstantiation when explaining what happens in the Eucharist.

Not all Anglicans so clearly distanced the Eucharist from the Incarnation in this way. George Herbert's teacher, the influential divine Lancelot Andrewes, wrote several Christmas sermons and liturgical prayers in which he seems to consider, in the tradition of Bernard of Clairvaux and John Chrysostom, the consecration and reception of the Eucharist as a re-enactment of the Incarnation and Nativity. For example, conflating the sacrament with the sign the angels told the shepherds they would find at the stable, Andrewes wrote:

> Of the Sacrament we may well say, Hoc erit signum. For a sign it is, and by it invenietis Puerum, "ye shall find this Child" [Luke 2:12]. For finding His flesh and blood, ye cannot miss but find Him too. And a sign, not much from this here. For Christ in the Sacrament is not altogether unlike Christ in the cratch. To the cratch we may well liken the husk or outward symbols of it. Outwardly it seems little worth, but it is rich of contents, as was the crib this day [the sermon was preached on Christmas Day] with Christ in it. For what are they but infirma et egena elementa, "weak and poor elements" [Galatians 4:9] of themselves? Yet in them find we Christ. Even as they did this day in praesepi iumentorum panem angelorum, "in the beast's crib the food of angels," which very food our signs both represent and present unto us.[59]

Although Andrewes says "our signs both represent and present unto us" the "food of angels," in what way "in them we find Christ" remains obscure. His teaching is complicated by his inclusion of what appears to be a paraphrase of the Gelasian Sacramentary in Latin as an authority.[60] Thus Andrewes relies on a similitude for clarification but does not define his terms.[61] Andrewes shows the same care to avoid definition of the manner of Christ's becoming present in a prayer he composed for the consecration of the Eucharistic elements, bread and wine:

> We beseech Thee, O Lord, that with the witness of our conscience clean, receiving our share of thy hallowed things, we may be united to the holy body and blood of thy Christ, and receiving them not unworthily may have Christ indwelling in our hearts.[62]

Andrewes is, on the other hand, very clear about rejecting the option of transubstantiation because it is extra-biblical:

> Christ said, "This is My body." He did not say, "This is My body in this way." We are in agreement with you as to the end; the whole controversy is as to the method. As to the "This," we hold with firm faith that it is. As to the "this is in this way" (namely, by the Transubstantiation of the bread into the body), as to the method whereby it happens that it is, by means of In or With or Under or By transition there is no word expressed. And because there is no word, we rightly make it not of faith; we place it perhaps among the theories of the school, but not among the articles of the faith ... We believe no less than you that the presence is real. Concerning the method of the presence, we define nothing rashly, and, I add, we do not anxiously inquire, any more than how the blood of Christ washes us in Baptism, any more than how the human and divine natures are united in one Person in the Incarnation of Christ.[63]

And Andrewes rejects transubstantiation explicitly here:

> But there is no mention there of a change in the substance, or of the substance. But neither do we deny in this matter the preposition trans; and we allow that the elements are changed (transmutari). But a change in substance we look for, and we find it nowhere.[64]
>
> ...
>
> At the coming of the almighty power of the Word, the nature is changed so that what before was the mere element now becomes a divine Sacrament, the substance nevertheless remaining what it was before ... There is that kind of union between the visible Sacrament and the invisible reality (rem) of the Sacrament which there is between the manhood and the Godhead of Christ, where unless you want to smack of Eutyches, the manhood is not transubstantiated into the Godhead.[65]

Andrewes's witness is very important for our understanding of George Herbert in particular: when Herbert was eleven, he was Andrewes's student at Chiswick, and Herbert held Andrewes in the highest esteem all his life. And Andrewes declares the manner of Christ's presence in the Eucharist adiaphora – among the things indifferent. Donne and Herbert both are aligned with Andrewes in this regard, as Robert Southwell could never be and as Crashaw probably was not even before his conversion to Rome. As the manner of Christ's presence becomes a thing indifferent, I would argue that there is visible evidence of its losing its centrality in English belief and imagination. By concomitance, Christ's physical body, especially in his babyhood, seems to disappear.

Donne, for instance, articulates his own preference for enjoying the liberty of ranging among opinions when it comes to the adiaphora. He says so himself in his preface to *Pseudo-Martyr*, his 1610 pamphlet arguing that Catholics could and should take the oath of allegiance to the king:

> My natural impatience not to dig painfull in deep and stony and sullen learnings; my Indulgence to freedom and libertie, as in all indifferent things, so in my studies also, not to betroth or enthral myself to any one science, which should possess or denominate me; my easiness to afford a sweet and gentle interpretation to all professors of Christian Religion, if they shake not the foundation wherein I have in my ordinary communication often expressed and declared myself, hath opened me enough to their malice.[66]

Like Calvin and Melanchthon, and unlike the Roman Catholics as a body and Luther as well, the Anglican poets tend to believe that Christ's body and blood are present and entering into their hearts, but they do not wish to define how because it is not stated directly in the Bible and is thus among the "things indifferent."

Herbert, like Donne, believed in the Real Presence but denied transubstantiation as an explanation. Many critics have discussed his belief, but let me present the essential evidence here. In *The Country Parson*, George Herbert's manual for Anglican priests, Herbert advises a posture of reverence to the sacrament at a time when kneeling was a controversial gesture, implying to many adoration of the bread and wine:

> Thirdly, For the manner of receiving, as the Parson useth all reverence himself, so he administers to none but to the reverent. The Feast indeed requires sitting, because it is a Feast; but man's unpreparednesse asks kneeling. Hee that comes to the Sacrament, hath the confidence of a Guest, and hee that kneels, confesseth himself an unworthy one, and therefore differs from other Feasters: but hee that sits, or lies, puts up to an Apostle: Contentiousnesse in a feast of Charity is more scandall then any posture.[67]

Thus, kneeling is not an act of worship but of humility; the focus is on the attitude of the recipient, not the nature of the thing received. Likewise, when speaking of the sacrament itself, Herbert revolves from the question of what it is to the worthiness of the minister:

> The Countrey Parson being to administer the Sacraments, is at a stand with himself, how or what behaviour to assume for so holy things. Especially at Communion times he is in a great confusion, as being not only to receive God, but to break, and administer him. Neither findes he any issue in this, but to throw himself down at the throne of grace, saying, Lord, thou knowest what thou didst, when thou appointedst it to be done thus; therefore doe thou fulfill what thou didst appoint; for thou art not only the feast, but the way to it.[68]

After stating that the sacrament is God and that God will be broken and administered in it, Herbert prostrates himself interiorly before God and throws the issue of understanding back upon God: he, God, knows; he is the feast and the way to it – but in what way God is the feast becomes murkier here, once Herbert has trodden perilously close to seeing the species of the sacraments as God and worthy of adoration. Thus, for the most part in *The Country Parson,* Herbert focuses on the priest as teacher rather than officiant, much less *alter Christus.* The parson must make sure that only the finest elements are used for the consecration, the most wholesome and most refined bread and wine. And his care must be for the exhorting of his flock to worthy reception; he skirts the issue of the substance of the instruction to be given, although he recommends early reception for children:

> The time of every ones first receiving is not so much by yeers, as by understanding: particularly, the rule may be this: When any one can distinguish the Sacramentall from common bread, knowing the Institution, and the difference, hee ought to receive, of what age soever. Children and youths are usually deferred too long, under pretence of devotion to the Sacrament, but it is for want of Instruction; their understandings being ripe enough for ill things, and why not then for better?[69]

What Herbert considers necessary is understanding that allows for distinguishing "the Sacramentall from common bread, knowing the Institution and the difference," a tall order, it might seem to us, but he thinks a child capable of this understanding. If his teaching was as frank as his description of impanation (the belief that Christ's body comes into the bread but does not replace it) in "The H. Communion," we may be sure his congregation did have a clearer knowledge than this instruction offers: "I could believe an Impanation / At the rate of an Incarnation / If thou hadst died for bread."[70] Mocking impanation, transubstantiation, and consubstantiation, Herbert makes it clear that he distances himself from any belief in the substantial presence of Christ's body in the sacrament. The phrase is sarcastic in a way Herbert almost never is, but the point he is making is important: if bread is elevated in this way by physical contact with Christ, redeemed, as it were, then Christ became incarnate to ennoble and divinize bread, an obviously absurd suggestion.[71] As James Bromley asserts, in contradistinction from Ryan Netzley's view, "Herbert is keenly aware of the absence of Christ's body in both historical and theological terms; consequently, his model of salvific intimacy with God is based in desire for that which is absent or lacking."[72]

"Salvific intimacy" is one of the things at stake when we look at the Nativity lyrics of these poets and search for an embodied Christ Child. Where the Roman Catholic might expect a portrayal of the fleshly child, a child who, incarnate, can thus be held, or kissed, or touched, the reformed writer might find such a portrayal beside the point, since Christ's whole aim was to create a new heart in the faithful and reside there, and his being a child was simply a step to that end. The Roman Catholic would be perfectly at ease with the idea of Christ in the heart; it is an image that arises in the Middle Ages and has many manifestations in art and literature, devotional narratives, and sermons up through the Counter-Reformation and beyond. But during the Reformation, particularly in those countries more inclined to Calvin than to Luther, the raising of the heart to Christ in the "Sursum corda" before the Words of Institution became the pattern for the only way in which intimacy could be imagined. Whereas for the Catholic it is a question of both/and, for the reformed poet it is becoming a choice of only one route to contact with the divine presence.

The young Milton was clearly raised in the anti-Roman sentiments of his father, but what he thought of Christ's potential physical presence in the sacrament at the time he wrote the Nativity Ode is something we can only guess at. He must have leaned more toward Calvin than to Hooker or Herbert. Later in life, by the time he writes the *Christian Doctrine*, Milton explicitly condemns Catholic and Lutheran teachings in the strongest terms: "Consubstantiation and particularly transubstantiation and papal ανθρωποφαγια or cannibalism are monstrous doctrines."[73] Of all the poets treated in this study, Milton most fully spiritualizes and de-materializes the sacrament, bypassing the material medium of the flesh. As Ulreich puts it, he "relegat[es] transubstantiation to one of the 'ordinary physical processes' ... in fact seculariz[ing] the sacred mystery of the Mass; at the same time ... exalt[ing] the ordinary physical process of digestion into a sacramental act."[74] The middle-aged Milton certainly rejects the notion that the sacrament of the Lord's Supper can unite the recipient bodily with Christ. The Nativity Ode may foreshadow such a rejection, but it is important not to read the more youthful poem too retrospectively.

Richard Crashaw, like George Herbert, grew up in the Anglican faith and wrote his Nativity poems for the most part before his conversion to Catholicism; however, he did revise the "Hymn in the Holy Nativity of Ovr Lord God" after his conversion. His revisions reflect a new emphasis on sacrifice and the Proleptic Passion. Although sacrificial references remained in the Anglican liturgy of the Eucharist, Cranmer's *Book of Common Prayer* reflected his belief that the sacrifice in the liturgy was one of praise and was offered by the body of Christ represented by the worshipping faithful. Since Crashaw translated Aquinas's Eucharistic hymns "Adoro te devote" and "Lauda Sion Salvatorem" (also before his conversion) and wrote other poems on the Eucharist, he clearly understood Roman Catholic doctrine on it, and even if he believed he could give a Laudian spin to Aquinas in his Eucharistic hymns,[75] Crashaw inevitably knew going over to Rome meant accepting precisely this doctrine. Recently, Kimberly Johnson and Ryan Netzley have written extensively on Crashaw's refracting of his belief in transubstantiation in his difficult and at times graphic poetry on the Eucharist.[76]

The Christ Child and *Storge*

Criticism in the age after Freud and his followers, Levinas, Lacan, and others, is filled with considerations of erotic love, but has as a result impoverished the understanding of other types of love and hence our ability to talk about them intelligently and with historical accuracy. The medieval lyrics and dramatic speeches I cited at the beginning of this chapter in general portray *storge* rather than *eros*, familial love rather than a love that arises in an adult from nature's urging to reproduce. In considering the Christ Child, the adult poets of the period often portray a parental or paternal protective love in the speaker. Not that this perspective is always the case: sometimes in Southwell the child is so powerful he does not seem to need the poet's tenderness, and at other times, as in Herbert, he is not there to receive it. But as Miri Rubin's and Rachel Fulton Brown's work on Marian themes has shown, medieval artists and poets often become rapt in the maternal qualities of the

Virgin Mother's perspective.[77] I would argue that the male perspective of these academic poets merits similar attention.

God and Poet

The poets of the Tudor and Stuart periods (in this study more narrowly defined as the 1590s through 1650) were deeply concerned with matters having to do with their own personal faith and the faith of the kingdom. They were highly skilled rhetoricians, adept at all manner of wordplay and knowledgeable about the poetic conventions and concerns of the past as well as of their own day. Yet they were also real flesh and blood human beings who almost all struggled with their own beliefs and had a relationship with someone other than their readers, which they expressed in their religious poetry: that someone else is God. All the poets in this study treat the Christ Child in the womb or newly born as the divinity they themselves worship and in whom lies their hope for salvation from sin and death. As Gary Bouchard has pointed out, all the Metaphysicals (and I would add Milton too, who displays some of the same tendencies) are aware of a pattern set by Southwell at the end of the previous century, the creation of a group of poems meditating on the Incarnation and birth of Christ. As I have mentioned, it is Southwell who probably makes the Nativity poem a popular subgenre, when poets of Henry's court were almost exclusively concerned with Petrarchan themes.[78] However, though the Metaphysicals turn to the events of the Incarnation recounted in the gospels, none of them evoke a scene purely based on the account in the Gospel of Luke. They play in a highly individualized way with the theme before them.

In all these poems, the craft is devoted to a mimesis of presence and to evoking wonder, joy, concern, trepidation, affection, and awe, or a combination of several of these emotions, depending on the particular poet. By the middle of the century, this blazing star dissipates, and even the later Metaphysicals are more concerned with following Jonson and Herrick out to the fields to gather holly, ivy, and bay, recording the rustic celebrations and at the same time protesting the Commonwealth's quashing of Christmas celebrations, than themselves celebrating the child in the manger. Bouchard notes a general lessening of devotional poetry at the end of the century, although the hymn begins to flourish as low church movements spread. The decline of the learned Nativity lyric seems to form part of this more general movement as we approach the eighteenth century.[79]

The close relationship between the Incarnation and the presence of Christ in the Eucharist seems one important trigger of the growing divide between Catholic and Protestant poetic cultures: Catholic poets imagine a physical and temporal union with the child in the manger and associate the sacrifice of Calvary with the sufferings of the Christ Child, whereas the Protestant poets seem less interested in creating any temporal or spatial collapse between themselves and the incarnate Christ Child, and tend to use the occasion of the Nativity to focus on their own interior illumination by divine wisdom or power. To put it briefly, as we trace the development of the Nativity lyric as a genre through the seventeenth century in England, the fleshly presence of the baby or child Jesus seems to vanish, until he is hardly to be seen and certainly not to be touched or held by the speaker contemplating his birth. This trend is a far cry from the mystical desire to behold and touch the Lord, articulated in the famous passage from St. Bernard of Clairvaux's *Commentary on the Song of Songs*: "But anyone who has received this mystical kiss from the mouth of Christ at least once, seeks again that intimate experience, and eagerly looks for its frequent renewal. I think that nobody can grasp what it is except the one who receives it. For it is 'a hidden manna,' and only he who eats it still hungers for more."[80]

The Metaphysical Poets on Christ as Cradled or Disembodied

In the following chapter (two), I examine "The Burning Babe" and "New Heaven, New Warre" by Robert Southwell, SJ. Here I introduce to the reader the conflation of time between the Incarnation and the Passion in Southwell's imagination of the Nativity (the Proleptic Passion I have already mentioned). The Christ Child's descent to earth is a military engagement with the forces of evil in which he triumphs even as a baby, a baby who can appear right before the eyes of the believer even in the present day. The Christian's role is to remain by the cradle, the "surest ward."

Chapter three concerns Donne's early sonnet from the *La Corona* cycle, "Immensitie cloysterd in thy deare wombe," or "Nativitie." Here I argue that the poet conflates the use of personal pronouns and vacillates between Mary, the poet's soul, and St. Joseph as addressees, creating an intimate Holy Family of which the speaker forms a part, and that the sonnet gestures toward the Eucharist with the image of the kiss.

In chapter four, Herbert's lesser-known lyric "The Starre" manifests what will be a growing movement away from fleshly contact with the Christ Child toward more spiritual and future-oriented images of union as the reformed poets, mostly educated at Cambridge, become the major voices in the Nativity tradition. I also briefly discuss the same characteristics of spiritual closeness but physical and temporal distance in Herbert's other Nativity poems.

Chapter five moves to John Milton's youthful ode, "On the Morning of Christ's Nativity," and discusses the possible state of Milton's belief in the divinity of the Son at the early age at which he composed the poem and also the purport of invoking Virgil in the depiction of the Christ Child's smile. In Milton too, the Christ Child's body puts in only a minor appearance.

The last chapter discusses Crashaw's Nativity and Epiphany hymns, which he meaningfully revised after his conversion to Roman Catholicism to reflect the connection between the Nativity and the Eucharist. His editorial changes emphasize the real fleshly presence of Christ and the belief in the whole life of Christ as part of the Eucharistic sacrifice.

In the conclusion, I enumerate several avenues for further research and speak of the later Metaphysicals, Traherne and Vaughan, and the waning of the tradition of the Nativity lyric with the rise of different forms of Protestant devotion as Calvinism begins to dominate in England.

Chapter Two

The Christ Child on Fire: Southwell's Mighty Babe

I am come to cast fire on the earth: And what will I, but that it be kindled?
Luke 12:49

The Immolated Christ Child

The last half of the sixteenth century in England saw continuing change in the religious climate that had fostered an image popular in the Middle Ages, that of the Christ Child suffering from the wounds of the crucified adult Christ: the Proleptic Passion.[1] Exegetes, artists, and poets depicted the Christ Child suffering from the wounds of the crucified adult Christ. Although in linear time, the Christ Child could not and did not have these wounds, the medieval Christian imagination perceived no incongruity in such an image. Participation in the liturgy had accustomed Catholics to the idea that they had access to the God who exists outside of time. They understood that both the Incarnation and the Passion were present in the Eucharistic Christ. The more rationalized view of sacrament and immanence that was growing with the Reformation probably accounts for the increasing rarity of images of the Proleptic Passion in the poetry of post-Reformation England. And yet, though they are increasingly rare, we do find a small handful of these images in Southwell, Donne, Crashaw, and Milton.[2]

The survival of the Proleptic Passion image in the works of the Jesuit writer and missionary Robert Southwell is noteworthy, not least because his poetry was surprisingly popular even though the English government condemned his faith and his priestly activity. Southwell's imaginative envisioning of events in Christ's life, most famously the Incarnation, provided devotional material for both Catholics and Protestants. His most well-known poem, "The Burning Babe," first circulated in manuscript but came out in its first printed edition in 1595, the year Southwell was hanged, drawn, and quartered on Tyburn Hill.[3] "The Burning Babe" is a poem of the Renaissance, with Ignatian composition of place, Counter-Reformation floods of tears, and Elizabethan extended conceits. But it remains an anomaly in the English Elizabethan canon. Like Southwell's other Nativity poems, it is a poem with strong roots in the medieval lyric and perhaps even in popular prose works such as tales of Eucharistic miracles or Malory's description of the apparition of the fiery Christ Child in the Grail.[4] Certainly Southwell's description recalls this episode with its strong sacrificial overtones and its language of immolation (that is, of the total destruction of a sacrifice in fire for the purpose of offering it to the deity). That connection between the Christ Child and the language of immolation is my focus here. In the language of the Passion, of the fire consuming the sacrifice, Southwell also finds a means of expressing the immense power of the mighty babe, the Christ Child at whose presence "All hell doth … quake, / Though he himself for cold do shake. / For in this weak, unarmed wise, / The gates of hell he will surprise."[5] It is through this power that he makes himself present to the speaker.

"The Burning Babe" has been highly praised from Southwell's day to our own. Shakespeare's contemporary Ben Jonson famously wished to have been its author; in a classic study, critic Louis Martz attributed to it "a subtle fusion of passion and thought" and claimed that it "feel[s] and know[s] the fact of the Incarnation with every faculty that man can muster."[6] This fusion that Martz finds so compelling arises at least in part from the density of the governing image, which collapses temporal sequences in Christ's life, merging his birth and death, and makes his sacrifice present and applicable to the meditating poet. Southwell's image serves a deliberate meditative purpose: it produces a mimesis of divine eternity by invoking the Christ Child as the nexus of time and eternity, man in time and yet God outside of time.

A Roman Catholic understanding of the Real Presence and a sacramental sense of time were intimately tied to the artistic representations of Christ in England before the Reformation; reformed understandings of Christ's potential presence on earth would come to affect artistic renderings of his Nativity and other points in his life on earth. Thus, as the century wore on, the image of the suffering Christ Child would fall into disuse. Right worship of the Eucharist as the true body and blood of Christ was a central issue in capital trials of Protestants under Henry and Mary, and brutal persecution also awaited those who maintained the Roman Catholic belief under Elizabeth. As Melanchthonian and Calvinist views of the Eucharist gained ground, further legal restrictions were imposed on Catholic practice, in particular on education and on the ability of lay devotional societies to assemble. Roman Catholic belief waned or went underground.[7] The governments of Edward and Elizabeth promulgated the codes replacing Catholic doctrine in the Forty-Two and Thirty-Nine Articles. The earlier codes under Henry had remained close to Catholic thought and practice, if leaning toward Lutheranism, and the two later codes, both written in the main by Thomas Cranmer, clearly delineated the English Church's differences from Catholicism and leaned toward Calvin. The securing of most posts in higher education for men who upheld the rejection of Roman Catholic doctrines also played a part in excising once-familiar images and language from the English religious and artistic vocabulary. These men were not only the priests and teachers of the lay faithful, but also the poets and artists of their age.

Nevertheless, medieval images of Christ did not immediately die out. Though representation in the pictorial arts was more strictly controllable, poetry, song, and drama remained plentiful storehouses of earlier ideas and images. A great many of the Middle English lyrics collected in the twentieth century in the well-known works of R.S. Greene and Carleton Brown[8] remained in the English repertoire past the break with Rome that began in 1532. Many were recorded in sixteenth-century manuscripts. It is very likely that some were still heard or sung up to the Puritan repression of the celebration of Christmas on 23 December 1644 and beyond. Moreover, the Corpus Christi cycles and other biblical plays that linked the Eucharist and the Nativity were so popular that they had to be forbidden by law repeatedly throughout the entire period.[9]

Like Malory's vision of the Holy Grail, these works present us with possible sources for Southwell's imagery (though he was a very bookish young man, it is hard to estimate how much he would have known of popular literature and entertainment). In addition, Southwell went to Europe at a very young age – fifteen – to study, eventually for the priesthood. Though his boyhood may have been saturated with English poetry and drama, European models may well have had more immediate and lasting influence, and in fact criticism on the poet has for the most part emphasized the latter influence over his work. Yet the experiences might not have been entirely dissimilar; in France and Flanders, where the young Southwell studied, the *Mystères* and other forms of popular entertainment enshrining Eucharistic miracles and celebrating the visions of saints were still in their heyday.[10]

European or English, as Southwell scholars such as Sadia Abbas have long recognized, Southwell's fund of imagery and concepts is basically medieval, although he was much influenced by Marinism and *concettismo* in the European portion of his education.[11] The images of the Nativity and the Eucharist that we find in the works of Bede and other early British writers were part of Southwell's mental vocabulary too: in his *Epistle of Comfort*, Southwell recalls the miracles of the Eucharist, many including the apparition of a child in the host or in place of the host reported by the Venerable Bede, Gregory the Great, Cuthbert, Dunstan, and others "registered by the same St. Bede and our own chronicles."[12] In addition to his familiarity with many authors who spoke of child-host miracles, there is also his knowledge of John Damascene, John Chrysostom, Augustine, and Tertullian, all of whom made reference to the Eucharist in terms of the Incarnation or presented the concept of time's collapse in the Eucharist and the Nativity.[13] Their understanding of the Eucharist enters into Southwell's representation of the infancy of Christ.

Thus this most baroque of England's poets created one of the most famous English images of the Christ Child out of a very traditional mode of representation, which he had inherited from the Middle Ages. Andrew Harnack, in his study of the typology of Christmas and "The Burning Babe," says that, "while 'The Burning Babe' contains undeniable intimations of the fast-approaching seventeenth-century English metaphysical sensibility, it is also – if not more so – a near-final expression of an older and more venerable tradition, the roots of which are planted in the theological vision which reaches all the way back in spirit and memory to the earliest experiences of God's people as described in the Old Testament."[14]

Harnack convincingly explains the medieval – in fact, biblical – background of the image of the immolated Christ Child. In terms of providing the reader with a reliable sense of the provenance of Southwell's imagery, Harnack's article, like Sadia Abbas's study specifying Southwell's debt to medieval and patristic sources, is indispensable to Southwell scholars. However, Harnack's essay is not concerned specifically with the collapse of time between the Nativity and the Passion inherent in the image. Thus we will, after looking carefully at "The Burning Babe," move on from the sources of Southwell's image to consider how the traditionally violent images of the Proleptic Passion figure in the portrayal of time and immediacy in Southwell's works and, in particular, in his view of the Christ Child as warrior. I also argue that, in spite of his popularity among readers of both faiths, Southwell's treatment of the Christ Child in some way marks the beginning of the end for a medieval way of conceiving of Jesus in his infancy.

The most recent studies of Southwell have focused on reintegrating technical analysis of his poetry and assessment of its status in the canon with an understanding of Southwell's own expressed artistic mission. Southwell understands that mission, the mission of a religious poet, to be alerting the reader to the presence of God and urging the reader to admit that presence.[15] Thus, he deliberately enforces the primacy of divine eternity over human time in "The Burning Babe" and other poems, as did many medieval artists before him. Southwell manifests in his imagery his poet's credo. In his "To the Reader," he says:

> Prophane conceites and fayning fits I flie.
> Such lawlesse stuffe doth lawlesse speeches fit:
> With *David* verse to vertue I apply.
> Whose measure best with measured wordes doth sit.
> It is the sweetest note that man can sing,
> When grace in vertues key tunes natures string.[16]

This final stanza of the poem echoes his earlier words in "The Author to his loving Cosen," the apology for poetry that introduced his collected works. Above all, when Southwell articulated his theory of poetry here, he had clearly formed that theory within the larger theological concept of nature perfected by grace. We should consider what this approach implies about the writer's use of language and, in our case, imagery. Just as for Philip Sidney, for Southwell nature is not the measure or model that art follows; nature must be tuned and measured by grace. Such a premise calls into question the primacy of the measures of human time, the authority of human proportions, and makes possible the collapse of historical time. This conviction questions a privileging of linear perspective as a norm, a tendency that, as we have seen in chapter one, also informed theological debates over the Eucharist and the probability of the Real Presence.[17]

No such norms constrain "The Burning Babe." In it, the description of the child born at a certain time is tuned to perfection by the use of language that overpasses temporal constraints, that is, language that recognizes God's perspective. Such language is representative of a certain mode of conceptualization. I say "mode of conceptualization" because the Proleptic Passion, the image of the Christ Child as suffering Redeemer, cannot be synthesized merely from word order or patterns of sound, those devices that characterize rhetorical figures. Even the ordering of presentation of concepts, which constitutes some figures, is not sufficient to create this effect. Rather, a familiarity with certain images, doctrines, and approaches, a conviction about the power and ends of language or art: these constitute the mode of conceptualization.

"The Burning Babe" narrates a traveller's vision of the newborn Christ. The solitary speaker stopping in the middle of nowhere is already a reminder to us of the medieval lyrics that recount a traveller's experience of overhearing a dialogue between a mysterious mother and an even more mysterious baby, wherein the mother laments her knowledge of the child's dreadful destiny and the child comforts his mother with a prediction of his resurrection. In medieval literature, a lone (sometimes lost) speaker is also generally a figure of mankind on its earthly pilgrimage, the goal of which is union with God. Witnessing the Incarnation in some sense bridges the temporal gap between man and his goal. In this poem on the Incarnation, Southwell locates the moment of man's confrontation with God on Christmas day. His first intimation of the child's presence is a heat that enkindles his heart while he stands "shivering in the snow":

As I in hoarie Winters night
   Stoode shivering, in the snowe
Surpris'd I was with sodaine heate,
   Which made my hart to glow;

And lifting upp a fearefull eye,
   To vewe what fire was neare,
A pretty Babe all burning bright
   Did in the ayre appeare;

Who scorched with excessive heate,
   Such floods of teares did shed,
As though his floods should quench his flames,
   Which with his teares were fed;

Alas (quoth he) but newly borne,
   In fierie heates I frie,
Yet none approach to warme their harts,
   Or feele my fire, but I;

My faultlesse breast the furnace is,
   The fuell woundinge thornes;
Love is the fire, and sighs the smoake,
   The ashes, shame and scornes;

The fewell Justice layeth on,
  And Mercie blowes the coales,
The metall in this furnace wrought,
  Are mens defiled soules;

For which, as nowe on fire I am
  To worke them to their good,
So will I melt into a bath,
  To washe them in my blood.

With this he vanisht out of sight,
  And swiftly shrunk away,
And straight I called unto minde,
  That it was Christmasse day.[18]

What the visionary's fearful eye sees is a kind of New Testament version of the burning bush, and the parallel is no coincidence. V. Sethuraman has written about the importance of the image from Exodus 3 – its connection to readings from Deuteronomy 4:24 ("Because the Lord thy God is a consuming fire"), which is repeated by Paul in Hebrews 12:29, and its resonance throughout the Hebrew scriptures.[19] Southwell does more than make vague, subconscious connections between these ideas; the scripture and figuration are at the heart of his poem. Moses's experience, recalled here in a Christian setting, was "liminal": he stood at the threshold of the divine, the place where God and man meet. Southwell's traveller is a new Moses who also experiences a time of God's visitation and whose mission is to bring God's message back from that threshold. He chooses the perfect moment to recall the image of Moses's encounter, for in patristic tradition Mary, especially at the Annunciation and Nativity, is called the burning bush: "What was prefigured at that time in the name of the bush was openly manifested in the mystery of the Virgin ... As on the mountain the bush burned but was not consumed, so the Virgin gave birth to the light and was not corrupted."[20] Mary is pregnant but remains *intacta virgo*; she brings the power of God into the world but remains unscathed; the word of God comes to man through her.

The Virgin Mary is not the only person to whom this figure applies, however; Andrew Harnack took the important step of recognizing the patristic association between the Incarnation and the image of the burning bush. Citing Irenaeus, the Great "O" Antiphons, and several Elizabethan sermons, Harnack reminds us of this connection:

> Along with ... its Marian associations, the manifestation of God in the burning bush lays equal and certainly more ancient claim to its figural

importance as type of the Incarnation itself. Thus before its assumption of Marian antitypes, the revelatory burning bush was first described as one among a number of memorably significant Old Testament events which adumbrated the antitypal birth of Christ. Frequently, for example, the early Church Fathers announce the theophany of Exodus 3 as but an early instance of God's preincarnational familiarization of Himself in his Second Person – that is, as the pre-existent Christ – who in the unconsumed bush makes himself known to his prophet prior to his descent and translation into the flesh. Thus Irenaeus (c. 130–c. 200) in *Adversus Omnes Haereses* claims that the Old Testament, especially in those portions written by Moses, repeatedly makes prevenient mention of the Son of God and so foretells his advent and passion.[21]

This episode from the Hebrew scriptures acquires even greater typological force when Southwell applies it, in good medieval style, to the appearance of the infant Christ. The images of immolation are the first intimation that there is a collapse of time in the depiction of the child; the theophany and the Passion are one event. The words "glow," "fire," "burning," "scorched," and "flames" have particular significance in this context. Images of fire are often associated with Christ's coming, in works as disparate as liturgical texts and mystical writings. Lactantius wrote of the Easter Vigil:

> This is the night that we shall celebrate watching for the advent of our king and God … [H]e is a deliverer, judge, avenger, king and God, and we call him Christ. Before he descends he will give the following sign. A sword will suddenly fall from the sky, so that the just may know that the leader of the holy army is about to descend, and he will come with angels accompanying him to the centre of the earth, and in front of him will go an inextinguishable flame.[22]

The intimations of the Second Coming are clear here; the quotation could easily apply to the descent of the Word in the Incarnation.

In addition to signifying the light of Christ and the flames of divine justice, fire also signifies divine love; Sethuraman has suggested this theme in his essay mentioned earlier. A writer favoured by the Jesuits of the period, the mystic Catherine of Siena, spoke of this love in her *Il Dialogo della divina provvidenza*:

> You are a fire always burning but never consuming; you are a fire consuming in your heat all the soul's selfish love; you are a fire lifting all chill and giving light … This light shows you to me, and in this light I know you, highest and infinite Good … You who are the angels' food are given to humans with burning love.[23]

Here we have the same linking of warming fire, the fire of love, and the immolation of the sacrifice that becomes the Eucharistic food that we see in "The Burning Babe."[24] These characteristics are related to the concept of union through love, which Southwell also garnered in part from secular poetry, as we will see more fully later.

Like so many religious poets, Southwell also borrows the language of love poetry to describe the emotional effect of this mystical experience. Here, the imagery of fire and sacrifice is a very common element. Bruce Wardropper has shown that Southwell's poem "What Joy to Live?" – a *contrafactum* (that is, new words set to older music) – is based on Petrarch's "Pace non trovo" (*Rime*, no. 134), whose second line is "E temo e spero, et ardo e sono un ghiaccio."[25] Here we have the images of burning and freezing – "ardo" and "ghiaccio" – which appear not only in Southwell's *contrafactum* but also in "The Burning Babe." Southwell, however, is not simply interested in echoing love poetry to evoke the theme of love; in the latter poem, he is using the imagery to collapse the time frame of Christ's Nativity (when, historically, only the intention to redeem man existed) and his death, indicating that both acts proceed from the same love and the same will. Noteworthy is Southwell's separation of the experience of the extremes; instead of the lover burning and freezing, we have the soul freezing and the Christ Child consumed by fire: "In fierie heates I frie"; "Yet none approach" to "feele my fire, but I"; "My faultlesse breast the furnace is."

Southwell takes apart the oxymoron to make the fire of love and sacrifice normative; it is the freezing that is unnatural, though it is the natural world that seems to cause it and though the fire is supernatural. And it is the fire that peremptorily calls the speaker into the present, into awareness: "as now on fire I am / To worke them to their good." The "wounding thornes" that fuel the fire consuming the babe are present; they are not a vision of the future. His faultless breast is the furnace, even though the babe at the same time predicts a future dissolution. He is on fire "now," and now he is newborn.

In this poem Southwell fuses the language of sacrifice and the language of love to collapse the distance between God and man, in particular, to collapse the distance between man's temporal life and Christ's historical birth and death. The heat and fire that signify both love and violent death warm and light up the heart of the solitary speaker: "Surpris'd I was with sodaine heate / Which made my hart to glowe." The "fire" is "neere," and the fire is the Christ Child. The fire, a portent of dissolution, at the same time dissolves every distance between man and the newborn Christ Child: it is indeed "Christmasse day," the day of the Mass of Christ, and his heart glows with the infectious heat.

Southwell is drawing on ancient literary and theological associations between the infant Christ and the sacrifice of the Mass. These echoes come not only from the literature on Mary and on the virgin birth, but also from the language of prayer and submission to God as sacrifice from the scriptures: "My hart is become like wax, melting in the midst of my bowels" (Psalm 21:15, psalm for Good Friday); "Sacrifice and oblation thou didst not desire ... Burnt offering and sin offering thou didst not require: Then said I, Behold I come" (Psalm 39:7–8, psalm for Good Friday). Paul applies the latter psalm to Jesus: "Therfore comming into the world he [Jesus] saith: Host and oblation thou wouldest not: but a body hast fitted to me: Holocaustes and for sinne did not please thee. Then said I, Behold I come: in the head of the booke it is written of me: That I may doe thy wil O God" (Hebrews 10:5–7, reading from the Vigil of Candlemas). The infant's immolation in Southwell's poem is evocative of such biblical analogies between the coming of the Saviour and his self-offering.

In popular literature, the most obvious example of a text with the image of the Christ Child as sacrifice that was still familiar to the older Catholic families but coming under increasing fire from Protestant scholars like Elizabeth's tutor Roger Ascham was Malory's *Morte Darthur*.[26] The image therein of the fiery Christ Child emerging from the chalice at the summit of the Grail Quest also owes its existence to the typological associations I have been discussing. Southwell probably would have heard and read stories as well as sermons in his youth, and Ascham's own words attest to the unusual pre-eminence of the *Morte Darthur* in his generation. Of course, we are only speculating that Southwell might have known the story (or some version thereof), but clearly, the connection it makes between the immolated Christ and the babe of Bethlehem was not unusual. In a Catholic home, he would have heard the old Christmas songs, and as a youth in France and in Italy, he would have seen many works of art that would familiarize him with the ancient image, which remained popular on the Continent while it was more and more associated with an abominated religion in England.

Because of his education abroad, Southwell had many opportunities to learn of the image, not only in England but also and especially in Flanders, France, and Italy. A number of his poems, including "The Burning Babe," "New Heaven, New Warre," "Christs returne out of Egypt," "The Nativitie of Christ," and "His Circumcision," conjoin these sacrificial associations with the depiction of Christ's infancy, manifesting both characteristics of the collapse of time one can see in many medieval Nativity lyrics: the provocation of an intellectual response by means of theological paradox and the reliance on the emotional sting provided by the image of the suffering child.

Such Eucharistic imagery appears even more vividly in "Beholde the father, is his daughters sonne." This poem revels in its paradoxes and at the same time directs them toward a conclusion that unites Eucharistic and Nativity imagery in the participants' renewed humanity:

Beholde the father, is his daughters sonne:
The bird that built the nest, is hatched therein:
The olde of yeares, an hour hath not out runne:
Eternall life, to live doth now beginne.
The word is dumme: the mirth of heaven doth weepe:
Might feeble is: and force doth faintly creepe.

O dying soules, beholde your living spring:
O dasled eyes, behold your sonne of grace:
Dull eares, attend what word this word doth bring:
Up heavie hartes: with joye your joye embrace.
From death, from darke, from deafenesse, from dispaires:
This life, this light, this word, this joy repaires.

Gift better then himselfe, God doth not know:
Gift better then his God, no man can see:
This gift doth here the gever geven bestow:
Gift to this gift let each receiver bee.
God is my gift, himselfe he freely gave me:
Gods gift am I, and none but God shall have me.

Man altered was by sinne from man to beast:
Beastes foode is haye, haye is all mortall flesh:
Now God is flesh, and lies in Manger prest:
As haye, the brutest sinner to refresh.
O happie felde wherein this fodder grew,
Whose tast, doth us from beasts to men renew.[27]

Here Southwell employs his favourite rhetorical structures of paralleled antitheses, chiasmus, and anaphora and the image of the Eucharistic Christ Child to speak of the *renovatio* of man that accompanies the new age Christ's Incarnation initiates. By fashioning the traditional paradoxes into a poem whose momentum builds both in terms of rhythm and of the development of the images toward the saving reception of Christ in the Eucharist, Southwell melds rhetoric with content.

The first stanza deals with time and the manifestation of the Word in time: "Eternall life, to live doth now beginne." The first use of polyptoton (the use of multiple words with the same root) in the poem focuses our attention on this last line of the quatrain, summing up the mysteries relating to time and generation. The couplet works on the related concept of the limitation of the illimitable: Christ the Word is "dumme" (the literal translation of *infans*); Christ the wellspring of joy "doth weepe"; Christ the power of God is "feeble"; and, in the phrase that ends the stanza, Christ the all-powerful "doth faintly creep." In these images, Southwell presents the Christ Child almost as an abstraction: "life," "word," "mirth," "might," and "force." To end the stanza with the image of "force" crawling as a baby crawls, becoming a baby, is a finely planned reversal of the anti-incarnational tonalities of the language in this stanza. This sense of real, human babyhood significantly colours a poem that may not seem to bear much resemblance to the lullaby meditations we call affective poetry. In fact, while employing so overtly the rhetor's tools, whose visibility is generally considered in later poetry to be a sign of insincere emotion, Southwell carefully preserves a sense of the incarnational, fleshly aspect of the event.

This sense holds true even though the second stanza returns to the more imagistic nouns of "spring," "sonne," "word," and "joye," for even this stanza with its exploration of parallelism and assonance calls for hearts to "embrace" their "joye." The word "embrace" implies a physical action demonstrating closeness.

Southwell's use of parallelism in the second stanza, moreover, invites comment. The couplet in orderly fashion, using alliteration, repeats the conceit of the stanza point by point: Christ's birth is a freeing event – "From death, from darke, from deafenesse, from dispaires." Southwell speaks of the liberation of the senses, the rehabilitation of which is of course important to a follower of St. Ignatius, whose exercises centre very much on the evocation of sense experience and, through this evocation, interior change.[28]

The third stanza begins the heightened rhetoric that leads to the culminating line of the stanza and then to the final stanza. The play on the words "gift" and "God" is at the same time a move toward greater ornamenting by means of polyptoton and toward the most crucial point of the poem: we are alerted that we are "entering the sanctuary," so to speak, by the increase in decoration. As Brian Oxley says when discussing the relation between ornament and God the craftsman in Southwell's poetry, "Southwell's sense of the artifice of holy things, and indeed, of the holiness of artifice, is central to his life and work."[29] By the heightening of the rhetoric, our path is illuminated to the union of

God and man in the manger/altar. The poet moves by the use of *gradatio* from the acknowledgement that man has through sin followed his basest instincts to become a beast, to the image that evokes the mortality of the body – "hay is all mortal flesh," to the image of hay as food. It is a transforming food for this man/beast who, through God's taking on the very physicality that makes him part animal, is able to consume a "hay" that makes him a man once more. Christ who lies in the manger is also lying in a ciborium, already giving himself as food to the human beings whom the beasts gathered around the manger represent. Southwell is drawing on the traditional iconography of Nativity paintings; the beasts whose presence is not recorded in the gospels were often seen as representations of fallen man waiting to be restored to human life by the consumption of the body of Christ.[30]

This association of the child Jesus with the Eucharist would not only have been familiar to Southwell from the art he viewed while in Rome, but also as a student in Douai in 1576, and again when he returned from Paris in 1577 (he had been sent to Paris by his superiors because of the political unrest in Douai). He almost certainly knew of the famous *miracle du Saint-Sacrement*, which took place in Douai in 1254. A priest dropped the consecrated host, which then miraculously elevated itself and reposed on the corporal (a square white linen cloth upon which the chalice and the consecrated host are placed during Mass), at which time those assisting at the Mass saw it take on the form of the Christ Child. The host was preserved afterwards in one of the main churches of Douai; the fifteen-year-old Southwell may even have seen it. However, if Southwell did not witness the miracle first-hand, it is highly probable that he learned about the renowned transformation soon after his arrival. The atmosphere of religious controversy prevailing in the city makes it all the more likely that the miracle was under discussion in the years Southwell lived in Douai; in fact, the printed edition of the medieval text through which we learn of it came out in 1617, within a generation of his death.[31]

Southwell's childhood before his departure for the Continent took place in an England focused intently on the issue of where Christ's body was in the Eucharist, if anywhere, and in what way it could be present. Three hundred years before Southwell, the priest, philosopher, and Catholic reformer John Wycliff suggested a naturalistic approach to the question of the sacrament, which finds the miraculous absurd because it does not conform to human reason. In his *De Eucharistia*, Wycliff had claimed that "God could not annihilate time and space" in the Eucharist but had to maintain the natural distance between the moment of the crucifixion and the multitudinous celebrations of the Eucharist.[32]

In Southwell's England, this view was increasing in popularity, with its main arguments repeated by the great names of the Reformation, particularly John Calvin and Huldrych Zwingli. For the reformers, the distance in historical time of Christ's life on earth was a true impediment to the possibility of a corporeal Real Presence in the Eucharist. Even the Roman Catholic community, of which Southwell was a part in England, Douai, and Rome, held different views of the way Christ's body related to time and space.

Additionally, Southwell would have had access to Thomas Aquinas's discussions on the Eucharist, specifically his theory of concomitance, which can be seen as a foundation for the ancient relationship between the Eucharist and collapse of time. Aquinas reasons that the whole Christ is present in any particle or drop of either Eucharistic species. In other words, if a person receives only the host, by concomitance the blood of Christ is also present, although the communicant has not received the consecrated wine. If Christ is in any way really present, then he is entirely present. His being is one and therefore cannot be divided.[33]

A near contemporary of Southwell and the head of the Franciscans in Strasbourg, Kaspar Schatzgeyer, reiterated Aquinas's position that Christ is one indivisible body and dwelt on the collapse of time in the Eucharist. In 1525, Schatzgeyer stated:

> Christ, as the Apostle testifies, is the same yesterday, today, and for ever. Therefore, there is no past or future for Christ the head and his mystical body (which is the Church with all and each of its members). So the sacrifice of Christ on the cross was present to the Church under the Old Testament spiritually and virtually and by sure promise, and was represented by many pre-figurative sacrifices; and it is present to the Church under the New Testament by a commemoration and representation which is not merely figurative but real, in the Mass.[34]

During the Council of Trent, this belief influenced Schatzgeyer's contemporary, the famous Polish cardinal Stanislaus Hosius, who headed the discussions about the Mass and composed the decrees on the Eucharist.[35] Southwell would have been well versed in the documents of the council, and there is no doubt that he would have known of another difference between the Catholic apologists and the reformers during his lifetime.

Whereas the reformed versions of the Lord's Supper restricted the commemoration enacted in the Eucharist to the Passion, the Catholic Mass had from ancient times referred to the Incarnation and, in the offertory, to the Resurrection and Ascension of Christ.[36] A prayer invoking the Nativity is to be found in the *Book of Common Prayer*, but only on Christmas and during its Octave:

> **PROPRE PREFACES.**
>
> ¶ *Upon Christmas daye, and seven dayes after.*
>
> BECAUSE thou diddest geve Jesus Christ, thine onely sonne, to be borne as this daye for us, who by the operacion of the holy goste, was made very man, of the substaunce of the Virgin Mary his mother, and that without spot of synne, to make us cleane from al synne. Therefore, &c.[37]

The day of the Nativity is referred to as "this day," but the Incarnation is in the past tense, and the priest does not make contact with Jesus or speak to him. Ridley gives us a clear view of why the Incarnation no longer has as prominent a place in the reformed liturgy:

> But all things are here to be understood spiritually. For that heavenly Lamb is (as I confess) on the table; but by a spiritual presence, by grace, and not after any corporal substance of his flesh taken of the Virgin Mary. And indeed the same canon doth very plainly teach, that the bread which is set on the table is material bread.[38]

Such was the difference in the English liturgies of the late sixteenth century. Since the Sarum Use manual I cited in the previous chapter was last reprinted by the Jesuits in Douai in 1604, after Southwell's death, and the missal was in use among the seminary priests in exile as well as among recusants in England, it is not only probable Southwell himself was very familiar with the Sarum Rite (as well as the Roman) but also that he celebrated Mass mostly in that use.

It is with such distinctive attitudes toward time, sacrifice, and eternity in mind that Southwell can write "His Circumcision." Although the Feast of the Circumcision was commemorated in the *Book of Common Prayer* and thus formed part of the liturgical cycle of the Elizabethan Church, Southwell clearly associates the shedding of Christ's blood with his salvific sacrifice on the cross, whereas the *Book of Common Prayer* speaks of Christ's obedience and asks that the congregation be granted "true circumcision of the Spirit."[39] Without the title, in fact, it would be difficult to judge that Southwell's poem commemorated the occasion of Jesus's presentation in the Temple rather than his Passion: "The head is launst to worke the bodies cure, / With angring salve it smarts to heal our wound."[40] Only the delicately worded phrase "blood runnes from wounded place" and the detail of the knife ("The knife that cut his flesh did pierce [Mary's] heart") assure us that this suffering is taking place in Christ's infancy. Southwell sets the first two stanzas in the present tense, which in some way is already taking us out of the temporal framework of history, but the shift into the past tense in the last stanza does not seem sufficient to create a confusion of tenses. Without relying solely on this specific technique to collapse time (which Milton uses, for instance, in his "On the Morning of Christ's Nativity"), Southwell still introduces sacramental time into the poem. How does he do it?

Southwell collapses the Presentation with the Passion by five different means: He depicts the rabbis performing the circumcision as the Roman soldiers who scourged Christ before he received the death sentence: "To faultlesse sonne from all offences pure / The faulty vassals scourges do redound." He speaks of the pain and bloodletting of the circumcision as redemptive: "The vein of life distilleth drops of grace." He also speaks of it as sacrificial and as Eucharistic: "This sacred dew let angels gather up, / Such dainty drops best fit their nectared cup." The image of the cup to gather blood recalls medieval and Renaissance depictions of the Church in the form of a woman or an angel using a chalice to gather the blood of Jesus as it flows from his pierced side. Southwell also recalls Simeon's prophecy of Mary's compassionate suffering at the death of her Son, a prophecy made at the Presentation in the Temple:

With weeping eies his mother rewd his smart,
If blood from him, teares ran from her as fast,
The knife that cut his flesh did pierce her heart,
The paine that Jesus felt did *Mary* taste,
His life and hers hung by one fatall twist,
No blow that hit the sonne the mother mist.

The fifth means is another collapse of time operating concomitantly: Southwell conflates the Feast of the Circumcision, 1 January, with the Feast of the Presentation in the Temple, 2 February (both observed in the Sarum Use and the former in the *Book of Common Prayer*).

Southwell ties the concepts of Eucharist and collapse of time and space together in his Thomistic meditation, "Of the Blessed Sacrament of the Aulter." This poem does not speak of the Nativity, but is based in some part on the translations Southwell had put into verse of St. Thomas's Corpus Christi hymns, "Lauda Sion" and "Tantum ergo Sacramentum," and, indeed, on the office for the day composed by Aquinas.[41]

In the last five stanzas, Southwell in effect exfoliates Aquinas's question about the multiplicity of hosts. The mystery of the presence of the body and divinity of Christ in the small host is seen refracted through the not-quite-sufficient analogues of God's omnipresence, the non-localization of the soul, and so forth. The closing lines, despite their undramatic and teacherly tone, effectively encapsulate the theme of the whole poem and the nature of the mystery: the miracles of the wedding at Cana and of Moses's staff to which Southwell refers would have been accepted by Protestant and Catholic alike as historical occurrences. By alluding to the wedding at Cana and the miracle performed before Pharaoh's magicians without invoking exegesis, Southwell sets in motion an intellectual process that expands outside the bounds of the poem. The miracles are mentioned with the historical rather than the moral, anagogical, or allegorical interpretation. Invoking the historical sense of the miraculous, Southwell flies in the face of the most popular, Wycliffite argument against the doctrine of transubstantiation: that it ludicrously twists the merely symbolic sense of Christ's words of consecration into a historical or literal sense. And yet the two miracles mentioned have a further significance: from at least the patristic period onward, Christ's miraculous transformation of water into wine was seen as a prefiguration of the later changing of wine into blood. Additionally, the transformation of Moses's staff into a snake that eats the serpents Pharaoh's magicians conjured was explained by Theodore the Studite and other commentators as a prefigurement of Christ's death on the cross swallowing up death itself.[42] Southwell does not mention the exegetical valences of the miracles; in a poem on the Eucharist he need not – they are understood by virtue of being used in his summation. The last stanza declares that this Eucharistic poem stands firmly within the non-symbolic tradition and, at the same time, demands of its audience a logical working through of the problem of the miraculous and its connection with the Eucharist and the Redemption. Of the varieties of collapse of time and space in such poetry, the Eucharist forms the nexus.

Southwell's knowledge of Aquinas (and not merely Aquinas) on this point translates for the poet into an ability to present visionary or miraculous occurrences as historical; time is conflated, but not deleted. The suffering is real, not symbolic. "The Burning Babe," "The Nativitie," and "His Circumcision" do not contain the cryptographic combination of details that characterize the ahistorical landscape of emblems or the emblem poems. The choice of non-symbolic language reflects Southwell's interest in accessibility as well as his theological position on the sacrament.

The Warrior Babe

Southwell is clearly thinking about the way cotemporalizing infancy and the Passion can produce a sense of presence in other poems as well. Another image that creates the same effect dominates in "This Little Babe so few Dayes Olde" (or "New Heaven, New Warre": some scholars consider the two poems one).[43] The power Christ exhibits in his death and resurrection is evident even at the moment of his birth; as a baby, he musters his troops and fights evil actively. Here Southwell draws on the tradition of representing Christ as a warrior going to his death and victory but applies it to the Nativity. This application has ancient precedents. Athanasius (AD 295–373) quotes from Isaiah 8:4: "Before the child knows how to cry 'father' or 'mother,' he will take the power of Damascus and the booty of Samaria in front of the king of Assyria"; and in a later section of this discourse (36) he says: "Who then is there who almost before his birth was reigning and despoiling his enemies?"[44] Even earlier than Athanasius, commentators and liturgists applied the source of this image, Book of Wisdom 18, to the Incarnation and to Christmas. In fact, it was and is used in the Christmas liturgy:

> For while al thinges were in qviet silence
> and the night was in the midst of her covrse,
> Thy almighty word leapt down from heauen
> from thy royal throne, as a fierce conqveror
> into the midst of the land of destrvction.
> WITH a sharp sword carrying thy vnfeigned commandment.
> … and standing on the earth reached euen to heauen. (Wisdom 18:14–16)

The image was also popular throughout the Middle Ages: Langland, for instance, says in *Piers Plowman* that the Christ Child was ready to have "yfoughte with the fend" in his infancy;[45] the fourteenth-century lyric "Somer is comen and winter gon" asserts that the Christ Child is "milde and wlonk [splendid] / and eke of grete munde [might]" and that "he brak the bond / That was so strong / Wit wunde."[46] So the tradition of Christ the warrior babe is well over 1400 years old when Southwell writes his famous treatment of it, "This Little Babe so few Dayes Olde."[47]

This poem emphasizes the closeness of the Nativity to the Passion and the Harrowing of Hell in terms of its redemptive value. Here Christ's victory over death is already beginning to take effect: "All hell doth at his presence quake." These words recall the earthquake that the gospel records as occurring at the times of Christ's death and his resurrection (Matthew 27:54; 28:2), as well as the Harrowing of Hell familiar to us from the apocryphal Gospel of Nicodemus, the cycle plays, *Piers Plowman*, Dunbar's "Done is a Battell on the Dragon Blak," and many other works. Without details of the Passion or overt Eucharistic references, the poem does not present us with a Christ Child suffering the wounds of the crucifixion, but it does present him as suffering and yet sure of victory: "And thus as sure his foe to wound, / The Angells trumps alarum sound." The angelic Gloria is not so much an announcement of his birth as a triumphant declaration of the imminent defeat of the enemy – death or sin. It is by associating the moment of Jesus's birth with redemptive suffering and the victory over sin that the poet begins to play with historical time. Southwell hovers between writing a "prophetic" poem and a poem that collapses time itself. That Jesus will surprise the gates of hell is a statement about the future, but that he wins the field with his tears, that he is at the moment using his naked breast as a shield – these actions are in the present. The building sense of rushing movement seems to whirl around the reader and impel them toward the moment of possible union "within his crib."

We find an analogous description of Christ's incarnation in Ephrem's "Sermon on Our Lord": "Death could not devour our Lord unless he possessed a body, neither could hell swallow him up unless he bore our flesh; and so he came in search of a chariot in which to ride to the underworld. This chariot was the body which he received from the Virgin; in it he invaded death's fortress, broke upon its strongroom and scattered all its treasure."[48] In this image, as in Southwell's, the body itself is the weapon Christ uses to invade his enemy's territory and seize back what is his own. I scarcely need to point out the other important parallel: the juxtaposition of the Incarnation and the Harrowing of Hell. Within this framework, Ephrem's text adopts Eucharistic implications. The consumption of Jesus's body, as Paul says in the First Epistle to the Corinthians (11:27–9), brings life or death to the one consuming: "Therfore whosoeuer shal eate this bread or drinke the chalice of our Lord vnworthily, he shal be guilty of the body and of the bloud of our Lord. But let a man proue him self: and so, let him eate of that bread, and drinke of the chalice. For he that eateth and drinketh vnworthily: eateth and drinketh iudgement to him self, not discerning the body of our Lord." In the case of death itself, consuming life causes death to explode.

If Southwell is drawing on this specific tradition, which seems likely, then the crib that is the surest ward against the enemy can be read as the altar of the Eucharistic sacrifice. The crib as trench may indeed signify this reading: the word that means a ditch dug as a defence against the enemy could be a pun on the word "trencher," the carved-out wooden dish in which bread was dipped at meals. Southwell might also have known the derivation of the word was from the French "tranche," or "slice, piece." This line of thinking is perhaps little more than speculation, but the ubiquity of the manger/altar image makes it very possible that Southwell was aware of the overtones in the specific lexis he chose for the poem.

Southwell uses other techniques to collapse time in this poem. The final stanza is an urgent call to immediate response, maintaining the sense of careering forward that Southwell has given the poem by using enjambment and ellipsis, along with numerous strong and vigorous verbs, especially in stanza two's military action. By making this battle something that happens in the present, by making the warrior the infant Christ, Southwell collapses the temporal distance between Christ's birth and the Triduum (the three-day celebration of the Passion and Resurrection), between the first century and the moment in which the reader reads the poem.

That Southwell wrote such poems at that particular moment in history may seem to us an uninteresting exercise in conservatism. The significance for his society of the warrior babe, the child on the altar, the child being immolated was ceasing to be conventional, however, and thereby gained in significance.

When Southwell writes about the arming of Christ in *An Epistle of Comfort*, Third Cause, we hear echoes of "New Heaven, New Warre":

> Aman a most ambitious and haughtye mynded man, thought it the greatest honour that a prince coulde doe to his subiect, to make him ryde on his owne palfrey, attyred in his most royall and statelye robes. If therfore tribulation be the most precious garment that Christ did weare, and the Crosse his palfrey, we are greately honoured, whyle he aduanceth vs to the same prerogatiues ... Christes cloutes comfort not those that walk in robes, the stable and maunger comforte not those, that loue the highest roomes in the sinagoges ... Let vs looke on the sacred coate, not of our sonne, but of our father & redeemer, of whose humanitye it is sayde ... Why is thy garment redd, and thy apparell lyke theirs, that tread in the winepresse: and who is this that cometh from Edome with stayned attyre? Let vs cast our eyes vpon this cote, dyed in his owne innocente bloode.[49]

The garment Christ put on in the manger, in the stable, is his flesh. This tradition has been well documented. Theresa Coletti has traced the image of Christ making a tunic – that is, a body – for himself from the Virgin Mary through the Holy Spirit to, among others, the sermons of

Anthony of Padua, the *Stanzaic Life of Christ*, and the Towneley Cycle's *Crucifixion*. Coletti maintains that the image of the Virgin Mary weaving is an image of both the Incarnation and the Passion because it suggests both the swaddling clothes of the infant Christ and the *tunica inconsutilis*, the seamless garment for which the Roman soldiers cast lots.[50] Rosemary Woolf has noted that, in the tradition of Christ as the lover-knight, his "aketoun," or battle-tunic, was "the human flesh which the virgin gave him in her womb."[51] Leo Steinberg has more recently spoken about the idea of the body as a garment, which he finds in a homily by the ninth-century bishop of Constantinople, Photius, but of course Photius was deriving it from much older authors.[52]

The Incarnation is thus the taking on of the bloody garment, the readying for battle. But so is the beginning of the Passion, the Last Supper:

> Remember howe often you haue bene with Christe at his Supper, and reasone nowe requireth you shold folowe him to *Gethsemanie* not to sleepe with *S. Peeter*, but with him to sweate bloode. Your lyfe is a warfare your weapons, patience, your Captayne Christe, your standerd the Crosse. Now is the larum sounded, and the warre proclaymed, dye you must, to winn the fielde.[53]

Southwell here repeats in measured prose the logic of "New Heaven, New Warre" in his chapter on the Tenth Cause of Comfort. " With Christ join thou in fight," he urges his soul in the former; in the latter he tells his correspondent, Philip Howard: "Let us carry the shield of faith to repair us from our enemy's shot."[54]

> The souldiers of Christ are most honourable, not, when they liue in deyntynesse, pompe, and maiestye, not when they murder impiously, cruelly and brutishly: But when they suffer, humblye, stoutly, and patientlye in his quarell ... So lett them [our adversaries] drawe vs vppon hurdles, hange vs, vnbowel vs alyue, mangle vs, boyle vs, and sett our quarters upon their gates, to be meate for the byrdes of the ayre, as they vse to handle rebels: we wil aunswere them, as the Christians of former persecutions haue done ... Such is the manner of our victorye, such our conquerous garment, in such chariotes doe we triumph. What maruayle therefore if our vanquished enemyes mislyke vs.[55]

Southwell returns to the image of the body itself as a weapon or armament when he refers to John Chrysostom's comparison of martyrs' bodies to the emperor's own armour.[56] The interrelation between martyrdom – the use of one's own body as the armour of Christ – and the

Passion is explicit. It is, moreover, related to the Last Supper, which Southwell refers to as an event at which the audience has been present. Again, the Eucharist is seen as the point where all times converge, the point at which imitation of Christ the warrior becomes possible.

Southwell is doing more in his Nativity poems than linking a martyr's death to the death of Christ. The image of the sacrificed Christ Child, the sacrifice to be consumed, was a reminder of his divinity and of his representation of eternity in the midst of the *saeculum*. As England moved toward the Enlightenment and away from the Roman Catholic view of the presence of the body of Christ in contemporary time, "rational" or "historical" time would come close to having sole authority in the imagination of the country's religious poets. But for Robert Southwell, the image of the Proleptic Passion was inextricably linked with his longing for eternity. In the image of the burning babe, of the warrior babe, he promoted the fundamental Christian connection between love and sacrifice, and declared his belief that the shivering child in a manger was in fact the Lord of the universe, who had all power and authority. He saw firm intention and command in the plaintive face and victory on the wounded brow.

Chapter Three

"Kisse Him, and with Him into Egypt Goe": John Donne and the Christ Child of "Nativitie"

Eternity is not an everlasting flux of *Tyme;* but *Tyme* is a short *parenthesis* in a longe *period*.

John Donne[1]

La Corona and the Incarnation

Like Robert Southwell, John Donne is also interested in the poet's power to create a sense of presence through prolepsis in his poems on the Christ Child. These poems occur in the sequence known as *La Corona,* a group of seven sonnets thought to have been written before Donne's conversion to Protestantism but presented in July 1607 to a Protestant patroness, Lady Magdalen Herbert, mother of George Herbert. Although time and its relationship to eternity was a preoccupation throughout his poetic career, Donne can be seen to treat temporal conflation in a particular way in his poems that deal with the Incarnation. He shows himself to be aware of the usefulness of liturgical time as well as the historical present; but in all these works Donne exploits some of the attributes of sacramental time, that is, time collapsed by virtue of actual contact with the eternal perspective of the incarnate deity.[2]

Constance Furey has written of the "relational dynamic" in Donne's (and Herbert's) poems.[3] She discusses, in regard to this dynamic, Ryan Netzley's and Regina Schwartz's locating Donne's expression of desire for union in a verbal performance meant to mimic Eucharistic presence.[4] As I have said earlier, Eucharistic presence is not a clear, unequivocal concept in Donne's day. Although her work focuses on Donne's later religious poems, Judith Anderson negotiates between an apophatic and kataphatic understanding of how God attains this union with the speaker. She points to the way Donne interprets Calvin's rhetoric of ascent and descent so that language becomes a medium of "exchange of value" between what goes up to God and what comes down from him.[5] I argue that, in addition, Donne negotiates between Christ's bodily presence and his present absence by imagining himself as a contemporary of the Holy Family, mediating his own wish to kiss the Christ Child through Joseph's paternal physical closeness to the babe.[6]

The intensified sense of physical presence that we find in "Nativitie" leads to the most intimate expression of closeness with the Christ Child, a kiss. Donne allows the speaker access to the moment in sacred history by means of Joseph's presence as interlocutor and substitute. In the Nativity sonnet of the *La Corona* sequence, John Donne continues the task we have seen Robert Southwell undertaking: to investigate the question of who the Christ Child is and how he may be represented poetically. Like Southwell, Donne will eschew apocryphal representations from folklore and popular tradition; and like Southwell, Donne will end up creating his own legend of the Christ Child. Unexpectedly, however, Donne will make use of the recently popular Counter-Reformation cult of St. Joseph to do so. Before proceeding to the sonnet itself, let us consider its place in the *La Corona* sonnet sequence.

Of the affinities between Southwell's and Donne's works, none is perhaps more marked than the common love for the paradoxes associated with the Incarnation of Christ. *La Corona* is a sequence of seven sonnets unified, in part, by its attention to those paradoxes. As already noted, Donne probably wrote it before his conversion to the Anglican Church, although that is not certain. Nonetheless, the sequence has often been relegated to the position of inferior or early work, as Helen Gardner already noted in her brief defense of *La Corona* in the early 1960s.[7] The single most important reason previous scholars have dismissed the *La Corona* sonnets as inferior to the later Holy Sonnets seems to be the sense that the poems in this circular grouping are more conventional, less personal than the other Holy Sonnets, a reaction most modern readers would share. J.B. Leishman lamented: "His [Donne's] attitude, whatever it may actually have been, appears in these poems strangely external and detached. He seems, as it were, to be trying to stimulate his faith by means of his intellect, trying to make himself feel the reality of these mysteries and paradoxes by displaying them to himself under as many aspects as he can."[8]

Leishman is looking for sincere emotion in *La Corona* and not finding it. This articulation of the modern reader's problem with the sonnets is helpful: Leishman's disappointment with stimulating "faith by means of the intellect" and with the speaker's making "himself feel the reality of these mysteries" reminds the reader to consider our cultural distance from Donne. Donne might not himself have found such attempts in the least problematic or in any way imagined the charge of insincerity. These phrases may represent exactly what the poet intends to do, for "Nativitie" and "Temple" are poems in which Donne attempts a mimesis of presence and a representation of both the eternal and temporal aspects of the incarnate Christ Child.

La Corona does not stop there, of course: the speaker crying "Lo!" in "Crucifying" and "Behold" in "Ascension" is pointing to something going on as he speaks, directing the reader's attention to Christ on the Cross, like John the Baptist in the Isenheim Altarpiece, or to the ascending Christ, as radiant clouds part above his head, like the dumbfounded apostles in Raphael's *Ascension*. For the speaker, these events are not in the past – and the Last Judgment is not in the future, conflated as it is with his own personal moment before God's judgment as he offers his *Corona* to God as a testament to his "Muse's white sincerity." And one could argue that the most intense sense of presence or identification with a sacred event occurs in Holy Sonnet XI, "Spit in my face, you Jewes," which borrows some language from *La Corona* ("God clothed himself in vile man's flesh, that so / He might be weak enough to suffer woe") but appears to be speaking *in persona Christi* in its initial line. Nonetheless, the sonnets on the Christ Child merit a separate consideration because they demonstrate that Donne's belief in the Incarnation underlies his evocation of the eternal in his poems about Christ.

In "Nativitie" in particular, Donne presents the Christ Child as an object of love, establishing an important and so far unrecognized register in his poetic voice, a language of tenderness.[9] The effect in this sonnet results in part from Donne's attention to ways to demonstrate his participation in God's communicability. Jeffrey Johnson has argued convincingly that Donne views the Incarnation as God's best means of creating the kind of unity God always desires; even the Trinity keeps the one God from being singular, to use Donne's term.[10] Johnson cites a 1624 sermon to the Earl of Exeter:

> And still our large, and our Communicable God, affected this association so, as that having *three Persons* in himselfe, and having *Creatures* of divers natures, and having collected all natures in *man*, who consisted of a spirituall nature, as well as a bodily, he would have one liker himselfe, than man was; And therefore he made *Christ*, God and Man, in one person, Creature and Creator together.[11]

Donne thinks of Christ's Incarnation, quite traditionally, as the means by which God creates a link between his image on earth, mankind, and himself. Donne has many ways of poetically representing this linkage, this function that Christ performs. In the *La Corona* sonnets, and in particular in "Nativitie," the poem that is the focus of this chapter, he emphasizes the seemingly self-contradictory mysteries of the Incarnation. He deliberately confuses pronoun references, and the speaker speaks to and identifies emotionally with Mary, Joseph, and Christ himself. Donne's purpose here is not to investigate his own doubts, as he does elsewhere, but to show his participation in the life of God as a Christian: the "crown of prayer and praise" is about unity, not anxiety.

Donne's interest in portraying oneness extends to the immediacy with which he has the events in Christ's life occur before the speaker: he consistently draws us into an atemporal world where the birth and passion of Christ have not yet happened, but yet are happening now before our very eyes. Moreover, he invites the reader to become one with him, adding yet another layer to the manifold conflations. In arranging his material in this way, Donne shows that he is not restricted to metaphors of union but is interested in "performing" it. Barbara Lewalski numbered the *La Corona* sonnets among Donne's works that employ Catholic meditative practices rather than Protestant because the "power of the imagination and analysis ... focus upon a scene or personage ... until the affections are moved to appropriate response and active participation."[12] This technique may be true of all the sonnets in *La Corona* to differing degrees, but is especially and specifically true of "Nativitie."

"Immensitie Cloysterd in Thy Deare Wombe" or "Nativitie"

The poem "Nativitie" is the third in the *La Corona* sequence, following "Deign at my hands this crown of prayer and praise" ("La Corona") and "Salvation to all that will is nigh" ("Annunciation"). Donne deliberately loads this particular sonnet with techniques representing and creating unity. Such a decision on his part is not surprising: as Leo the Great had pointed out centuries earlier,[13] the grace of union is *the* gift of the Incarnation, and it is the source of every other grace. Donne also encourages an affective intimacy between the reader and the Christ Child, attempting to make the newborn child present to his audience. He does so by emphasizing not only God's stooping to man, but also man's movement toward God:

> *Immensitie cloysterd in thy deare wombe,*[14]
> Now leaves his welbelov'd imprisonment.[15]
> There he hath made himselfe to his intent
> Weake enough, now into our world to come;

But Oh, for thee, for him, hath th'Inne no roome?
Yet lay him in this stall, and from the Orient,
Starres, and wisemen will travell to prevent
Th'effect of *Herods* jealous generall doome.
Seest thou, my Soule, with thy faiths eyes, how he
Which fils all place, yet none holds him, doth lye?
Was not his pity towards thee wondrous high,
That would have need to be pittied by thee?
Kisse him, and with him into Egypt goe,
With his kinde Mother, who partakes thy woe.[16]

In a poem on the Incarnation, we might expect the addressee to be the Christ Child himself, but Donne eschews this obvious strategy in favour of continuing his address to the Virgin Mary from the previous sonnet, "Annunciation." The confusion of pronoun reference, however, is perhaps more marked here than in any of Donne's lyrics: thy, his, he, himselfe, his, our, thee, him, him; thou, my, thy, he, him, his, thee, thee, him, him, his, thy: twenty per cent of the poem is made up of pronouns, simply pronouns. And to whom do they refer? As just mentioned, the addressee of the poem, following the "Annunciation," is the Virgin Mary, at first, and yet only two of the seven references to the second person singular clearly refer to her. The next four instances refer almost certainly to the speaker's soul, and yet, when we arrive at the end of the sonnet, it is impossible that his soul should kiss the Christ Child except in some kind of mystical fashion. If we read further to the next sonnet, "Temple," or "With his kinde mother, who partakes thy woe, *Joseph* turne back," we realize that the partaker of woe at the end of the poem is none other than Joseph. But how did "thou" turn into him? The pronoun references can confound readers: Elizabeth Hodgson actually deletes Joseph from her reading of "Nativitie" to assert that the speaker is merging with the feminine persona of Mary, but in doing so she misrepresents Donne's structuring of the poem. She asserts: "The merging of Mary and the poet's soul throughout this poem builds on the identities of the speaker/poet and Mary in the previous sonnet, and precipitates the moment at which the two human-creators join forces as the 'soul' appears at Mary's side and thus enters, is born into, the world he has been imagining." In attributing the final kiss to Mary, who appears in the same sentence in the prepositional phrase "with his kinde mother," Hodgson does violence to Donne's syntax and his meaning.[17]

Recently critics have focused a great deal on Donne's complex syntax with a view to a kind of deconstructive reading. Ryan Netzley, for instance, claims that Donne's ambiguous grammar drives "readers to focus not on what the poem means, but the syntactical, structural, grammatical, even possessive relations that obtain within it."[18] However, Donne attempts to achieve an effect systematically through such deployments of rhetorical strategy, even in works originally presented orally where meditation upon syntax might not be possible: his sermons. Eiléan Ní Chuilleanáin has shown that Donne uses precisely this technique of pronoun confusion in his sermons to conflate himself with his audience – with unity in mind.[19]

Donne's end of unity brings us back to the rhetorical aims of this pronoun confusion. In "Nativitie," the profusion of pronouns revolves around the trope of apostrophe, that poetic technique employed to address the absent, the inanimate, or the dead. By speaking to Mary first and foremost, Donne follows a very ancient tradition of identifying with and appealing to Christ's mother for a closer intimacy with Christ himself. Moreover, by addressing the Virgin, he violates a prime principle of Tyndalian and Calvinist Christianity. Calvin had remarked of the (to him) preposterous Catholic usage of the angelic salutation in their prayers: "Their silly ambition leads them into a second blunder, for they salute a person who is absent."[20] For Calvin those persons who are in heaven are always absent from those who still dwell on earth. There can be no closeness with the saints, no intimate colloquies. This view was shared by Tyndale.[21] Richard Hooker offered a softer approach in *Of the Laws of Ecclesiastical Polity*: "Notwithstanding thus much we know even of Saints in heaven, that they pray. And therefore prayer being a work common to the church as well triumphant as militant, a work common unto men with Angels, what should we think that but that so much of our lives is celestial and divine as we spend in the exercise of prayer?"[22] Yet Anglican usage was divided, and the Thirty-Nine Articles eventually forbade prayer to the saints. Moreover, as Itrat H'usain pointed out, in 1630 Donne publicly condemns prayer to the saints in heaven: "Though they have a more personall and experimentall sense of our miseries than Angels have, we must not relie upon the prayers of Saints."[23] If the composition of *La Corona* predates Donne's abandonment of the Catholic Church, there is no problem, but if it does not, we must nonetheless concede that apostrophe is not prayer and that Donne publicly commends the saints in his sermons and even preaches about them on the feasts of All Saints, although he considers turning to them for help to be idolatry.

In what way and for what reason, then, does he speak to Mary? Unlike many medieval poems on the Nativity, Donne's sonnet is not a prayer at all; it is, rather, an announcement of the event followed by an intimate and direct comment on it, not to the reader at first, but to Mary and Joseph. Donne is not asking for Mary's intercession; he is speaking to her as if she were before him, needing to understand the events befalling her the night of Christ's birth.[24]

Mary is not invoked for her aid, but as an object of the speaker's solicitous love. He manifests an ethos of tenderness and sympathy in the phrases "thy deare wombe," "welbelov'd imprisonment," "for thee, for him, hath th'inne no roome?" as well as indicating the tenderness and closeness of the relationship between mother and Son, a closeness he appears to adopt. He is perhaps also thinking of the likeness between Mary and all mothers, or Christ and all children, in the paradox of the womb being a "wellbelov'd imprisonment": as he says in Sermon IX of 1619, "Wee are all conceived in close Prison; in our Mothers wombes, we are close Prisoners all."[25] In *La Corona*, Donne's point is not the human inheritance of sin and suffering, except tangentially, as the motivation inducing the Christ Child to execute his plan. He needs to tell Mary about that plan, which leads him to place himself by her side, commenting on the events of Christmas Eve. This stance is a kind of immediacy, of entering into the gospel story, that even Southwell does not imagine, however close he is to the Christ Child in his Nativity poems.

Exclaiming "But Oh, for thee, for him, hath th'inne no roome?" Donne arrives at the apex of the poem's emotional trajectory; the use of multiple caesurae and the interjection "oh," as well as the asyndeton, indicate real agitation in the speaker. His dismay is a reaction of surprise as well, and we find ourselves in the "now" of the second and fourth lines, as if Donne has only just realized that Christ is in a stable, not a traveller's lodging place. However, Donne's play with pronouns does not stop here. By calling the world "our world" when speaking to Mary, he includes her as well as Christ in the bond of humanity: "There he hath made himselfe to his intent / Weake enough, now into our world to come." Donne explicitly ascribes "intent" to the babe in the womb as the second person of the Trinity who exercises his divine power to weaken that power.[26] Christ's life in the womb of course is an even greater mystery than his hidden years in Nazareth, and Donne is drawing on well-established tradition in indicating that Christ has not renounced one iota of divine omniscience in becoming incarnate. In fact, this aspect of the poem is worthy of more extensive comment, since it partakes of a tradition that saw Christ as starting out in Mary's womb perfectly formed, without need of passage from embryo to fetus.[27] Christ is in control; he knows just how long it will take himself to become weak enough. Reversing the biological path of development until whole and strong enough for birth, this fetal Christ is reducing himself until he can accomplish his mission to suffer and die. The speaker recognizes that we live in a world that cannot hold God in his power – that he must diminish himself for the purpose of saving man; however, the additional point Donne makes is that it is *our* world, the speaker's, Mary's, Christ's, and, in an at first almost unnoticeable move outward, the reader's. Remarkably, the many layers of address and perspective are almost all there by the end of the first quatrain.

The sense of immediacy produced by direct address to Mary and to us deepens and then dissipates somewhat in the second stanza. The speaker maintains his solicitous demeanor with his direct command to the Virgin Mother to lay the Christ Child in the stall, as if it were *his* solution to the Holy Family's predicament and they were in need of his directions. The speaker's relationship with the Virgin seems less protective, however, when we consider he is asking her to accept the frightening vulnerability of her child's position – after all, she is to lay him in the stall simply to await the unfolding of events that might imperil his life.

The speaker turns his attention to this peril: when Mary lays the Christ Child down, the Wise Men and the mystic star[28] will arrive, and they will keep the terrible consequences of Herod's decree from affecting the infant: "Starres and wisemen will travell to prevent / Th'effect of *Herods* jealous generall doome." At this moment, the physical picture the speaker is imagining seems to fade somewhat, and the immediacy diminishes. The relationship between the "I" and "thou" disappears as third-person narrative dominates. The "prophetic" voice of the poet tells Mary what will happen, but begins to seem as if he is merely telling us. Mary fades out, and the speaker advances.

It is at this point that Donne's address turns inward, and he commands his own soul to respond to the sight of Mary laying the Christ Child in the manger. His last command was to Mary herself, however, so the new "thou" seems almost as if it could be she and not he. The specificity of the word "thou" begins to melt away. By the end of the poem, the familiar pronoun has been used to speak to Mary, the poet's soul, the reader, and Joseph. The unclear distinctions between the addresses have the effect of drawing two of those "thou's," the soul and the reader, into union with the others. The Holy Family no longer seems a distant or even separate entity, but has melded, now indistinguishable, into the "I" that is never an "I" in the poem. And this union is a union of love, for in the couplet the addressee must show love in the most immediate and physical way ("Kisse him") and act upon it in haste ("with him into Egypt goe"), joined with the family ("with his kinde Mother") who share "thy woe."

Confounding the pronoun antecedent also confounds the meaning of this "woe." Whose woe is it that Mary partakes? Christ's? Donne's? The reader's? Joseph's? The answer is, finally, all four; Donne intentionally crafts the work to create multivalence. It is left to the reader to deduce that Mary, in union with Christ in his humility, shares in the sorrows of his poverty and sacrifice; in union with Donne and the reader in their position as children of God, she shares in their sorrow at the predicament into which God's love for them has led him; she certainly, in union with Joseph as a guardian of the Christ Child, shares in his grief and anxiety at the departure from their homeland and, in the next sonnet, in the loss of the young Jesus in Jerusalem. The obliqueness of the speaker's references forces the reader to think of the possible allusions, yet another way of engaging the reader in the poem.

We might also note that the speaker's identity at the end of the poem may be merging with that of the angel who warned Joseph in a dream to take the child and his mother to Egypt (Matthew 2:13). The tone of the command and, of course, its content make it likely that Donne is thinking of precisely that event and inserting himself into it, which makes the poem take on some of the qualities of a vision.

At this point we encounter the potential problem, for a reformed writer at least, with the composition of a poem on a biblical subject, however carefully the poet might have avoided praying to the persons named within it. Such a poem almost inevitably engages in a process similar to what Evelyn Birge Vitz has called apocryphogenesis – the creation of apocrypha from the canonical texts of the Bible.[29] Donne is creating a new gospel story of the moment when John Donne, poetic persona or admonitory angel, intervened on behalf of the Holy Family and advised Joseph to depart into Egypt. One detail above all cannot be found in scripture, and that is the direction for Joseph, the speaker's soul, or the reader to kiss the child. Reformation as well as Counter-Reformation writers, at least those trained for the priesthood, knew about the early medieval Gelasian decree concerning the Apocryphal Gospels and the more recent decrees of the Council of Trent on appropriate subjects for representation (1563). Both sideline the apocrypha, and almost all the traditional stories about Christ's childhood and fables about the flight into Egypt come from apocryphal texts. The mysterious silences of Luke on these matters somehow seem to invite readers' curiosity to know more and thus the poets' later imaginative expansion of them. Donne is aware of this dynamic in a sermon, as he himself says of God's providential provision even in the Apocrypha of the Catholic Bible of the knowledge of his destructive punitive power: "And because God foresaw, that mens curiosities would carry them upon Apocryphal books also, it is repeated in almost every book of that kinde, in Ecclesiasticus, in Tobit, in the Maccabees."[30] In other words, God makes sure his message about his ability to punish sinners is included even in those non-canonical books that men will read because they are curious (*curiositas* not being a virtue, however, in Donne's time). Donne, in contradistinction to his homiletic pronouncements (but in keeping with his homiletic practice, we might add), expands the biblical narrative from the Gospels of Luke and Matthew. In "Nativitie," these additions consist of personal interaction and displays of affection.

The address of the poem gathers all the paradoxes Donne emphasizes into one intimate society. This society is a Holy Family, which extends beyond its centre, God, to embrace Mary and Joseph, and beyond them also to embrace Donne. With Donne are included all those who respond to the invitation of the lowliness of the Nativity to give their love to the God who has made himself weak enough to "need to be pittied." God creates this need so that he may accept the same sort of compassionate love he gives to his children and so that the audience may be urged to go with him wherever he goes (Revelation 14:4), although the "star fades, and the brilliance turns to shadow."[31] In choosing the dramatic voice he does, with its ethos of anxious tenderness, Donne seeks to enact the effect God sought: he would "have need to be pittied by thee." The reader is not just to feel pity, but also to put his devotion into action: "with him into Egypt goe." Donne's poetic additions to the biblical text are not a festooning of the infancy narrative with description or ornate language; rather, he intensifies the sense of the narrator and the reader as present at the side of the Christ Child, as close as Joseph and Mary.

Donne might have proceeded in this way without a literary or meditative model to guide him, but it is probable he had three main sources in mind. It is generally thought that as a youth John Donne performed Ignatius's *Spiritual Exercises* under Heywood, although there is no concrete proof that he did. Even if he did not, he surely read them, and therein would have found the meditation on the infancy narratives in versions that largely excluded the trappings of the popular view of Christmas – ox and ass, the Magi – to concentrate on the child himself.[32] Ignatius says the person wishing to contemplate the Nativity should proceed as follows (and it is noteworthy that he later adds that one should cover both the presentation in the Temple and the flight into Egypt in one's meditations):[33]

> **First Point**. The first Point is to see the persons; that is, to see Our Lady and Joseph and the maid, and, after His Birth, the Child Jesus, I making myself a poor creature and a wretch of an unworthy slave, looking at them

and serving them in their needs, with all possible respect and reverence, as if I found myself present; and then to reflect on myself in order to draw some profit.

Second Point. The second, to look, mark and contemplate what they are saying, and, reflecting on myself, to draw some profit.

Third Point. The third, to look and consider what they are doing, as going a journey and laboring, that the Lord may be born in the greatest poverty; and as a termination of so many labors – of hunger, of thirst, of heat and of cold, of injuries and affronts – that He may die on the Cross; and all this for me: then reflecting, to draw some spiritual profit.

Colloquy. I will finish with a Colloquy as in the preceding Contemplation, and with an OUR FATHER.[34]

In the *La Corona* sonnets, we find the Christ Child in a world with few buildings and no landscapes or animals, uncoloured by imaginative renderings of nature such as one would find in Lope de Vega's popular "Cantarcillo de la Virgen," written within the same decade.[35] He seems to be in a world that almost lacks geography, a world of theological paradoxes without warmth or any sensory reality. However, Donne chooses to render the Christ Child sensibly present – "to draw some profit," as it were – in this verbal world by several interesting means. We now turn to the last of these means: the presence of Joseph as interlocutor.

Devotion to Joseph was receiving some encouragement after the Council of Trent, though it would not reach its full flourishing until the twentieth century, when Pope John XXIII ordered the inclusion of Joseph, husband of Mary, in the canon of the Mass.[36] But the roots of this devotion can be traced back to the Middle Ages. In fact, the earliest extant Christian hymn honouring St. Joseph is by the fourth-century Syrian deacon, St. Ephrem.[37] A favourite medieval source of Donne's, Bernard of Clairvaux, lauded Joseph in his second homily in praise of the Virgin Mary, identifying him as the second biblical Joseph in salvation history: the first was an interpreter of dreams, but the second not only knew "heavenly mysteries but even participated in them."[38] St. Bernard is one source Donne probably had in mind in composing the sonnets concerning Christ's childhood in the *La Corona* sequence, for it is in Bernard that we find the encouragement not only to guard the child but to hug and kiss him, perhaps accounting for the highly unusual mention of kissing in "Nativitie." Bernard famously admired Joseph's immense privilege of interacting intimately with the Christ Child: "To him it was given not only to see and to hear what many kings and prophets had longed to see and did not see, to hear and did not hear, but even to carry Him, to take Him by the hand, to hug and kiss Him, to feed Him and to keep Him safe: *non solum videre at audire, sed etiam portare, deducere, amplecti, deosculari, nutrire, et custodire.*"[39] McGuire believes that the second half of this observation, dealing with the affection Joseph must have shown to his foster son, is original to Bernard,[40] while the first, more general half comes from Jesus himself in Matthew 13:17.

Donne's second probable source is Jean Gerson's famous *Considérations sur St. Joseph* of 1413, which drew on Bernard's encomium.[41] Dzon cites the following passage, so reminiscent of Bernard's: Joseph "fuest gouuerneur dudit enfant Jhesus, le porta souuent, le baisa souuent, laraisonna souuent plus familierement quaultre homme quelconques" ("was the guardian of the infant Jesus, he carried him often, kissed him often, and spoke to him more familiarly than any other man").[42] As Carolyn Muessig states, "Bernard's writings permeate almost the whole of the Gersonian corpus."[43] In contrast to those who preferred an old and feeble Joseph, Gerson in the *Considérations* presents Joseph as a "young, strapping man who did not take on his important role in redemptive history reluctantly, but actively and willingly."[44] Gerson also petitioned for a feast day in honour of the marriage of Joseph to the Virgin Mary and preached on Joseph at the Council of Constance.[45] Donne was very familiar with Gerson's work, studying at least his *De laude scriptorum* closely and replicating some of the arguments therein.[46] Anthony Raspa argues that Donne's *Pseudo-Martyr* also reveals a profound familiarity with Gerson's work.[47] Gerson is also one potential source for the images of violent love in Donne's more famous Holy Sonnet (XIV), "Batter my heart, three-person'd God."[48] Since Gerson's name was so tied to the developing cult of Joseph, it is likely Donne also knew of his labours on Joseph's behalf.

A third source for devotion to Joseph that Donne would probably have known well was Teresa of Avila. In her famous *Autobiography*, she writes about Joseph's intercession for her and wishes others would also seek his help:

> Would that I could persuade all men to be devoted to this glorious Saint, for I know by long experience what blessings he can obtain for us from God. I have never known anyone who was truly devoted to him and honored him by particular services who did not advance greatly in virtue: for he helps in a special way those souls who commend themselves to him. It is now very many years since I began asking him for something on his feast, and I have always received it. If the petition was in any way amiss, he rectified it for my greater good …
>
> I ask for the love of God that he who does not believe me will make the trial for himself – then he will find out by experience the great good that

results from commending oneself to this glorious Patriarch and in being devoted to him.[49]

Notable here is the difference between Bernard's and Teresa's descriptions of their interactions with the saint. Although Teresa looked upon Joseph as the father and guardian of herself and her fellow nuns, Teresa's enthusiastic endorsement of her patron is not of the same emotional order as Bernard's (or Gerson's) evocation of Joseph's paternal caresses and care. Donne's depiction of Joseph seems to derive more specifically from Bernard's meditation on his paternal role, or perhaps from Gerson's reformulation of the same. The physical contact with the child is similarly affectionate.

Donne was the father of a very young family in the years after his secret marriage, the decade in which we usually situate *La Corona*, and his own contact with his babies and toddlers might also have inspired him. Other sources in devotional writing and art were of course available; Donne could have been exposed to actual devotional practices growing up in a Catholic home – his mother's picture of the Virgin hung in his dining room all through his life, and perhaps there were other images, too. He also no doubt saw artworks during his travels to Europe; representations of Joseph in art in Donne's time often showed Jesus and his foster father interacting affectionately.[50] Thanks to Molanus's arguments against the apocryphal imagination of Joseph as aged (influenced by Gerson's earlier condemnation of the same), more youthful representations of the foster father of Jesus were beginning to appear.[51] "Nativitie" offers the Christ Child a loving and perhaps hasty kiss as the Holy Family departs to escape "th'effect of *Herods* jealous generall doome." The looming danger intensifies the emotion that provokes Donne's use of words like "doome" and "woe": this embrace is prompted by protective love that the speaker commands his soul or the reader or Joseph to give. Donne is encouraging an attitude of *storge* toward the child Jesus.

Whichever of the likely candidates is Donne's real source for placing Joseph in these two scenes, what readers have not noticed until now is that it is exceptional that Joseph should be there at all. We modern readers are so used to the presence of an often youthful and active Joseph in Nativity scenes or Christmas cards or scenes of the flight into Egypt that we forget that, in Donne's day, the saint was only recently coming into greater eminence and was almost never portrayed as a young man. Apocryphal texts attested to his being of advanced age, doubtless because then one could imagine a chaste marriage to the Virgin Mary more easily and could also attribute to him an earlier marriage that produced the so-called brothers of Jesus mentioned in the gospels.[52] There was still suspicion about the new devotion to him, even among the Jesuits, who were important proponents of the cult of Joseph.[53] It is possible that Donne knew of the controversy from his exposure (presumed) in his youth to instruction from his uncle, Catholic priest Jasper Heywood. At that time, the most significant challenge to Joseph's new popularity was being circulated. Some even considered the new young Joseph indecorous, because the image of Joseph as a slightly baffled or even jealous old man, suspicious of the Virgin Mary, was so widely accepted as historically accurate.[54] We find that Donne, writing in *Ignatius His Conclave*, is aware and dismissive of an apocryphal work thought to elevate Joseph.[55] The 1611 date of Donne's book puts it very close to the presumed date of the *La Corona* sonnets: "And so I thinke did he, which dedicated to *Adrian 6*, that Sermon which Christ made in prayse of his father *Joseph*: for else how did they heare that, which none but they ever heard?"[56] Here as elsewhere Donne is deeply sarcastic about apocryphal stories of the saints,[57] but in "Nativitie" he is, as we have seen, creating his own apocrypha. In this story, the only extra-biblical action of Joseph is the kiss itself. Donne chooses a male interlocutor who is being increasingly recognized within the Catholic Church in his time as the sole male, outside of Simeon, privileged to show affection to the Son of God in his infancy. In other words, Donne is deliberately choosing a male model of affection within the Holy Family, and he is in step with what was in the first decade of the 1600s a relatively new trend that would leave its characteristic mark on Counter-Reformation art.[58]

Joseph does appear in other English Nativity poems of the century, notably in Robert Southwell's "Behold a silly tender Babe" or "New Prince, New Pompe":

> Weigh not his crib, his wooden dish,
> Nor beast that by him feed;
> Weigh not his mother's poor attire,
> Nor Joseph's simple weed.

But he does not play such a dynamic role as he does in the *La Corona* sonnets. And he will not appear in what most critics believe are Donne's more mature poems. Neither will the Christ Child.

By means of such play with the identity of the speaker, Donne makes the event of the flight into Egypt contemporary with himself. But more, he moves rapidly in the course of the sonnet from the "now" of Christ's birth to the foreseeable future of the massacre of the Holy Innocents and the "now" in which the child can be kissed as a final preparation for the journey into Egypt. This sophisticated manipulation of temporal sequences, drawing us closer and closer to physical contact with the Christ Child, should remind us of Louis Martz's theses on the meditative tradition, defended again in *Doctrine and Devotion in Seventeenth-Century Poetry* by R.V. Young.[59]

The effect is a reaching toward unity with the Holy Family in the speaker's attempt to tutor his soul in an appreciation of God's love and mercy. Donne accomplishes the effect deliberately, aiming toward an identification between himself and Jesus's foster father. P.M. Oliver, in arguing this thesis in *Donne's Religious Writing*, states that "the ending of a Donne poem is the acid test," and he cites Donne himself to this effect: "In all metrical compositions … the force of the whole piece is for the most part left to the shutting up … The last clause is as the impression of the stamp, and that is it that makes it current."[60] Donne knows what he is doing when he ends this poem as he does, with a line he repeats as the introduction to the next poem in the sequence. The impression that makes this piece "current" is what Oliver calls "a bizarre gesture of affectionate allegiance."[61] What is that bizarre gesture, that stamp? It is something the reader of Donne's works would never expect, given the closure of every other poem among his works: "Nativitie" is Donne's *only* poem that ends with a kiss.

Chapter Four

"My Saviour's Face": George Herbert's "Starre" and the Vanishing Christ Child

When George Herbert writes his Nativity lyric "The Starre" in his sequence *The Temple* (1633), he speaks of his "Saviour's face" being surrounded by beams, a sight he desires to travel to Bethlehem to see, but, as in his other Nativity poems, Herbert never shows the reader an image of the Christ Child, not even of his face. The goal of Herbert's pilgrimage is not the face of God but a kind of dissolution of the self into God's light. Herbert's speaker longs for union with Christ, but it is a Platonized, Johannine light he seeks, not a child in a manger. Thus this poem, like his other Nativity lyrics, meditates on the mystery of Christmas to acquire spiritual ascent for the speaker, not access to the physical babe of Bethlehem. Herbert represents a turning point in the history of the Nativity lyric in England, and though poets who preceded him also described access to the Christ Child through spiritual and not physical proximity, Herbert most clearly chooses to depict an exclusively spiritual rather than physical closeness. Herbert's powerful influence on the next generation of metaphysical poets in particular will help shape poems written on the subject of the Incarnation and Christmas during the Interregnum and the Restoration.

In his Nativity lyrics, Herbert uses mediating figures to approach the Christ Child, as Donne does, but differs from Donne in that those figures keep the child at a remove from the speaker rather than enabling him to draw near. Both Herbert and Milton perhaps understand mediation differently than Donne (Southwell, of course, does not use an interlocutor); Herbert and Milton owe debts to Edmund Spenser and his Pseudo-Dionysian concept of mediation by the angels of all knowledge of God, for instance. This abstruse concept, practically unknown to modern readers, was far from unfamiliar to any of the poets we are considering, but of special interest to Herbert and Milton. To put it simply, it means the human being never knows God directly, but only through the angels. Other beliefs about sacraments, time, and immanence also play a role in what will come to be the increasingly disincarnate celebration of the Incarnation in the latter half of the seventeenth century in England.

"The Starre" affords us a multifaceted glimpse into Herbert's approach to the Incarnation and Nativity of Christ. It draws on alchemical and mystical literature in brief but uses specific allusions and metaphors to demonstrate the suffusion of the speaker by the divine light. Significantly, Herbert does not imagine the Christ Child as a real infant, nor does he approach him with any gestures of physical affection, unlike John Donne's more traditional representation of the Nativity. Donne needs little to no hermeticism and nary a nod to Platonism. By contrast, readers need not look into Herbert's understanding of the relationships within the Holy Family, because he gives us no fleshly evocation of the newborn Christ. With Herbert we clearly step from one mode of representing the Christ Child to another. Even though the last poems this study treats, the Nativity and Epiphany hymns of Richard Crashaw's *Carmen Deo Nostro*, published posthumously in 1652, postdate Herbert's poems and show clear signs of Herbert's influence on his admirer, in this respect the two differ, and it is Herbert and not Crashaw the later Metaphysicals will continue to imitate.

Without a portrayal or even intimation of physical affection or loving wonder at the beauty of the Christ Child or at the marks on his body of his Proleptic Passion, Herbert's Nativity lyric nonetheless offers an engaging image of the effect of Christ's presence on the sinner. Herbert's great achievement in this poem is his deft creation of the sense of charming sweetness and friendliness, of trust and yearning, that permeates what could in other hands have been a fearsome philosophical treatise. There is nothing heavy, overbearing, or tendentious in this poem, as mind-boggling as the appearance of a phrase like "our trinitie of light, motion, and heat" is in a Nativity lyric. The idea of the speaker as a star and as a bee has a childlike and natural quality no matter how rooted both images are in the philosophical tradition. This work is Herbert at his best, engaging multiple levels of literary allusion and allegory in a dressing of the greatest simplicity and plain speech, with great beauty conveyed by the aural qualities of the poem and the images evoked.

To read "The Starre" with full understanding, we should bear in mind that Herbert often envisions union with Christ as an ascent to Real Presence.[1] Unlike his predecessors in the genre of the Nativity lyric, however, Herbert does not connect that divine presence with the reception of the Eucharist (although he certainly imagines the interior transformation of the Christian as effected by the real reception of the body and blood of Christ).[2] Nonetheless, unity with God is clearly a concern in this poem:

Bright spark, shot from a brighter place,
Where beams surround my Saviours face,
Canst thou be any where
So well as there?

Yet, if thou wilt from thence depart,
Take a bad lodging in my heart;
For thou canst make a debter,
And make it better.

First with thy fire-work burn to dust
Folly, and worse than folly, lust;
Then with thy light refine,
And make it shine:

So disengag'd from sinne and sicknesse,
Touch it with thy celestiall quicknesse,
That it may hang and move
After thy love.

Then with our trinitie of light,
Motion and heat, let's take our flight
Unto the place where thou
Before didst bow.

Get me a standing there, and place
Among the beams, which crown the face
Of him who dy'd to part
Sinne and my heart:

That so among the rest I may
Glitter, and curle, and winde as they:
That winding is their fashion
Of adoration.

Sure thou wilt joy, by gaining me
To flie home like a laden bee
Unto that hive of beams
And garland-streams.[3]

Although for a Nativity poem it is a little unusual in approach, Herbert certainly imagines some kind of union with God. It is a union of light with light, rather than of worshipper with child; the medium of flesh is absent, and thus from a Roman Catholic or Lutheran point of view it is desacramentalized. Such a preference for spiritual over physical union is the hallmark of Calvinist and Anglican poetics and sacramental theology, as we have seen in previous chapters. This poem functions much as Herbert's poem "Christmas II" does; as Robert Whalen explains, "divine / human union consists in the interpenetration of the speaker's music and God's light: 'His beams shall cheer my breast, and both so twine, / Till ev'n his beams sing, and my musick shine.'"[4] Martin Elsky contrasts a liturgical "making present" in Robert Southwell's "Burning Babe" with "Protestant liturgical 'remembrance'" in Herbert's "Good Friday" to make the following point: "The metaphorical image [of Christ as the poet's clock or 'sunne'] has been used in service of a characteristically Protestant way of meditating on Christ. Unlike Southwell, Herbert has rejected a contemplation of Christ as an external object and instead has incorporated the event into himself, becoming himself the measurement of God's grace," a strategy that is apparent in "The Starre" and his other Nativity poems.[5]

This kind of incorporation into the self is nevertheless not consumption and therefore not Eucharistic in the metabolic sense; rather, the speaker claims to share in the powers of his addressee and asks for elevation, such as we see in the Calvinist concept of mystical Real Presence.[6] Helen Vendler, one of two major commentators on the poem, mentions the insistent use of the pronoun "our" for the terms "trinitie" and "flight," though the unity the speaker imagines here is with the star and not with the Christ Child. Nonetheless, as Vendler points out most importantly, in the parallels between stanzas four and six, "he [the speaker] then offers a startling equation of Jesus and the star: since the star 'disengaged' Herbert's heart from 'sinne,' and since Jesus is defined as the one 'who dy'd to part / Sinne and my heart,' Jesus and the star become temporarily indistinguishable, and the descent of the star becomes momentarily a parable of the Incarnation."[7]

Vendler also asserts quite rightly that "as a messenger, the star remains separate, in that function at least, from Jesus, and acts at the end more like an angel."[8] She might not be thinking of angelic mediation in the sense that I have mentioned earlier; rather, Vendler may merely be probing Pseudo-Dionysian elements in "The Starre." She closes her analysis of this poem by noting the separation of the speaker from the star at its end: "These proposals … amount to a separate installation in heaven of Herbert and his star, a formal leavetaking by those who had briefly been twinned, allowing the poem to subside."[9]

Vendler's analysis of this poem is both the lengthiest and most significant to date. She claims that "The Starre" attains "not only equilibrium, but expansion, trust, and even rest."[10] At the same time, she seems to indicate that the poem would have been more successful if the disjoining of Herbert and the star, the star and Jesus were not so emphatic. In the poem she primarily notices a descent that echoes the Incarnation. However, as we shall see, the speaker imagines more clearly an ascent for himself as well as a linear motion that seems, early in the poem, to go backward in time. I would argue that the central trope of the poem is this ascent, both Platonic and Dantesque.

James Boyd White, the other major commentator on the poem, sets the image of the star in an important context: Herbert's "star" language, his habitual references to stars throughout *The Temple*. He sees the poem as helping to unify the entire project of *The Temple*, no little feat: "Perhaps more fully than any we have read, this poem expresses the possibility of happiness, touched with feelings of longing."[11] White helpfully enumerates three sets of images in the poem: the bees returning to their hive, the spark, and curling or winding. Whereas our other poets address the Christ Child himself or describe his actions, White notes that "most striking of all" in this lyric is the "tone of intimacy and confidence ... that allows the speaker to talk to the star, a mediator between him and his God, as to a friend."[12] The exceptionally buoyant quality of the poem invites us as readers to examine the speaker's stance. Given both White's and Vendler's responses to the poem, their impressions of its intimate tone, it is worthwhile examining how Herbert creates this sense of intimacy when the Christ Child himself rapidly recedes from centre stage after the second line.

One reason the poem feels intimate is precisely because of Herbert's use of apostrophe. The addressee of the poem is ostensibly the star of Bethlehem, but as Donne does with the Holy Family in "Nativitie," Herbert obscures the identity of his addressee, purposefully it seems.[13] Bruce Johnson has shown that Herbert is indubitably aware and deliberate when he shifts between audiences, citing a paragraph from Herbert's *The Country Parson*.[14] Herbert says the preacher should

> turn ... often and make many apostrophes to God, as Oh Lord, blesse my people, and teach them this point: Or, Oh my Master, on whose errand I come, let me hold my peace, and doe thou speak thy selfe; for thou art Love, and when thou teachest, all are Scholars. Some such irradiations scatteringly in the Sermon, carry great holiness in them.[15]

Helen Vendler also investigates Herbert's use of apostrophe. For her, this trope is the poetic element that "contrives its web of relation with another person ... The tones summoned up characterize not only their utterer but also his relation to his addressee, creating on the page the nature of the ties between them."[16] Since the identity of the star shifts during the poem, as we shall see, this trope indicates closeness, but it is sometimes unclear to whom.

Examining Herbert's Nativity poems allows the reader to assess levels of tenderness and expectation with regard to Christ in his infancy and to consider Herbert's Christology. My argument is that Herbert's emotion is displaced from the infant to the star and then to the second person of the Trinity who is light from light. Cherishing, caressing, or wondering at the newborn Jesus are not at all a part of the approach, even though we are led to believe that is the direction of the poem in its first stanza. The poem offers a sense of spiritual intimacy with a fellow gazer upon divine glory and a positive, hopeful expectation of rising to the sphere of fire beyond the sinful constraints of an earthly dwelling place. The etherealizing of closeness is not the absence of closeness.[17] However, the physical world that Herbert depicts is elemental – all fire and air and earth – and lacks form, shape, and individuality. That Herbert chooses to eschew the material presence of Christ when he emphasizes the material world in other poems is interesting, given that his theme is the Incarnation.[18]

One of the most important questions to ask when we approach Herbert's only portrait of the Christ Child in his poems is, "What is the I-thou relationship in this lyric?" Is he speaking to Christ himself? If the star is in some way conflated with Christ, embodying the idea of Christ as divine light, source of illumination for the believer, why is it distant from Christ? The poem's rich biblical allusions and metaphysical conceits allow us to investigate this mystery. Rosemond Tuve once remarked that "Herbert writes poetry like a theologian,"[19] and Heather Asals comments on this assertion: "He [Herbert] bravely undertakes to deal in those unique predicates of God. He understands well the logical impropriety of 'de-fining' the 'in-finite' in the predication of God, and so he undertakes to 're-fine' the material of the predication of God in the 'fine-ness' of language itself."[20] The language of refinement in this poem registers this relationship Asals articulates so well: the star, which is "thou" to Herbert, is a heavenly fire, both Jesus and not Jesus, both united to his "I" and not united, as the speaker is drawn back to the source of his being but returns as a laden bee to the hive, not to an identity with the source of the purifying light and fire. Because Herbert is amalgamating both biblical allusions and neo-Platonic concepts of union and purification in this lyric, we should turn now to the texts he has in mind.

Indeed, like his fellow Nativity poets of the century, Herbert connects the Incarnation not with folk motifs but with the scriptures. The title of the poem, "The Starre," equivocates between the meaning of the star of Bethlehem and the bright beaming face of the infant Jesus. Thus, not only does it start out talking about the face of the Christ Child, but it also alludes to Christ's identity as the star from Jacob rising (Balaam's last prophecy in Numbers 24:17):

> I shall see him, but not now: I shall behold him, but not near: there shall come a Star out of Jacob, and a Scepter shall rise out of Israel, and shall crush the forehead of Moab, and destroy all the children of Sheth.

The prophecy could not be more clear about placing the event in the future, and Herbert's allusion could account for why the speaker's gratitude refers to an event occurring after the Nativity, the Passion: "I shall behold him, but not near." However, it is not really justifiable to think of the whole verse as intertext; the poem unfolds in another direction. From the initial bright spark, it goes straight from the stable to Herbert's heart:

> Bright spark, shot from a brighter place,
> Where beams surround my Saviours face,
> Canst thou be any where
> So well as there?
>
> Yet, if thou wilt from thence depart,
> Take a bad lodging in my heart;
> For thou canst make a debter,
> And make it better.

Herbert in two stanzas has jumped to the Pauline image of the indwelling Christ of Galatians 2:20 and to God's removing a heart of stone and replacing it with a heart of flesh in Ezekiel 11:19 and 36:26, not to the destruction of Moab and Sheth. (It is possible that the spiritual improvement could amount to the same thing allegorically.) Christ's payment of man's debts also moves us out of the Book of Numbers and into Isaiah 53:4–6: "Surely he hath borne our griefs, and carried our sorrows: yet we did esteem him stricken, smitten of God, and afflicted. But he was wounded for our transgressions, he was bruised for our iniquities: the chastisement of our peace was upon him; and with his stripes we are healed." Herbert's allusions probably also include 1 John 2:2: "And he is the propitiation for our sins: and not for ours only, but also for the sins of the whole world"; and 1 Peter 1:18–20: "Forasmuch as ye know that ye were not redeemed with corruptible things, as silver and gold, from your vain conversation received by tradition from your fathers; But with the precious blood of Christ, as of a lamb without blemish and without spot."

Herbert's seemingly simple, short-line stanzas are packed with numerous biblical intertexts, but very few of these are to the actual biblical texts of the Nativity. The star of Bethlehem is biblical, but Herbert begins the poem with a metaphysical conceit that is not biblical. This conceit, which will extend through its entirety, is that the star of Bethlehem (Matthew 2:1–2) is a light that departs from the face of the infant Jesus to transform into the refiner's fire (Malachi 3:3), burning the heart of the sinner to purify it. The applicability of the image of the refining fire to the Incarnation had long been recognized.[21]

The speaker in Herbert's verses envisions himself as joined to the burning star to be purified by fire; he inserts himself into the event of the Nativity to internalize the light: "First with thy fire-work burn to dust / Folly, and worse than folly, lust; / Then with thy light refine, / And make it shine." Herbert's very language implies ascent. Even the shift in vowel sounds between the dullest of them, the short, thudding "u" of "dust" and "lust," and the highest and brightest, the long "i" of "refine" and "shine," illustrates the purification's effect as a rising.

One could fruitfully compare Herbert's "The Starre" as refiner's fire with Southwell's "The Burning Babe," which makes use of some of the same biblical texts for its imagery and may have provided inspiration to Herbert. Southwell's Christ Child says "the metal in this furnace wrought are men's defilèd souls," and Herbert thinks of himself as one of those souls. If no one approaches the child on fire in Southwell's poem, Herbert at least seems to have listened to the Redeemer's lament.

Interestingly, the light from the Christ Child is not in the biblical narrative of the Nativity in Luke (or Matthew, of course), though from very early on in Christianity it became usual to talk about the light of Christ illuminating the night of his birth, since he is the "Sol splendissimus."[22] The initial stanza is deliberately elusive, not clearly indicating the source of the light in the poem, but instead denoting "a brighter place / where beams surround my Saviours face." The star seems to originate in the stable and is a symbol of Christ as light. The beams surrounding the Saviour's face are the beams of light (Vendler thinks of them as sun beams), but Herbert puns subtly on the word "beams," as his later use of the word in the poem indicates: he imagines the stable with beams, presumably of wood, suggesting the beams of the cross. Referring to the child as his Saviour seems to bring up the Passion by association, a use of the Proleptic Passion we saw earlier in Southwell. Nevertheless, the light coming from the child Jesus's face lacks both biblical authority and the full authority of the poet. Herbert rather carefully constructs a sentence indicating that the light of the star originates from the stable, but, interestingly, he does not say directly that the light emanates from the baby's face. Herbert distances the source of light from the child himself, perhaps deliberately avoiding referring to a medieval visionary text we shall examine later. Herbert perhaps considered that vision to be pure fiction, yet some readers at least would infer that the infant Jesus is the source of the light he mentions.

Modern audiences, accustomed to the convention of heavenly light illuminating the stable, would never notice it as an accretion to the biblical account, but it has its roots in only patristic and medieval texts. St. Jerome stated that the night was as bright as day at Christ's birth. Late medieval texts such as Ficino's *De Stella Magorum* (1482) mention Psalm 138:12 as a prediction of the light that enveloped Christ at his birth: "But darkness shall not be dark to thee, and night shall be light as day: the darkness thereof, and the light thereof are alike to thee" (Douai).[23] Mary Dzon has discussed the imagery of light in depictions of the Nativity.[24] However, this light only becomes a characteristic feature of images of the Nativity in the late sixteenth and throughout the seventeenth century, particularly notable in the followers of Caravaggio, who loved to paint night scenes with the baby's face illuminating the stable.

Herbert may also have been influenced by the medieval visionary St. Birgitta of Sweden (c. 1303–73), however suspiciously he might have regarded her. Her account of a vision of the Nativity she had on a pilgrimage to Bethlehem was immensely popular throughout Europe, and was responsible for the increasing inclusion of this miraculous light the Christ Child exudes (or with which the stable is somehow filled). Birgitta's revelations ensured the spread of this configuration of the participants at the Nativity in art for centuries to come. It remains a mystery what art Herbert might have been exposed to, given the thoroughness of the iconoclastic depredations that went along with the English Reformation, but Nativity scenes or illuminations from before the time of Birgitta would have posed the actors in the drama much differently. Her vision gives the following rendering of the Nativity:

> When I was present by the manger of the Lord in Bethlehem I beheld a Virgin of extreme beauty wrapped in a white mantle and a delicate tunic through which I perceived her virginal body. With her was an old man of

> great honesty and they had with them an ox and ass. These entered the cave and the man having tied them to the manger went out and brought in to the Virgin a lighted candle which having done he again went outside so as not to be present at the birth … When all was thus prepared the Virgin knelt with great veneration in an attitude of prayer; her back was to the manger, her face uplifted to heaven and turned toward the East.
>
> Then, her hands extended and her eyes fixed on the sky she stood as in an ecstasy, lost in contemplation, in a rapture of divine sweetness. And while she stood thus in prayer I saw the Child in her womb move; suddenly in a moment she gave birth to her own Son from whom radiated such ineffable light and splendour that the sun was not comparable to it while the divine light totally annihilated the material light of St. Joseph's candle. So sudden and instantaneous was this birth that I could neither discover nor discern by what means it had occurred. All of a sudden I saw the glorious Infant lying on the ground naked and shining, His body pure from any soil or impurity. Then I heard the singing of the angels of miraculous sweetness and beauty. When the Virgin felt she had borne her Child immediately she worshipped Him, her hands clasped in honour and reverence saying: "Be welcome my God, my Lord, my Son" … She and Joseph put the Child in the manger, and worshipped Him on their knees with immense joy until the arrival of the Kings who recognized the Son from the likeness to His Mother.[25]

Although Herbert's emphasis on light might have owed something to this popular vision, in his portrayal of the Nativity, even the biblical Mary and Joseph, swaddling clothes, manger, and stable are all absent, effaced to place the speaker amid the beams emanating from the child's face.

In fact, the natural characteristics of the stable that John Donne imagined causing discomfort to Christ's tender flesh in a Christmas sermon of 1626 are also absent.[26] In their place is an imaginative whorl of dust motes or sparks swirling in the radiance that "glitter, and curle, and winde" like fire: "that winding is their fashion / of adoration."[27] They are not completely insubstantial, but come close to being so. Ann Astell, commenting on the physical qualities of sight in Eucharistic adoration, has observed that sight too was thought of as physical touch in the Middle Ages; the rays thought to radiate from objects enabling sight were not spiritual but material.[28] John Riggs records that medieval Christians in some places even thought that a sinner's contacting the Eucharist only with his or her sight could lead to divine condemnation.[29] Herbert may be thinking of the divinization of the material world in this way.

Alchemical influences also play into the imagery of light that displaces the traditional focus on the baby himself. With its conviction that "the Spirit of Man is descended not only from the Stars and Elements, but there is hid therein a Spark of Light and Power of God,"[30] "astral magic" is an important element in Paracelsus and other early modern hermeticists' figuration of the soul's ascent to God.[31] It may be that for Herbert, the alchemical factor is merely a metaphor for the action of grace, but in this poem it almost seems to crowd out the function of the biblical star of Bethlehem, which was to lead the Magi to the child, at whose feet they worshipped. Rather than that event, the light imagery hints to the reader that the poem is about the transmutation of the speaker. Indeed, he imagines merging with the star and sharing its "trinitie of light, motion, and heat." Those qualities shared by all stars suggest to Herbert the three persons of the Trinity and the three powers of the human soul. Such elements are a part of the natural world, but the pronoun "our" that implies the star of Bethlehem is unified with the speaker could well indicate that only the spiritual part of man ascends.

The lyric is concerned more with a metamorphosis in the speaker than with the fleshly reality of the incarnate God, although vestiges of the flesh or at least of a material world remain. The sense of amity and joy that Vendler and White detect in the poem is connected with the speaker's friendship and brief union with the star and, of course, with his hope for illumination and salvation. Herbert wishes to adopt the "light, motion, and heat" of the star to imitate its motion, very much in the vein of "imp[ing] his wing" on Christ in "Easter Wings." The metamorphosis is partly Ovidian – desire transforms one into an object in nature – but its aim is Christian: ascent to the heaven of light from which all lights emanate, by implication the Holy City whose light is Christ.

The fiery imagery assimilates the star of Bethlehem into the sphere of fire, and the mystery of the light around the baby's face is revealed:

Bright spark, shot from a brighter place,
Where beams surround my Saviours face,
Canst thou be any where
So well as there?

The "brighter place" is probably the stable, which is imagined as a sphere of fire instead of a building or cave belonging to an inn (Luke 2:7). The originality of the conceit is stunning, and its ability to assimilate with the Birgittine notion of the stable alit with Christ's light is also remarkable. But the speaker's first question is whether the star is most decorously and fittingly located only in the "brighter place / Where beams surround my Saviours face." The speaker really desires to have the illumination move from Bethlehem to his own heart, but this movement only seems possible if he, too, is present at the Nativity.

Then with our trinitie of light,
Motion and heat, let's take our flight
Unto the place where thou
Before didst bow.

Get me a standing there, and place
Among the beams, which crown the face
Of him who dy'd to part
Sinne and my heart.

The trinity of light, motion, and heat will lend the speaker the power to travel through not only space, but also time. It is a strange locution, considering the imagination does not need them to move the mind's eye to first century Judea, and the speaker's actual physical self is not going there either. The request is phrased somewhat like a request for a place at court, and briefly, attendance at Christ's birth sounds like political advancement.[32] But the motion upward is spiritual; as Mario Di Cesare observed about the affinities between Herbert and John's Gospel, "both works make use of vertical imagery (up-down as well as down-up) … both are grounded in a major pattern of 'return.'"[33] If there is a sacramental union imagined or imitated in "The Starre," it is the Calvinist one where the "Sursum corda," the "Lift up your hearts," enjoins the congregation to unite spiritually with Christ who is in heaven. If Herbert situates Christ in the sphere of fire, then the stable ceases to be the stable of Bethlehem very early on in the poem and becomes a metaphor for heaven, beyond the sphere of fire. The speaker then is never asking to go back in time to the moment of Christ's birth, but always forward to the moment of his union with God. The trinity of light, motion, and heat are his motive force.

Herbert thinks of motion itself when he thinks of the star of Bethlehem. Stars and motion are inextricably linked in Aristotle's *De Caelo*. Simplicius commented on the text, which was known, via his commentary and Aquinas's, to Robert Grosseteste and other English academics in the Middle Ages. The three terms appear together in the following passage of Aquinas: "Aristotle states that 'heat and light are produced by the stars, and friction in the air by their movement.'"[34] Aquinas of course was read at Cambridge well into the seventeenth century, and his *De Caelo* was of particular interest to the hermetically inclined poets graduating from England's two major universities.

The sphere-of-fire element of the argument and, indeed, the language of the entire poem seem to echo book ten of Marsilio Ficino's *Platonic Theology*, in which Ficino discusses the significance of light, motion, and heat to the incarnate nature of the soul and the soul's ascent to God. For "the sphere of fire has three kinds of quality: heat, light, and the levity that always aims at things above ... [I]n addition to heat and light, it imparts to the least material bodies the levity that lifts to things supernal."[35] "God has an appointed goal it can someday attain; and this goal is none other than that rest in God, which the rational soul will not enjoy until it has abandoned its abode here."[36] If Herbert has this passage in mind, and it is so close to his imagery it seems most likely, the star is seeking rest in God, and the motion of the star is toward "things supernal."

The trinity of powers Herbert describes has its roots in early Christian, and perhaps Augustinian, Platonized terminology. Herbert's reference to the "trinitie" of "light, motion, and heat" may be the first occurrence of this image as analogue of the Trinity, though Herbert means the trinity that propels the star and himself, not the Triune God. But if the star is, albeit briefly, both Christ and the speaker, which trinity is this trinity? Herbert is also probably familiar with Augustine's use of the term "tripotens" to describe God and perhaps even with Augustine's source, Victorinus, who was a neo-Platonist before his conversion to Christianity.[37] The poem is not a discussion of the role of the Trinity in the Incarnation; Herbert's choice to use it as his image of those things that are able to help his mortal self to ascend bespeaks a fascination with things other than the Word assuming flesh. He does not imagine himself bowing before the manger, but sees a star-like version of himself accompanying the star of Bethlehem to the stable as source of interior illumination. This trinity is not God but some kind of reflection of God within the poet.

The other dominant simile for the self approaching God in this poem is that of the bee:

> Sure thou wilt joy, by gaining me
> To flie home like a laden bee
> Unto that hive of beams
> And garland-streams.

Famous pagan sources used the bee as an image of ascent, as in Porphyry's Cave of the Nymphs and Virgil's Elysium in *Aeneid* VI.[38] Nicholas Horsfall discusses the various sources of bee imagery:

> Many thought of the soul as a bee ... According to the distinguished neoplatonic philosopher Porphyry (c. AD 3), men of old – οἱ παλαιοί – gave

> the name of "bees" to souls awaiting rebirth and to prove the point Porphyry cited a verse of Sophocles: "the swarm of the dead hums and passes upwards." A scholiast on Euripides confirms this image: "the bee means, allegorically, the soul."[39]

Porphyry was a professedly anti-Christian author, but his allegoresis of bees clearly shows why later generations of Christians would co-opt the image:

> All souls, however, proceeding into generation, are not simply called bees, but those who will live in it justly and who, after having performed such things as are acceptable to the Gods, will again return (to their kindred stars). For this insect loves to return to the place from whence it first came, and is eminently just and sober.[40]

Virgil similarly associates the bee with the human soul and uses his bee simile in the episode of the descent to the underworld, where Anchises will tell Aeneas about the mystery of transmigration (6.707–11). In the *Paradiso*, Dante transforms Virgil's beehive from a place of transmigration, where personality and individuality are lost, to the home of the soul compelled by desire to seek its loving maker.

The allegorical valence of bees changed under Christian treatment.[41] The bee symbolized wisdom, diligence, chastity, and preaching in the Church.[42] By the Middle Ages, the bee would be considered a fitting image of Christ himself,[43] and this tradition might also account for Herbert's conflation of himself and the bee: "In Christian art, the bee's tirelessness is taken as a symbol of hope for the Christian, the sting serving as a reminder of Christ as judge. Belief in the bee's parthenogenesis led to its being a symbol of the Virgin Mary and the Immaculate Conception."[44] Most famously, Chrysostom in his twelfth homily on the Statutes says: "The bee is more honoured than the other animals; not because she labours, but because she labours for others."[45] Additionally, St. Birgitta of Sweden compared Christ to a bee (chapter forty-five) and Mary to a beehive (book six, chapter twelve) in her *Revelations*.[46]

The bee, significantly, is featured in the *Exultet*, one of the most important liturgical prayers, not of the Christmas season but of Passiontide. Although Cranmer deleted the *Exultet* along with most other sequences from the *Book of Common Prayer*, Herbert would certainly have known this ancient hymn of the Easter Vigil, not least because the concept of the *felix culpa* that it enunciates was the source of important discussions by reformers such as Beda (Strasbourgeois theologian Noel Bédier). The bees whose wax makes up the Easter candle are thus associated with the Resurrection. The poem then hums with a long tradition of bees and their association with immortality, purity, rebirth, ascent to heaven, and Christ. Herbert's brief stanza predicts the return to its home, or Herbert's, to heaven, its "hive of beams / and garland-streams."

Herbert's use of neo-Platonic elements may prompt us to examine the tenets about representing the divine that governed neo-Platonic thought: "We dare not speak or say anything about the superessential and hidden divinity apart from what has been divinely revealed to us by the sacred Oracles, for ignorance of its superessentiality is beyond reason and intellect and being."[47] So said Pseudo-Dionysius, and it is in this direction that Protestantism in England in the seventeenth century moved, disenchanted with the constant searching for rational explanations of mysteries among the scholastics.[48] Sophie Read says of Herbert's Eucharistic poetry: "The poet retreats in humility from the need to formulate a consistent viewpoint, preferring rather to have faith in, than a precise understanding of, the mysteries of the sacrament."[49] Pseudo-Dionysius and mystical spirituality deriving from his works are clearly important to medieval and early modern Roman Catholicism, but grew in relative importance as Aristotelianism fell into some disfavour among the educated elite of England. As the seventeenth century progressed, language about divine union and the presence of Christ becomes notably less physical. Whereas medieval Christians freely enacted the mysteries of Christ's life in plays and imagined the domestic moments in the life of the Holy Family in art and poetry, the Cambridge men who mostly comprised the school of metaphysical poets were deeply affected by the claims of Plato and the later neo-Platonists regarding poetry; Protestantism in general concerned itself more with the indwelling of the Holy Spirit than closeness to the Holy Family generated by imaginative recreation of biblical scenes, partly because of the resultant problem of apocryphogenesis.

Although Herbert imagines a non-biblical trip to Bethlehem, and an ascent to the sphere of fire when he gets there, he may glitter and curl and wind, not kneel or kiss – for not only is Christ disembodied but the speaker, too, ceases to be a human being with a body. He is too weightless, too sparkling, to tread the earth a traveller, pilgrim, shepherd, or wise man.

"The Starre" describes the action he would take once freed from the power of sin with these beautiful lines:

So disengag'd from sin and sicknesse,
Touch it with thy celestiall quicknesse,
That it may hang and move
After thy love.

The sense of stillness and suspension in this stanza is permeated with the life and movement lent by the star: its "celestiall quicknesse" allows it both to "hang" and "move." And the star is clearly Christ again when Herbert indicates the goal of its movement: "thy love," although he is probably punning on the word and giving it its Thomistic and Dantesque sense of the motive power that leads a created being to its natural final cause. The crisp guttural consonants of "disengaged," "sickness," and "quickness" race toward the more resonant and prolonged "o" sounds of "move" and "love," and the hissing "s" sounds sound like sparks sizzling and popping before Herbert shifts to aspirants, nasals, and liquids in the more stationary second half of the stanza.

However, "The Starre" is not about baby Jesus. A photograph can be an amazing photograph, but if the parents who order an image of their baby are presented with an image of the photographer, they will not have a record of their child's appearance. Even poems like Southwell's "Christes childhood" and Donne's "Temple" draw the reader's attention to the contrast between the childishness of Jesus's appearance, his body, and the extraordinary wisdom he displays, and thus it remains important for Southwell and Donne that he is a little boy in their representations of him even after the Nativity.

The bodilessness of this poem is even more remarkable because "elsewhere in *The Temple,* Herbert uses images of personal contact."[50] If we look at "Church Music," a close analogue to "The Starre," we shall see the trajectory of Herbert's imagined ascent is nearly the same, as is the bodilessness of it:

CHURCH-MUSICK.

SWEETEST of sweets, I thank you: when displeasure
  Did through my bodie wound my minde,
You took me thence; and in your house of pleasure
  A daintie lodging me assign'd

Now I in you without a bodie move,
  Rising and falling with your wings:
We both together sweetly live and love,
  Yet say sometimes, *God help poore Kings.*

Comfort, 'Ile; for if you poste from me,
  Sure I shall do so, and much more:
But if I travel in your companie,
  You know the way to heavens doore.[51]

Metamorphosis, disembodiment, and ascent are connected together in a similar way here, and the destination is also heaven, where the speaker's musical guide can lead him.

So what is the nature or status of the fiction Herbert's persona creates when trying to imagine the Nativity and its import? Harold Toliver calls such an imaginative approach a "poetic supplement."[52] Herbert's supplement is Platonized and incorporeal, even if spatial relocation is important to the speaker's act of devotion. He bypasses the baby in the manger because he has transformed the stable to heaven. Southwell does the same in his "New Prince, New Pompe," but unlike Herbert, he focuses on the naturalistic details of the manger scene and the Christ Child himself.[53] Herbert's framework is Dionysian, as is the disembodiment and the emphasis on the angel/star.

Herbert does not imagine a wounded Christ Child as Southwell and Donne do, but he does evoke the traditional trope of the Proleptic Passion in all of his Christmas poems and in "Good Friday" as well.[54] We also see the tradition evoked in his Latin poem, "In Natales et Pascha Concurrentes."[55] Herbert knows of this important element in the medieval and earlier Renaissance Nativity lyric. It does not seem to function in quite the same way for him as it does in his two predecessors.

Richard Hughes asserts: "What Herbert felt about the Incarnation is, without question, the central issue of his poetry."[56] Yet for Herbert, the Incarnation is not a site of temporal collapse between himself and the historical life of Jesus in the manner of the earlier poets. Why did Herbert pass over the baby's actual body as of no consequence to his poem on the Incarnation? Of course, we could speculate that possibly the reason is biographical – perhaps because Herbert married later in life and seems to have been childless, he was not drawn to the child Jesus for his childlike qualities, nor, unlike so many saints, did he yearn to hold the Christ Child in his arms and kiss him. But more likely, because we shall see this retreat from the physical in other religious poets, worship of the Christ Child was not the only or even the preferred road to mystical union with Jesus for priests of the Church of England. Herbert accepted Calvin's and thus the Anglican divines' rationale for rejecting the belief in the substantial presence of Christ's body in the Eucharist. Their logic resisted portraying the Incarnation as a site of communion with that body: the conviction that the physical body of Christ after the Ascension could not be in two places at once and therefore could not be on earth again.

In addition, the Calvinist and Anglican English poets manifest a neo-Platonic reluctance to define and describe mysteries as they try to produce an alternative to scholasticism and medieval popular piety.[57] I would argue that their portrayal of the Incarnation is affected by a fear of appearing to ascribe to what, in their view, was an irrational Roman Catholic understanding of Christ's physical appearance in the sacrament. As Sophie Read asserts, "the gaps that the Reformation opened between words and their meanings allowed the latter a brief afterlife in a kind of conceptual limbo: a horrified shrinking from the magic and mummery of the Catholic rite did not, at least for some, preclude an imaginative participation in its twin promises of divine presence and the performative power of the creative word."[58] This point may be most particularly true of George Herbert, whose interest in depicting Christ's presence and his immediacy in poems like "Love (III)," with its invitation to the Eucharistic banquet, is well known. But even there, the Christ who invites the speaker to the Eucharistic banquet is little more than a voice, and the encounter seems to take place in the New Jerusalem, not here on earth.

The disembodied treatment of the Incarnation employed in "The Starre" appears also in Herbert's other poems on the Nativity. Unlike Donne, Herbert does not imagine the physical aspects of the Nativity such as the sharp hay wounding Christ's tender flesh or St. Joseph (or himself) kissing the Christ Child.[59] In the Nativity poems, Christ does not chide man for his lovelessness (as Herbert envisions him doing in other poems in *The Temple*) or speak directly to the poet; he does not play or show extraordinary wisdom; indeed, he is scarcely there at all. Let us examine George Herbert's better-known poems on the Christ Child in *The Temple*, "Christmas (I)" and "Christmas (II)," beginning by looking at pertinent elements other critics have noticed in these poems.

John Drury has observed that the sonnet "Christmas (I)" starts with an everyday hunting scene, but in a very few lines Herbert achieves "a breathtaking but modest mythopoeic stroke": the discovery that the inn he is staying in is the very same one in which Christ has just been born. The hunter experiences a vision of the Christ Child's "glorious, yet contracted light" stealing into the manger.[60] Herbert was more anxious than either Southwell or Donne before him to avoid fanciful fictionalizing of biblical events, but here he inserts himself into the Nativity narrative by relocating it to a contemporary rural English landscape. Drury's term "mythopoeia" shows he is alert to the extra-scriptural quality of the episode Herbert narrates.

Herbert's strategy, however, is not to get physically close to the Christ Child himself. He does not touch or embrace the child, and the child does not speak to him as Southwell's burning babe does. It is in fact very unclear in stanza two, where the speaker finds his "dearest Lord" is already at the inn, that his Lord is a child:

There when I came, whom found I but my dear,
My dearest Lord, expecting till the grief
Of pleasures brought me to Him, ready there
To be all passengers' most sweet relief?

Without reference to the Christ Child of any sort, we do not assume the "dearest Lord" is the babe of Bethlehem. Moreover, we would not really know the event is even taking place at Christmas without the title of the poem. The first quatrain merely states that "with full cry of affections, quite astray," the speaker has settled in the first inn he finds in order to take a break from riding "after all pleasures." Needless to say, the Gospel of Luke records that there was no room at the inn for Mary and Joseph, so they did not stay there.[61] Therefore, the speaker's staying at an inn does not indicate that he has come to the site of Christ's birth.

Herbert does not speak of the Incarnation until the third quatrain, which is the only mention of the Christ Child in the poem:

Oh Thou, whose glorious, yet contracted light,
Wrapt in night's mantle, stole into a manger;
Since my dark soul and brutish is Thy right,
To man of all beasts be not Thou a stranger.

In this single quatrain, Herbert evokes many traditions, though it is clear his focus is the coming of Christ into the soul of the believer, not a portrayal of the night of Christ's birth or of the child himself. Richard Strier points out Herbert's almost exclusive emphasis in the sonnet on this "second Advent of Christ," stressing the "possible conflict between history and postfiguration." He uses the poem briefly as an example of his assertion that "the inward and personal emphasis of Protestant tropology and typology could have radical implications when both the Old and the New Testaments were treated as merely 'typical' of events in the soul."[62] One of those radical implications was unfixing Christ's birth as the centre of Christian history and making his spiritual birth in the individual believer's soul the centre. Taken to an extreme, this habit could imply that the Incarnation was even to a certain degree beside the point. Herbert's description of the Incarnation – the wrapping in "night's mantle" of Christ's "glorious, yet contracted light" – is actually a subordinate clause, leading us to man the beast. It erases the flesh; it erases Mary; it erases body and history. It almost sounds as if a Platonic idea has descended into the allegorical cave.

When the speaker apostrophizes Christ, it is perhaps the Christ Child in his Nativity, but the manger remains as an allegorical image of the human soul, a traditional equation already in the Middle Ages but becoming the almost exclusive Protestant mode of thinking about the Nativity after Luther and Calvin.[63] The contraction of Christ from his omnipresent glory to the limited space of the manger shows Herbert is as aware as Donne is of Christ's power to manipulate space. However, the argument privileges the "second Advent," as Strier designated it, over the first.

In referring to the beasts, traditionally and logically brought into the scene from Luke (which does not mention them), Herbert demonstrates he knows the apocrypha or at least the commentaries by Fathers of the Church. Augustine, as one example, gave an allegorical reading to the beasts' presence in Isaiah 1:3: "The ox knoweth his owner, and the ass his master's crib, but Israel does not know, my people doth not consider."[64] Behind all this lies a recollection, presumably shared with the reader, of a traditional Nativity scene replete with all the human and animal actors. Nevertheless, the speaker does not imagine Christ's body when he imagines himself as Christ's lodging in the couplet:

Furnish and deck my soul, that Thou mayst have
A better lodging, than a rack, or grave.

Christ will come to his soul, and if it is not refurbished by Christ, it will be a Good Friday kind of lodging, not a Christmas one, an instrument of torture or the tomb sealed with the stone. At no point in this sonnet are the speaker and the Christ Child together.

In "Christmas (II)," the speaker merges himself with the shepherds of Luke's Gospel, but does so in their act of leaving the child in order to glorify and praise God. They still seek a sun that does not set to illuminate their artistic acts of praise, implying that the speaker cannot be unified with Christ yet:

The shepherds sing; and shall I silent be?
  My God, no hymn for Thee?
My soul's a shepherd too; a flock it feeds
  Of thoughts, and words, and deeds.
The pasture is Thy word: the streams, Thy grace
  Enriching all the place.
Shepherd and flock shall sing, and all my powers
  Outsing the daylight hours.
Then will we chide the sun for letting night
  Take up his place and right:
We sing one common Lord; wherefore he should
  Himself the candle hold.
I will go searching, till I find a sun

Shall stay, till we have done;
A willing shiner, that shall shine as gladly,
As frost-nipped suns look sadly.
Then will we sing, and shine all our own day,
And one another pay:
His beams shall cheer my breast, and both so twine,
Till ev'n His beams sing, and my music shine.

"Christmas (II)" is so emphatically leaving Bethlehem and searching still that there can be no doubt Herbert is deliberately shifting the reader's focus from an imagined presence at the Nativity to an eventual spiritual union. As R.V. Young noted of this poem, "the movement here and in virtually all of *The Temple* ... is toward deeply personal reflection. Herbert finds the significance of the Nativity in its application to an individual spiritual and moral condition."[65]

The same is true in Herbert's other famous poem on the Incarnation, "The Bag." Although Strier emphasizes the incarnational focus present in the final apostrophizing of Christ, aside from the "new clothes a-making here below" (line 18), there is no reference to the flesh of the infant Jesus in the poem.[66] The Christ who takes off his majestic robes and lays aside his weapons as he descends comes to an inn "as travellers are wont," but not as a baby:

Hast thou not heard, that my Lord Jesus di'd?
Then let me tell thee a strange storie.
The God of power, as he did ride
In his majestic robes of glorie,
Reserv'd to light; and so one day
He did descend, undressing all the way.

The starres his tire of light and rings obtain'd,
The cloud his bow, the fire his spear,
The sky his azure mantle gain'd.
And when they ask'd, what he would wear;
He smil'd and said as he did go,
He had new clothes a making here below.

When he was come, as travellers are wont,
He did repair unto an inne.
Both then, and after, many a brunt
He did endure to cancell sinne:
And having giv'n the rest before,
Here he gave up his life to pay our score. (stanzas 2–4)

Herbert's tendency throughout "The Bag" is to narrate the story in the past tense, further emphasizing the distance between the speaker's own day and the life of Christ on earth. However, we can see he is aware of the traditions we have observed in the previous chapters: "When he was come, / ... he did repair unto an inne. / *Both* then, and after, many a brunt / He did endure to cancell sinne." Herbert acknowledges that the Incarnation is part of the salvific suffering of Christ, but he never participates poetically in the tradition of marvelling at the wondrous smallness, the humility and sweetness, of the almighty God who has become a little child. The special tenderness and protectiveness due to a newborn do not colour his portrayals of the infant Jesus, an omission especially noteworthy because many of Herbert's other poems feature just those qualities of marvelling and sweetness. Neither does he wonder at the infant's paradoxical might.

Whatever the real reason, Herbert never evinces a desire to represent the Christ Child in poetry (or sermon, as far as we know). Robert Whalen's observations about Herbert's approach to the Eucharist seem apt here: "Belief in the centrality of inward spiritual life ... was reinforced by a theology in which the external elements are less effectual instruments than mere signs of a strictly invisible grace."[67] We could perhaps soften Whalen's expression by the removal of the word "mere," but his point that the external elements are not perceived as instrumental is worth considering. If, in "The Starre," Herbert imagines the Christ Child as present but bathed in an excess of light, à la Dante, he is unconcerned, because the effect is still attainable. The Christ Child in Herbert's Nativity poems is invisible, although he saw the child as God and as the pathway to the realms supernal. Thus, like the star of Bethlehem, he was moved to show the place where the child lay.

As we shall see in the next chapter, it is not only Herbert but also John Milton who shies away from the description of the physical child. Both poets concentrate on the effects of the Redemption yet to come to the world or to the self. Their focus on elements other than the actual person of the Christ Child begins to "disincarnate" the Incarnation. Speakers no longer voice any sense of concern, admiration, or affection for a Christ Child whose littleness or suffering were themes of the more traditional Nativity lyric, which insisted on the true physical babyhood or boyhood of the child Jesus. More curiously, both poets reveal a familiarity with the theme of temporal or spatial collapse. Both speak of it or use some variants of it in their Nativity poems, but both reject physical proximity to the Christ Child himself.

Chapter Five

"Wisest Fate Says No": Milton's Nativity Ode

How soon hath thy prediction, Seer blest, Measur'd this transient World, the Race of time, Till time stand fixt: beyond is all abyss, Eternitie, whose end no eye can reach.

Adam to Michael, *Paradise Lost* 12.552–6

On the Morning of Christ's Nativity
Compos'd 1629

I

This is the Month, and this the happy morn
Wherein the Son of Heav'ns eternal King,
Of wedded Maid, and Virgin Mother born,
Our great redemption from above did bring;
For so the holy sages once did sing,
That he our deadly forfeit should release,
And with his Father work us a perpetual peace.

III

Say Heav'nly Muse, shall not thy sacred vein
Afford a present to the Infant God?
Hast thou no vers, no hymn, or solemn strein,
To welcom him to this his new abode,
Now while the Heav'n by the Suns team untrod,
Hath took no print of the approching light,
And all the spangled host keep watch in squadrons bright?

IV

See how from far upon the Eastern rode
The Star-led Wisards haste with odours sweet:
O run, prevent them with thy humble ode,
And lay it lowly at his blessed feet;
Have thou the honour first, thy Lord to greet,
And joyn thy voice unto the Angel Quire,
From out his secret Altar toucht with hallow'd fire.

XVI

But wisest Fate sayes no,
This must not yet be so,
The Babe lies yet in smiling Infancy,
That on the bitter cross
Must redeem our loss;
So both himself and us to glorifie:
Yet first to those ychain'd in sleep,
The wakefull trump of doom must thunder through the deep.[1]

In "On the Morning of Christ's Nativity," written in 1629, Milton refers to the Christ Child by many titles. He is the "Son of Heav'ns eternal King," who sits "at Heavn's high Councel-Table," "the midst of Trinal Unity." He is the "Infant God," "thy Lord," whose "secret altar" is "toucht with hallow'd fire." He is the "Heav'n-born-childe," Nature's "Great Master" and "her Maker," the "Sovran lord" of kings, the "Prince of Light," the "Lord" of the stars, a "greater Sun," "the mighty Pan." He is "Heav'n's new-born Heir," both the "Babe" and the "dreadfull Judge," the "dreaded Infant" who shows his "Godhead true." Lastly, again, he is "[Mary's] Babe" and the "sleeping Lord" of "Heav'n's youngest-teemed Star." The "Elegia Sexta," written at the same time, pronounces the Christ Child, wonderfully, "caelifugam … deum" – the "Heaven-fleeing God."[2] If these descriptions constitute a sort of litany to Christ recited by the youthful Milton, it is a litany emphasizing both Christ's humanity and his divine power. It is orthodox and traditional. As Dayton Haskins and Anton Vander Zee have both pointed out, the poem even emphasizes the Virgin Mary's role in ways we might not expect from a Protestant.[3]

Yet the poem strangely resists traditional representations of the Nativity, dismissing the (unscriptural) ox and ass, emphasizing the military aspects of the attendant angels, and above all, focusing more insistently on the exorcism of the pagan gods from their altars than on the manger/altar image that goes back at least to John Chrysostom.[4] There is no St. Joseph, and it is part of the poet's design that the Magi should not arrive in time to be part of the representation. But someone is at this Nativity scene, someone who has never put in an appearance before – that character is "wisest Fate."

There are two lords of history in the Nativity Ode: the babe and fate. John Milton's "On the Morning of Christ's Nativity," with its impressive magnitude and a more ambitious scope than most Nativity lyrics had attempted in the long history of the genre, poses the question of who oversees salvation history, in the end deciding that it is not the Christ Child; the babe whom the Virgin has laid to rest smiles in ignorance of his coming Passion. This chapter focuses on three points Milton makes interdependent in his poem: the intervention of fate in the poetic collapse of time that the poet imagines between his own day and the birth of Christ; the mediation of the Heavenly Muse; and the infant's smile. Milton's invention of a character or force he calls "wisest Fate" moves the locus of power away from the Christ Child to something or someone else, whose identity remains a mystery. Thus, Milton's poem constitutes a decisive step away from the traditional view of the mighty babe, the Christ Child who governs, judges, and fights, and the all-wise but vulnerable infant, who knows why he has come into the world and is already beginning his salvific action.

The Nativity Ode occupies a signal place in the history of the Nativity lyric. Its grandeur and ambitious length seem to look forward already to Milton's later epic style and form. Its learnedness outshines the studied simplicity of some of his forerunners, and its proposal of a grand outline of human history gives it greater scope. Above all, since Milton's accomplishment in *Paradise Lost* will later grant him an authority and almost prophetic status among the English, his more youthful works bask in that reflected light. The dignity and august sobriety of the Nativity Ode set it off from the many other lyric treatments of the Incarnation of the century. Moreover, Milton's classicism will be adopted by his most important eighteenth-century literary descendant, Alexander Pope, who will increase the Virgilian echoes in his "Messiah." Between them, Herbert and Milton overshadow their earlier forerunners in the subgenre, and their representational choices prevail in the period during and after the Commonwealth. Few writers follow Southwell, and Donne's *La Corona* sonnets appear to have no imitators. We look in vain for Nativity poetry from Marvell, Cowley, or Dryden (who translated Virgil's Messianic Eclogue but, unlike Pope, did not attempt to Christianize it into a Nativity poem). Milton's desire to create a sense of presence in the poem harks back to the earlier Nativity lyric; his physical distance from the disembodied Christ Child is a waymark in the history of the Nativity lyric in England, pointing forward to the preoccupation with classicism of the eighteenth century.

Lowry Nelson helpfully notes Milton's confusion of verb tenses and frequent use of the present tense to create a sense that the Nativity is happening now, when Milton is writing it, celebrating his soberly poetic Christmas in counter-distinction to his friend Charles Diodati's more festive and food-filled Yule in 1629.[5] Milton is thinking about distinctions between pagan and Christian, Catholic and Protestant, medieval and (for him) modern theophany as he writes this great lyric. Many critics have noted the seemingly elegiac regret over the dismissal of the pagan gods, but have not much discussed the Virgilian smile of the infant, who has perhaps emptied out his divine knowledge and divine eternal perspective in taking on flesh. Although there are elements of the ode that make it clear that Milton's Christology at the age of twenty-one is Nicaean and traditional, Milton's assigning the phrase "smiling infancy" to describe the consciousness and power of the newborn Christ is a troubling new note in the history of the Nativity lyric.

Like other Nativity poets, Milton wants his poem to imitate in some way the immanence of Christ, to bring Christ down from heaven in a reiteration of the moment of the Incarnation. Milton is unlike any previous poet we have examined, however, and perhaps unique, in the meta-poetic conflict he foregrounds over whether or not to produce a poetic mimesis of presence in his Nativity poem. The presence that words may effect is of course always an imaginative, as opposed to a physical, one. Words can only reify by producing images of physical things or sounds that connote physicality (such as in onomatopoeia): they cannot make things; they are not magic spells or creative fiats. The mimesis may be, as Sidney claims, a mimesis of the poet's fore-conceit and not even of nature, but a poem cannot enable a reader to hold or kiss a child. One of the informing ideas of the poem is Milton's recognition of this fact: these are privileges he reserves for Mary, who perhaps, as Anton Vander Zee argues, has been nursing the Christ Child while the poet has engaged his imagination with the exorcism of the pagan gods.[6] The poet's ambition is only to lay his poem at the "blessed feet" of the Christ Child, to consecrate his poetry to him, not to touch him, although the mention of the baby's feet is a gesture in the direction of the incarnate flesh.

Milton's admirers often try to obviate the coldness implied by the neoclassical form of the Nativity Ode by claiming for it the ability to conjure, like Nativity poems of old, the devotion of the audience. Gordon Teskey says that the poem ends "in a beautiful stanza that emphasizes the humanity of the child, while the signs of his divinity – the star overhead and the angels guarding the stable – stand at a distance."[7] As we have seen throughout this study, the question of how the poets present the Incarnation has a great deal to do with their respective positions on Christ's divinity, humanity, and the ways in which he remains immanent in the life of the believer. Teskey believes Milton foregrounds the human and de-emphasizes the divine, a position we shall see not everyone agrees with. Along these lines, Ann Baynes Coiro even goes so far as to read Milton's imagery throughout the ode as a veiled description of the "act of birth," which would make Milton's poem the most insistent on the physical reality of Christ's birth of any of the lyrics I examine here, though she herself remarks: "[In] the Nativity Ode itself, as many critics have noted, there is a conspicuous absence of the bodily."[8]

In fact, many a reader has shared the sense that the poem distances us from the reality of the Incarnation. Rosemond Tuve observed long ago that the "Gospel narratives of the Nativity" are less important preparation for understanding the poem than are other gospel texts about the mystery of peace.[9] Martin Evans asserts that the ode participates in a traditional Pindaric stance of distance.[10] Ann Christina Fawcett goes even further in assessing Christ's immanence in the ode when she calls it a "supposedly Christian poem" and comments on the "oddly Herculean" Christ Child who controls the "damned crew" of pagan gods.[11] How is a reader to reconcile these completely opposing judgments on perhaps the most important Nativity poem in the English language? Is the answer only to be found in Milton's oscillation between extreme views in an unresolvable delirium, as Teskey has recently argued about Milton's entire oeuvre?[12] Taking a fresh look at several key cruces in the poem – the sources and analogues of the representation of the Christ Child's divine power, the well-rehearsed issue of Milton's collapse of temporal distinctions, the identity of wisest Fate, and the portrayal of the infant as smiling – will reveal that, although Milton's portrayal of the Incarnation is in some ways even more traditional than George Herbert's, it opens the door to his later, heretical Christology. But Milton at twenty-one is not Milton at fifty, as a comparison to the poem he wrote soon after the Nativity Ode, "Upon the Circumcision," will show: Milton's understanding of the Incarnation in his early twenties was probably orthodox, although he is troubled by issues of presence that resonate with Calvinist understandings of sacrament and immanence.

Milton's Italian Sources

Determining Milton's understanding of who Christ is and what the purpose of a Nativity lyric might be involves knowing something about the works that inspired him. Milton adopts techniques for collapsing time and producing a mimesis of presence from various Italian poets, among others. Torquato Tasso, whose favourite authors were Plato, Virgil, and Dante,[13] has long been thought an influence on the Nativity Ode: Grierson and Carey showed distinct parallels between Tasso's Nativity poem and Milton's.[14] Feinstein also convincingly argued for Gian Francesco Pico's *Hymnus ad Christum* as precursor and pattern for the young Milton's Nativity Ode.[15] In spite of the many beauties of Tasso's and Pico's poems, however, Milton's youthful work is more ambitious and more memorable. It is nonetheless worth noting that some elements on which we might base our assumptions about Milton's theological beliefs are in fact common to these Italian Catholic poems. Tasso himself was probably inspired by other baroque poets and by the great Nativity mosaic in Santa Maria Maggiore by Jacopo Torriti.[16] These poems manifest Byzantine, medieval, and classical influences, which perhaps one could say lie as a palimpsest behind Milton's great Nativity Ode as much as Milton's own more immediate inspirations. Tasso, for instance, mixes tenses in his poem much as Milton will do, while spanning the primitive Protoevangelium of Genesis and the overthrow of Satan at the end of time.[17] He also, like Milton, punctuates the temporal play with reminders of the line of time: in Tasso's poem, as in Milton's, it is the cross that achieves the salvation, which is only commencing at the Nativity. I believe Milton was interested in precisely this detail and adapted it to his own purposes in his Nativity Ode.

That Milton interrupts a vision of atemporal salvation or return to a golden age is unusual, but has an ancestor in Tasso's "Per il presepio," although there is no smiling baby in Tasso. Nor is this technique only to be found in Milton and Tasso, as Lowry Nelson showed in his comparison of the Nativity Ode to Góngora's *Polifemo*.[18] As for elements drawn from Pico's "Hymnus ad Christum," Feinstein says: "By favoring the routing of the pagan gods, by equating them with confusion, ugliness, error, and by drawing on a poet who is essentially antipoetic and starkly Christian, Milton demonstrates in the Nativity hymn-ode that early in his career he is strongly on the side of orthodoxy."[19]

Salvation History: Time as a Line versus God's "Nunc Stans"

What is innovative and perhaps unique in Milton's view of the Nativity is the intervention of "wisest Fate" in the middle of the poem. Milton thereby alerts us to the limitations of language and manifests a Calvinist or an Anglican concept of God's immanence. Although he plays with verb tenses, Milton interpolates reminders of the orderly passage of time, which, as we have seen, poets who wish to delete temporal distinctions generally do not do. Moreover, although he begins the poem by imagining that his ode can be laid at the feet of the newborn Christ Child, by the middle of the poem he denies the ode the possibility of joining with the angels' song. Since the Nativity is in the unreachable past, there can be no real union between time-bound man and the eternal God made flesh in the Incarnation. This division between man on earth and Christ in heaven constituted an essential tenet of Calvinism and of the more extreme Servetist and Waldensian views of the relationship between man and God. Milton's technique of imitation echoes the contemporary interpretations on the Lord's Supper as sacrament that most emphasized the lack of Christ's bodily presence.

First, it is important to acknowledge that Milton does in fact have an interest in making the past event of the Nativity present to the reader, and he exerts his powers to achieve this end. He uses some of the same techniques to collapse time that one sees in many medieval poems.[20] These are poetic tropes and schemes of order that we have seen in previous chapters. For instance, Milton begins and ends the poem in the present tense: "This is the Month, and this the happy morn" when "all about the Courtly Stable, / Bright-harness'd Angels sit in order serviceable."

Edward W. Tayler argues that, by the fourth stanza of the poem, the "'now' of Christmas 1629 has become the 'now' of the actual Christmas of the Nativity and not merely its calendrical commemoration" because the poet can run before the Magi, that is, take part physically in the scene.[21] "The 'Now' of the Nativity Ode may therefore also be considered a poetic 'nunc stans,' glancing simultaneously toward present and past and conflating the two events separated in Time as though viewed from the vantage of Eternity."[22] In fact, Lowry Nelson claims, "the birth of Christ and every Christmas are essentially the same,"[23] ascribing to the poem an imaginative effect achieved by this use of the historical present and the admixture of tenses similar to what we have earlier observed with the admixture of addresses in Donne's "Nativitie."

In addition to Tayler and Nelson, Gregory F. Goekjian and Ralph W. Condee have discussed the occurrence of the tense shifts and their effect in terms of what Auerbach calls "imitatio veritatis" – the imitation of God's eternal perspective, outside of time. Such a form of imitation points not only to the concrete future but also to something that has always been and always will be; it points to something in need of interpretation that will indeed be fulfilled in the concrete future but is at all times present, fulfilled in God's providence, which knows no difference in time.[24]

However, to draw a clearer distinction, Auerbach defines this "imitatio" as the representation in a figure of an event we perceive as being in the future, but which God perceives as being in the present. This type of imitation, according to Auerbach, does not describe a union between the author or reader and the God who does not dwell in time. The collapse of time Auerbach discusses points, but does not enact.

Milton also, like his Italian predecessors, devotes a great deal of the poem to subordinating the sun and the sun gods of old to the brightness of the newborn Christ.[25] This technique, too, denies the authority of linear time and subordinates its passage to the newborn Christ, who is eternal. Is Milton claiming for the poet, as Crashaw did in his "To the Morning: Satisfaction for Sleepe," the ability to "stand upon the shoulders of Old Time, and trace eternity"?[26] These factors in the Nativity Ode reveal that Milton already knows how to use the traditional techniques to create a sense of simultaneity; without his warning against the collapse of time in stanza XVI, his poem would be a pattern of temporal collapse. However, he also wants us to know that, though "holy Song" may have this power over the imagination, "wisest Fate" has decreed the temporal distinctions that divide the babe from the suffering adult, and both from us.

Once we acknowledge that Milton knows how to manipulate the reader into thinking everything is going on at once, we need to consider what he tells us explicitly about time in the text of the poem. Do we have an eternal present, when Milton expressly forbids the conflation of the Incarnation, the Passion, and the Golden Age?

> But wisest Fate says no,
> This must not yet be so,
> The Babe lies yet in smiling Infancy,
> That on the bitter cross
> Must redeem our loss;
>
> So both himself and us to glorify:
> Yet first to those ychain'd in sleep,
> The wakeful trump of doom must thunder through the deep.

The "fullness" and "perfection" of "our bliss" is impossible until the crucifixion, and now that we are in the present tense with the Nativity, the Passion is a distant future point on the line of time, as is the Last Judgment. Far from collapsing the two events of the Nativity and the crucifixion, Milton introduces the cross as the sign through which he can re-establish the linearity of historical time.

There are many medieval lyrics that carefully denote the distinctions between events in salvation history;[27] however, no other Nativity poem contains such a caveat to the reader. If we imagine ourselves in the "eternal present" because of his use of other traditional techniques, Milton soundly disabuses us of our illusion: our perspective is linear and earthly after all, for if we did have God's perspective, we would not have to put off the cross or the Last Judgment. The compression of time into the "momentaneous present" may be an attractive poetic device, but Milton affirms that it is neither real nor mimetic. Two things must happen before it can be real: the Passion (which has happened, but not in the present tense of Milton's ode) and the Apocalypse (which has not happened yet). We have no real, tangible link to the incarnate God that would make the real collapse of time possible until he returns.

The very centre of the "Hymn" – stanza XIV – contains the proposal, already hedged with an "if," that time might bring back the Golden Age through "holy Song," an image of temporal unity in its "ninefold harmony." But Milton very carefully puts all these possibilities into the future tense. They, too, do not belong to the present because his song only creates a fiction of presence. The poet is conscious of what tense shifts might imply, conscious enough to have "wisest Fate" say "No, / This must not yet be so." Milton makes it clear that the events of salvation history are, from our perspective, discrete points in time. They do not overlap or occur together as one mystery because "the Babe lies yet in smiling Infancy."

Having made this distinction, Milton can settle into the present tense for the rest of the poem (stanzas XVIII–XXVII) with no fear that his characters will step out of the frame of their painting, or that we will step in. The doctrinal distinction that hinges on this point may account for the stridency of tone in the beginning of the stanza, the abrupt intrusiveness of "wisest Fate." If all the emotion of the poem were tied up in its ability to evoke a "momentaneous present," the force of wisest Fate's intervention would destroy it. It would seem Milton introduced wisest Fate into the poem to do something along those lines.

Milton does not seem to wish to invest his poem or the moment of the Incarnation itself with the power to make eternity accessible to human beings. He refrains even though he uses the traditional image of the mighty babe that we have examined in Southwell's poetry. Does he not believe that the Christ Child whose birth he celebrates is capable of being the nexus of all points in time? If the Christ Child in the manger is not the Lord of time and eternity, if he is not the still spot in the temporal flux, a force directing his movements might be that Lord.

In spite of what I.H. Hanford argues in *The Youth of Milton*, it is possible the young Milton's views were not orthodox, if by orthodox we mean in full accord with the writings of the Fathers or with the contemporary beliefs of the Church of England.[28] Milton's own interpretation of the scriptures and his studies would eventually lead him to argue explicitly not only against sacramentality but also against the divinity of Christ and his co-eternity with the Father, but the habit of mind that will lead him to the views he will enunciate thirty-odd years later in *The Christian Doctrine* can already be seen in the Nativity Ode. Yes, Milton calls Jesus "the Infant God"; yes, he identifies the Christ Child as the second person of the Trinity (stanza II, line 11); yes, "Our Babe, to show his Godhead true, / Can in his swaddling bands control the damned crew" (stanza XXV, lines 227–8). But Milton sees the "perpetual peace" of line 7 as incomplete. Milton hesitates over the question of perpetuity, and this hesitation in itself is significant. If Christ as a newborn has the power to control the pagan gods, why can he not conquer time?

The earthly life of Jesus recounted in the four gospels without question plays itself out on the line of time, with a beginning at the Annunciation and an end at the Ascension. However, because the Christ Child was always considered as possessing all the powers of his godhead, hymns in the early ages of the Church discussed the incarnate Word at his birth as Lord of time and eternity, and as co-eternal with the Father. The Latin hymns of the Incarnation most probably known to Milton, such as "Corde natus ex parentis" (Prudentius) and "Veni, redemptor gentium" (Ambrose),[29] among others, assert the eternity of Christ without qualification.

Although there is nothing unorthodox in Milton's argument that the Golden Age cannot return (in fact, the opposite) and that evil is not fully conquered until the Second Coming of Christ as judge, there is something singular in his reasoning. That something is his insistence on Christ's limitation by time. Milton uses the Christ Child to make the distinctions between moments in human, linear time: because the Christ Child is still an infant, the cross and the Last Judgment are inaccessible to the reader. Because the Christ Child is still an infant, wisest Fate can intervene and put a stop to idle "fancy" of a union between heaven and earth. The young Milton's noteworthy innovation in the Nativity lyric is not a mere lack of interest in the eternal perspective of the Christ Child; it is a deliberate restriction of that perspective.

If the angels' music of stanzas IX onward bridges heaven and earth, bringing the music of the spheres and the poet's song (stanza IV) into the simultaneity of harmony, why does Milton refuse to see the gates of heaven open and Truth, Justice, and Mercy moving between heaven and earth (stanza XV)? It is because he doubts that the "crystal spheres" have the power so to "touch our senses"; he fears that "holy Song" should not "enwrap our fancy" to the point of confounding times. Music cannot yet "hold all Heav'n and Earth in happier union"; union will only come after the "horrid clang" announcing the Last Judgment.

By the time of the composition of *Paradise Lost* and *Paradise Regained*, Milton will resolutely disbelieve in the Trinity; his view of Christ as a creature subordinate to the Father is developed at length in both poems and in his prose works: "it seems to be altogether impossible that the Son should be either begotten or born from all eternity ... Since therefore the Son derives his essence from the Father, he is posterior to the Father not merely in rank (a distinction unauthorized by Scripture, and by which many are deceived) but also in essence."[30] Milton devotes much of his argument to proving that Christ cannot be "coeval" with the Father and avoids even mentioning Christ's declaration "Before Abraham was made, I AM" (John 13:58), the assertion that Milton certainly knew was the scriptural foundation for the doctrine of Christ's eternity as well as his divinity (because Christ ascribes to himself the name God pronounces as his own in Exodus 3:14–15 – "I am"). Milton's claim to knowledge of the arguments for Christ's divinity and eternity must be justified: we know from his "Prolusion Against Scholastic Philosophy" that his work at the university included theological arguments which, according to him, he already found very distasteful. The Nativity Ode itself shows a familiarity with the extensive literature on the Incarnation, written in the preceding centuries by men who did not hesitate to speak of the divinity of the Christ Child.

Wisest Fate as Lord of History

Although Milton manifests the traditional poetic desire to show his own devotion to the Christ Child in a mystical evocation of the birth's presence to his contemplative mind,[31] he also insists upon the unaccomplished task of redemption that the child in the manger is not yet master of. This insistence affects the poem's portrayal of Christ. Aligning himself with and competing against the angels and wise men, Milton in the Nativity Ode still has "wisest Fate" interpose to prevent premature rejoicing in Christ's victory. Thus the real question about time in the Nativity Ode does not devolve upon the poet's ability to manipulate verbal structures or to evoke the scene of Christ's birth compellingly. Milton inserted into this poem a question, Who governs time and history? – a question no other Nativity poet has asked because, previous to him, they all would have given the same answer. Whoever or whatever "wisest Fate" is, it does govern time, and it opposes the power of "holy Song"; it has the power to re-assert the dominance of linear time in a world that is tempted by the idea that Christ's birth means either immediate salvation or a Virgilian return to the Golden Age. On a first reading, the character wisest Fate might appear to belong to the classical world that forms such an important part of the ode, but in fact, Milton's wisest Fate opposes both pagan circularity and the deceptive "Fancy" of earlier Christian poets.[32]

What, however, is wisest Fate doing in the stable with the Christian God? The easiest answer to this question derives from Milton's later poem *Paradise Lost*. If Stanley Fish is right, that Milton never changes his ideas over his entire career[33] (an argument better Milton scholars than I have refuted), the Father's "What I will is Fate" in *Paradise Lost* explains the mysterious voice that intervenes in the Nativity Ode:

> Though I uncircumscrib'd myself retire,
> And put not forth my goodness, which is free
> To act or not, Necessity and Chance
> Approach not mee, and what I will is Fate. (*Paradise Lost* 7.170–4)

When he writes *Paradise Lost*, Milton makes God's providence "Fate," refuting Satan's claim that Fate is necessity. Walter Clyde Curry cites Ben Lumpkin's early study on Fate in *Paradise Lost*: "It may be recalled that in the *Christian Doctrine* (XIV, 7), Milton had shown impatience with those who, like some Neoplatonists, associate Fate merely with the workings of Nature and had concluded, 'Fate can be nothing but a divine decree emanating from some almighty power.'"[34] If Milton has determined in his college years what he asserts later, then wisest Fate is God the Father, who does not bow to any kind of necessity. Although one cannot legitimately turn to a later work to explain precisely what Milton means by wisest Fate in 1629, there is another reason for believing Milton had perhaps already defined fate for himself in this way. Milton's known familiarity with Epiphanius's *Panarion* against the heresies of the early Church had probably begun in his days as a student; it is likely he read it in his course of studies preparatory to receiving holy orders in the Church of England, which of course he never proceeded to do. However, a heavy dose of theology was part of a Cambridge education in Milton's day, and all students receiving a bachelor's degree and preparing to undertake the master's signed a document promising to continue on to the priesthood. Milton himself signed such a document. Epiphanius's *Panarion* was the sourcebook par excellence for the understanding of heresies of the early Church for these future priests.

Epiphanius takes on the problem of the definition of fate explicitly, and dismisses the concept of fate as opposed to the doctrine of free will and God's justice in judging the merit of saints and sinners.[35] These are the stances Milton will take toward the issue in *Paradise Lost*. It seems at first that this conclusion would be the simplest answer to this central problem in the Nativity Ode, though we are then left with the problem of why the Father has to correct everyone's false impression that the arrival of the Son on earth means sin is conquered.

It is also possible Milton has not yet developed his view of God's providence as fate at this stage of his career. After all, Crashaw speaks of fate in his poem on the Holy Innocents, "In felices Martyres":

> Nos miseri sumus ex amplo; spatioque perimus.
> In nos inquirunt fata; probabantque manus.
>
> Ingenium fati sumus, ambitioque malorum;
> Conatus mortis, consiliumque sumus.[36]

And Barbara Lewalski observes that John Donne in his poem "Crucyfying" (in the *La Corona* sonnets) says: "During the passion Christ's enemies 'prescribe a Fate' to Christ, 'Whose creature Fate is … / Measuring self-lifes infinity to'a span, / Nay, to an inch.'"[37] Donne, thinking of time and eternity himself, describes Christ as subject to fate, meaning a fatal death sentence, in the Passion. He does not think of fate as the will of God the Father in a poem written some fifteen to twenty years before Milton's. So was Milton's view in those early years the same as it was later, and how can we know?

Milton introduces in an "if" clause the potential power of "holy Song." Holy Song's power is able to inspire a return to the Golden Age; the time that is under the poet's control is therefore cyclical:

> For if such holy Song
> Enwrap our fancy long,
> Time will run back, and fetch the age of gold,
> And speckl'd vanity
> Will sicken soon and die,
> And leprous sin will melt from earthly mold,
> And Hell itself will pass away,
> And leave her dolorous mansions to the peering day.
> …
> But wisest Fate says "No." [133–40, 149]

A belief in time as a cycle rather than as a line is an attribute of classical culture, as various scholars have demonstrated. The basic pre-Christian, classical conception of time is represented by a circle.[38] The return of the Saturnian Age that Virgil speaks of in his Fourth Eclogue is perhaps an imagined and not a real return, but it represents the only way Virgil sees of reclaiming innocence and justice: going back to the beginning. Thus in the *Aeneid,* he imagines the gods of Troy returning to their native places in Latium, and the just race of Romans arising from the commingling of the bloods of the Latins, who still live in the Saturnian Age, with the Trojans, who wish to reconstitute it in the future. This example is but one famous example of the way in which return is rebirth in classical thought, but it is clearly a kind of renewal that Milton thinks is as impossible as it is imaginatively compelling.

Fancy, too, will later have a definition in *Paradise Lost* when Adam explains to Eve how it differs from imagination, and how little it is to be relied on (5.100–13). The problem Milton has introduced into this early poem is the inability of the reader to identify the voice: in the context of a Virgilian return to the Golden Age, the reader is perhaps lulled into thinking of wisest Fate as Virgil's "Fatum."

Milton, I would suggest, is thinking about the relationship of the newborn Christ Child to time. It occurs to him that Christ submits himself to time in some way through the Incarnation; how the eternal God can be confined by time and how he can grow, develop, and mature on the line of time is of course a mystery. As I have said, like Tasso and Pico, Milton imagines the sun realizing he has lost his authority over time. Jonathon Goldberg, writing of the traditional contrast between the earthly sun and heaven's newborn Son, says Milton complicates it through the presence of Hesperus/Lucifer, who "submits to the *stella matutina* assuming that the Apocalypse is at hand, but 'wisest Fate says no.'"[39] He concludes: "Nature errs by reading the first appearance of Christ in history as his last."[40] I would simply add that it is part of the overall design of the Nativity Ode that Nature should make this error, because Milton wants to correct it. When Lowry Nelson says that "the Christian idea of the circularity of time and the simultaneity of all moments under the aspect of eternity underline the innermost structure of the poem," I believe he confuses two different world views that Milton takes pains to differentiate.[41] Pietro Siniscalco, who collated the conclusions of theorists and historiographers on the subject, offered as the standard formulation Oscar Cullmann's thesis:

> E nota la tesi di O. Cullmann secondo cui per il cristianesimo primitivo, come per il giudaismo e per la religione iraniana, l'espressione

simbolica del t[empo] sarebbe la linea, mentre per l'ellenismo sarebbe il circolo.[42]

Oscar Cullmann's thesis is well known; according to him, for primitive Christianity, as for Judaism and for Iranian religion, the symbolic expression of time is the line, whereas for Hellenism it is the circle. (translation mine).

The Judeo-Christian concept of time is generally linear, not circular.[43] Milton, in any case, excludes the idea of return specifically. His sense of history, like that of Albert Schweitzer and Martin Werner,[44] seems to hinge on the Parousia, not on the coming of Christ. The "wisest" voice directs our attention to the Second Coming, away from the picture of prelapsarian innocence where hell has no human inhabitants, away from the fabulous "Saturnia regna" (line 4) of Virgil's Fourth Eclogue.[45] Even the fiction of poetry should not betray us with a false hope. Christ did not come to turn back the clock, nor is the eternal now of heaven available to those who dwell in history.

The Heavenly Muse

In another stroke against the creation of a sense of presence, Milton creates a mediator who does not bring him to the Christ Child, but who goes in his place: the Heavenly Muse. The possibility of seeing or touching the Christ Child is a part of the collapse of linear time in the poems of Robert Southwell and John Donne, but in Milton's poem the poet is not even present at the Nativity scene. Alison Shell speaks of "Southwell's audaciousness" "in doing away with neo-platonic machinery and other transitional figures between human and divine; his poetry seeks an apprehension of God with which even a heavenly muse would interfere."[46] However, in Milton's work, it is the "Heav'nly Muse" and not the speaker who runs ahead of the Wise Men to the stable:

Say Heav'nly Muse, shall not thy sacred vein
Afford a present to the Infant God?
Hast thou no verse, no hymn, or solemn strain,
To welcome him to this his new abode,
Now while the Heav'n by the Sun's team untrod,
Hath took no print of the approaching light,
And all the spangled host keep watch in squadrons bright?

See how far upon the Eastern road
The Star-led Wizards haste with odors sweet:
O run, prevent them with thy humble ode,
And lay it lowly at his blessed feet. [III–IV.15–25]

The pronoun "thy" has as its only logical antecedent the Muse, not Milton. In other words, the Heavenly Muse can overpass the constraints of linear time as the poet cannot. It is perfectly rational for Milton to appoint a Heavenly Muse as an allegory of memory or an angelic (or divine) traveller between the present and the past, but such an appointment is not conducive to the elimination of spatial distinctions.[47]

A strong case can be made for attributing the entire "Hymn" to the voice of this Heavenly Muse whom Milton has conjured in the two preceding stanzas. Whether the speaker of the "Hymn" is Milton or the Heavenly Muse, however, the fact remains that even at the close the speaker points to the scene for us, but does not participate in it:

> But see! the Virgin blest;
> Hath laid the Babe to rest.
> Time is our tedious Song should here have ending;
> Heav'n's youngest-teemed Star
> Hath fixt her polisht Car,
> Her sleeping Lord with Handmaid Lamp attending:
> And all about the Courtly Stable,
> Bright-harness'd Angels sit in order serviceable. [XXVII.237–44]

The poet or Heavenly Muse can see within and without the stable, an "omniscient narrator" rather than "first person." The poet himself does not kneel by the crib in this "Mystic Nativity," but, as Beverley Sherry says, "he writes around the picture frame"[48] or, like Da Vinci's angel in Vasari's *Baptism of Christ*, he looks at the viewer and points to the scene. This stance is a deliberate choice: he is a seer or a prophet,[49] not a participant. Nor are we.

The sense of the importance of the Incarnation in the "On the Morning of Christ's Nativity" rests, then, not on the evocation of the closeness and immediacy of God's presence but in an acknowledgment of the spiritual benefits that the Incarnation gained for the world and in the loveliness and evocative power of the language the Heavenly Muse fashions into a "solemn strain" of welcome. This language, however, is not powerful enough against the dictates of wisest Fate to arrest time in its course.

The Nativity and Kenosis

What the Christ Child's powers are then becomes a question. Milton seems to have some hesitation here too; the previous topics that arise in the poem might demonstrate his doubts over the power of poetry, but when we turn to the way he depicts "our Babe," we might notice some differences from the representations we have seen thus far. Examining what Milton thinks about Christ's self-emptying or "κένωσις" in the Incarnation is the next step to understanding his depiction of Christ in the Nativity Ode. Guy Jobin actually refers to Milton's *Paradise Lost* as an example of the continuation of the patristic idea of "kenosis": in Jobin's view, the mature Milton adheres to the traditional concept that Christ veiled his glory rather than enunciating a subordinationist position that would see kenosis as Christ actually renouncing his divine attributes while in human flesh. Jobin claims that *that* view dates from the nineteenth century and later.[50] It is, however, very clear that this understanding was already in the air before the middle of the seventeenth century in England. In a study of Crashaw's life at Cambridge, Kelliher provides the documents for a case brought against a Reverend Ellis in 1641 in which Crashaw witnessed that Ellis said Christ was limited by his taking on flesh. Ellis denied the charge that he had said in a sermon "Christ is Personally Limited" and added: "But this Sonne of God, Infinite as Himselfe, at this his Inanition (the Deity and Humanity making but One Person in him theanthropos God = Man) became Finite [viz: in our nature assum'd soe that Christ, as hee is Man or the Sonne of Man, cannot be in two, or many places together, Acts 3.21]."[51] Ellis's answer shows that he is influenced by Wycliff and Calvin's interpretation of Peter's words in Acts 3:21 about Christ, "whom the heaven must receive until the times of restitution of all things, which God hath spoken by the mouth of all his holy prophets since the world began. Or, be taken up into heaven" (Geneva Bible English translation). As I discussed in chapter one, this verse compelled Calvin to reject any sacramentology that embraced the concept of Christ's bodily presence as a substance in the Eucharist, and the Geneva translation earned Lutheran condemnation.[52] To refresh the reader's memory, Calvin argues in the *Institutes*,

> For as we do not doubt that Christ's body is limited by the general characteristics common to all human bodies, and is contained in heaven (where it was once for all received) until Christ return in judgment [Acts 3:21], so we deem it utterly unlawful to draw it back under these corruptible elements or to imagine it to be present everywhere.[53]

Clearly, though at first sight kenosis might seem not to have much relation to Christ's immanence in the sacraments, Calvinist-leaning Anglicans of Crashaw's day – and Milton's – believed that the self-emptying of the Incarnation prevented Christ's bodily presence in the sacrament after the Ascension. The rules applying to the physical limitations – geographical and temporal – of a human body apply to Christ even after he rises from the dead and ascends to the Father.

The debate over how one was to understand kenosis in Paul's hymn of Christ emptying himself to take on the form of a slave (Philippians 2:5–11) is central to understanding Milton's Christology. I include the text from the Geneva Bible here for those readers who might not be familiar with it, although Milton had no trouble reading New Testament Greek and probably even in his teens would have done so in preference to a translation:

> Let the same minde be in you that was euen in Christ Iesus, Who being in the forme of God, thought it no robbery to be equal with God: But he made himselfe of no reputation, and tooke on him the forme of a servuant, and was made like vnto men, and was found in shape as a man. He humbled himselfe, & became obedient vnto the death, euen the death of the crosse. Wherefore also God hath highly exalted him, and giuen him a name aboue euery name, That at the Name of Iesus should euery knee bowe, *both* of things in heauen, and things in earth, and things vnder the earth, And that euery tongue should confesse that Iesus Christ *is* the Lord, vnto the glorie of God the Father.[54]

The Geneva Bible might indeed have given rise to a kenotic theology that understood Christ's self-emptying as his surrendering his divine attributes: this version glosses the end of Luke 2 with its verse on Christ's submission to his parents and growth in wisdom thus: "Christ verie man is made like vnto vs in all things, except sinne." Although the commenter does not assert this idea, the ambiguous reference to another famous biblical passage at just this juncture seems to indicate that Christ learned like a normal human being, implying that he did not have omniscience.

Michael Lieb's work on the subject also argues that Milton, even at the time he wrote *Paradise Lost*, understood the Son's kenosis in the traditional way. That is to say, Milton followed Origen and Augustine in representing the Son's emptying of himself as setting aside his glory but not his divine knowledge and omnipotence: "the form of the servant was added, the form of God not subtracted."[55] Thus, Milton does not think of Christ as having surrendered his divine prerogatives in taking on the form of man. Yet we know that in *Paradise Regained* the Christ Child does not know he is God until he is twelve. Such ignorance of his mission and identity is impossible for the Christ Child in any Nativity poem we have studied thus far. But does Milton at age twenty-one think the infant Christ does not know who he is? We cannot presume that a poet thinks exactly at age sixty-three what he thought at twenty-one. But it is possible that even at that age he could have been more radical than the Puritans, just when readers would expect him to side with Calvin. That is, it might already have occurred to the young Milton that the assumption of a human body meant not only that Christ could be wounded and die in the Passion but that he might not be equal in power or knowledge to the Father so long as he possessed a human body.

Fate, Fatum, and the Smiling Christ Child

What power has Christ renounced in becoming a child? One of the most popular paradoxes in Nativity poetry and sermons throughout the Middle Ages and the Renaissance was the Verbum infans – the silent Word. Milton well knew that "fatum," the word for fate, had the same root as "infans: "But wisest *Fate* says no / This must not yet be so / The Babe lies yet in smiling *Infancy*" (italics mine). "Fatum" means what has been spoken; Christ is as yet "infans" – without speech. The Word is silent. This polyptoton draws our attention to the disjunction between wisest Fate and the Christ Child. If wisest Fate is the Father speaking, or another force speaking, or the Word himself looking upon himself as a child from his vantage point outside of time, that force is still not one with the babe lying in the Virgin's arms.

> The Babe lies yet in smiling Infancy,
> That on the bitter cross
> Must redeem our loss;
> So both himself and us to glorify.

Hence, Christ is not really here, before our eyes, nor is the redeemed world he will eventually perfect. God's eternal now is not for us, and it seems not to be for the child, either.

Milton told his friend Charles Diodati that he intended in the Nativity Ode to "sing the peace-bringing King of heavenly generation, / and the blessed times promised in the sacred books; / the crying of God" ("Paciferum canimus caelesti semine regem, / Faustaque sacratis saecula pacta libris; / Vagitumque Dei")[56] However, Milton's Christ Child does not weep; he smiles: "The Babe lies yet in smiling Infancy." As the reader will now recognize, the smiling infant Christ is another feature of the Nativity Ode that sets it apart from the poems of Southwell, Donne, and Herbert. The most obvious reason the child is smiling is because Virgil's infant smiles in the "Messianic" Eclogue, Eclogue IV:

"incipe, parve puer, risu cognoscere matrem." But what does Milton's use of the smile mean? No doubt something different from what Virgil meant: Peter Dronke argues that Virgil's child smiles because he is a god, unlike human infants who cry.[57] Dronke is commenting on Notker's description of a smiling Christ Child in his sequence on Mary's Purification:

Exulta, cui parvus
Arrisit tunc, Maria,
Qui laetari omnibus
  Et consistere
Suo nutu tribuit!

Exult, Mary, whose
Little boy then smiles,
He who with his nod confers joy
  And subsistence.[58]

Thus the smile "manifesta la sua appartenenza al mondo divino" – "manifests his belonging to the divine world."[59]

Leo Steinberg argues the same about pictorial and statuary depictions of the Christ Child smiling, which become more common between the thirteenth and fifteenth centuries.[60] He opines, but acknowledges he cannot prove, a connection between Virgil's depiction of a divine smile and the artworks he discusses. He dismisses Pope-Hennessy's assertion that images of a solemn Virgin Mary and smiling baby exemplify "the age-old relationship between the prescient Virgin and the unreflecting Child" for the historically accurate reason that "no Renaissance artist knew a Christ 'unreflecting,' whether living or dead, in utero or in infancy." He is right to observe that such a "want of reflection" would imply that "this Child's other nature" could be "subdued." He adds that the "Child's laughter, then, does not enter Renaissance iconography in mere imitation of frolicking children," and it seems an opportune moment to observe that whatever else the poems we are considering do, they do not tell us much about early modern understandings of natural children's behaviour, except in noting the ways in which the Christ Child's differs.

However, unlike in statuary and painting, the Christ Child rarely smiles in Nativity lyrics, and in medieval lyrics it is overwhelmingly the case because the child is telling his mother about his upcoming Passion.[61] He is certainly the prescient one in the mother-child relationship, and he is often telling a horrified Mary about his destiny to suffer.

Nonetheless, Notker's sequence makes a smiling Christ Child imaginable from the ninth century onward, and Milton might even have known some of Notker's hymns, so famous were they, but I would argue for a different interpretation of this smile, which would accord more closely with Pope-Hennessy's assertion (in that case almost certainly a misunderstanding) of the meaning of a smiling Christ Child in the plastic arts.

Virgil's child in Eclogue IV smiles in recognition; his is a knowing smile, a smile without which he would not be worthy of a goddess's bed. Milton transforms this smile, and in his hands it becomes a smile of ignorance:

> The Babe lies yet in smiling Infancy,
> That on the bitter cross
> Must redeem our loss;
> So both himself and us to glorify ...

The babe who lies in smiling infancy is no longer the mighty babe, but the Christ Child who, emptied of divine power, can smile at his mother, not knowing what the prophetic poet knows: that the bitter cross lies in his future – and that enduring it will mean his glorification. In fact, until the "wakeful Trump of Doom" thunders "through the deep," "our bliss" cannot be "full and perfect."[62] The smile is, like the infancy to which it is connected, a manifestation of childish impotence and weakness, a lack rather than a manifestation of superior knowledge. What the poet knows, the child he describes seems not to know.

The Mighty Babe, Kenosis, and the Question of Immanence

In the Nativity Ode it seems Milton wishes to teach the reader to avoid, as the speaker does, the temptation to say that there is or can be a continuing presence of this Christ Child. Milton's notable resistance to the tradition that collapses the temporally separate events of the Incarnation and the Passion (and the Eucharist) bespeaks an alertness to its implications in Protestant theology. Without this collapse, we do not have unity of time or space between Christmas 1629 and the birth of Jesus, between Milton and the Christ Child. Milton's more Puritan tendency to avoid indications of physical proximity and his employment of memory and imagination in the place of a "mimesis of presence" sets his poem apart from those that make use of sacramental time. Since he does not even ask the Christ Child to enter his heart or soul, he does not even imagine a Catholic spiritual communion or a Calvinist communion when he offers his hymn of adoration – via the Heavenly Muse – to the Christ Child.

Milton does not find in the Christ Child's ability to control the pagan gods by reaching out his hand a justification for attributing to the child an ability to reach out his hand to the author or the reader. No one touches this child (except Mary, if Vander Zee is right – and still, that happens offstage), no one kisses him, no one looks to sacramental union with him. At the beginning of the ode, although he has chosen "with us a darksome House of mortal Clay," he is not even in his mother's arms, but in the "rude manger." At the end of the poem his mother has just laid him to rest – yet, with the exception of Vander Zee, critics of the poem do not assert that she has picked him up. Only Osiris "feels from Judah's Land / The dreaded Infant's hand," and a strictly metaphorical hand it is, too.[63] In this meditation upon – or representation of – the effects of the Incarnation, then, Milton's avoidance of physical contact with the child actually strengthens an awareness of the doctrinal significance of the unrepeatability of the Nativity. There is to be no further physical bond between this child and us. We are to acknowledge a fact and, perhaps, be moved as the poet was to join our voices "unto the Angel Choir."

"Alas, How Soon Our Sin Sore Doth Begin His Infancy to Sease"

And yet it is going too far to say that the twenty-one year old Milton does not believe in the divinity of the Christ Child. In his poem "Upon the Circumcision," written shortly after the Nativity Ode, Milton evokes the emotional response of his reader and confirms the divinity of the child.

Ye flaming Powers, and winged Warriours bright,
That erst with Musick, and triumphant song
First heard by happy watchful Shepherds ear,
So sweetly sung your Joy the Clouds along
Through the soft silence of the list'ning night; [5]
Now mourn, and if sad share with us to bear
Your fiery essence can distill no tear,
Burn in your sighs, and borrow
Seas wept from our deep sorrow,
He who with all Heav'ns heraldry whileare [10]
Enter'd the world, now bleeds to give us ease;
Alas, how soon our sin
Sore doth begin
His Infancy to sease!

O more exceeding love or law more just?
Just law indeed, but more exceeding love!
For we by rightfull doom remediles
Were lost in death, till he that dwelt above
High thron'd in secret bliss, for us frail dust
Emptied his glory, ev'n to nakednes;
And that great Cov'nant which we still transgress
Intirely satisfi'd,
And the full wrath beside
Of vengeful Justice bore for our excess,
And seals obedience first with wounding smart
This day, but O ere long
Huge pangs and strong
Will pierce more neer his heart.[64]

This smaller lyric offers a good corrective to any overreading of the Nativity Ode. It does so in several ways. First of all, the temporal scope of the poem allows us to see that Milton is capable of evoking the divine perspective in brief: all he need say is "O ere long / Huge pangs and strong / Will pierce more neer his heart," and the time between the circumcision and the piercing of Christ's side with the lance is collapsed to a matter of days or hours rather than thirty-three years. The predominance of spondaic feet in these lines emphasizes the weighty, grievous injury. Second, Milton engages the reader's sentiments of compassion on behalf of the Christ Child, offering the bold and intriguing conceit that the fiery essences of the angels will need to borrow tears from the human followers of the Lord in order to make even a show of mourning. Thus the human ability to grieve becomes a power, higher than angelic intelligence, unifying the audience with the suffering Christ Child whose blood has been shed for the sake of the covenant. Third, the evocation of the covenant allows Milton to unite the fulfillment of the Mosaic law with the Passion that the circumcision prefigures. The Pauline concept of "kenosis" is present in compact form as well: "he that dwelt above / High thron'd in secret bliss, for us frail dust / Emptied his glory, ev'n to nakedness." One would be hard put to claim that Milton's presentation of the theme smacks of nineteenth-century heresy. Christ has exchanged bliss for nakedness and suffering. Milton does not enter further into more theological refinements. Last, Milton imbues the poem with emotional weight in a traditional way: he sees the Proleptic Passion taking place in the wounded body of Jesus, and that is what provokes the cry of pity: "O."

This is the same poet, the same child, with the same fate as the child in the Nativity Ode. Although the power that intervenes in the prematurely unitive song could very well be God the Father in the Nativity Ode's fiction, it is really none other than John Milton himself. He stolidly prefers the line of time of salvation history over the cyclical recurrence of a golden age before the mansions of hell had inhabitants. He is nonetheless a seer who, like Simeon, can see with fearful intensity that "ere long / Huge pangs and strong / Will pierce more neer his heart." Whatever distance the lofty language and temporal distinctions of the poem impose upon Milton's Nativity scene, he demonstrates in his poem "Upon the Circumcision" that the Proleptic Passion is still an image that has force to move his audience. Milton does not urge his reader to kiss the Christ Child as John Donne does, but he does want his reader to consider that this Christ Child has lost his infancy so soon because our sin has made him suffer, a suffering no child, even a divine one, should bear.

Chapter Six

"We Kis't the Cradle of Our King": Affection, Awe, and Abridging the Laws of Time in Crashaw

When we come to Crashaw, we find ourselves with a poet who clearly was indebted to George Herbert, but whose treatment of the Nativity in his lyrics is often strikingly different. We do not need to ask "Where is the body of this Incarnate God?" when we examine his poems, for the Christ Child as fleshly baby is there, a corporeal reality portrayed by the poet. He is sometimes so lost in admiration of the child that he in fact forgets himself. As the poets of the latter half of the seventeenth century in England will follow in Herbert's footsteps rather than Crashaw's (and in the eighteenth century, if they write Nativity poems at all, in Milton's), Crashaw does not constitute a link to the future so much as the triumphant and joyous climax of a lineage from the past, harking back to Southwell and Donne,[1] and to similar Continental voices like Lope de Vega and Luis de Góngora.[2] The large number of critics who evince polite disgust or visceral repulsion at Crashaw's ecstatic poetics is testimony to the changes in taste that accompanied changes in religious convictions in England, as Alison Shell, Maureen Sabine, Kimberly Johnson, and others have recently argued.[3]

Crashaw is, like Southwell, intently focused on the moment of Christ's coming to earth and on directing his reader's attention to that wonder that "lifts earth to heauen, stoopes heau'n to earth." In the 1930s, Helen White observed:

> The same wonder everywhere penetrates Crashaw's thought of the Incarnation. For him that was the central fact in the world's history. Not that Christ has died for man to satisfy God's justice and redeem his elect, but that God should have come into the world, stooping his glory to the meanness of earth, adding to his ancient cares the littleness of human life.[4]

White's perceptive designation of the Incarnation as Crashaw's central motivating belief prompts us to examine his Nativity lyrics carefully.

Her phrasing of the observation is telling, since she says he does not focus on the effect on the elect, but on the humility of the glorious divinity. Crashaw privileges wonder at the condescension, the stooping of God, over the condition of the sinner. Simply put, he looks more at Christ and less at himself. He is more concerned with *portraying* Christ than any poet since Southwell. Producing Nativity lyrics that are clearly aware of the theological – specifically Christological – ramifications of his use of imagery and poetic structures, he is nonetheless also unselfconscious in his emotional approach to the babe in the manger.[5] In Crashaw we find Southwell and Milton's glorying in the Christ Child's might, Donne's amazement at the classic paradoxes attending his birth, and Herbert's joyful expectation of paradisal vision. Unlike Southwell, Herbert, and Milton, however, and like Donne, Crashaw offers the human contact of a kiss, an embrace, as demonstrating the unity and joy that he associates with the Incarnation of Christ. Before the manger, natural affection and religious devotion combine to salute the Christ Child with this intimate gesture, confirming his closeness and his lovability. As R.V. Young pointed out, "nothing could be more striking than the divergence between Milton's treatment of the Nativity and the Catholic counterpart provided by Crashaw ... Even in the limited scope of a lyrical ode, Milton's 'On the Morning of Christ's Nativity' focuses on the epic action of the Redemption; and until the end of the poem, and then only in the most cursory fashion, the concrete scene of Christ's birth never materializes."[6] Young also noted in his book *Richard Crashaw and the Spanish Golden Age* that the tone of Crashaw's Nativity lyric owes more to the joyous rusticity of Lope de Vega than to the classicism of a Geraldini or the luxuriant baroque sensibilities of a Marino. The joy has a source other than the evocation of the pastoral scene and Crashaw's use of popular language, though these are significant factors Young has detailed; it is the immediacy of the scene that allows the joy to be felt and shared.[7]

Time and Immanence

Two seemingly disparate topics have, as we have seen in this study, much to do with each other in Nativity poems of this period: expressions of affection toward the Christ Child and belief in his immanence through the Eucharist. My argument about this connection culminates with an examination of Crashaw's attitudes toward collapse of time in his Nativity lyrics. He unites both the sacramental "Sursum corda" of the Calvinist, looking up to heaven, with the Catholic "Heaven itself lies here below."[8] We see both the idea of joining with Christ spiritually and the coming down of Christ to the altar, the sacramental entry into eternity that contact with the body of Christ permits. If the trajectory I have traced in the previous chapters seems to point toward an absent Christ Child less than straightforwardly, it is mostly the fault of Crashaw, who is certainly a bump in the road.

Crashaw's early works already display a confidence in his own poetic power to see temporal divisions in a unity, an adoption of a divine perspective, even when Christ is not his subject. A Laudian Protestant until his conversion to Roman Catholicism in the mid-1640s, Crashaw, even before his conversion, was steeped in Catholic devotional material – such as Francis de Sales's *Introduction to the Devout Life*, the possession of which led to his being disciplined as a college student.[9] When young, he also read Bernard of Clairvaux and perhaps Richard Rolle, Catherine of Siena, as well as Birgitta of Sweden's *Revelations*, with its portrayal of the Nativity before the very eyes of the visionary. He was familiar with Giambattista Marino (whose *Sospetto d'Herode* he later translated and, Praz says, improved) and the *concettisti*, as well as Petrarch and other Catholic poets.[10] His father, perhaps in his desire to confute Roman Catholic doctrine and tradition, had a supply of Continental poetry in the house, which Crashaw availed himself of as a youth.[11] As I have argued elsewhere, several of these writers provided justification for poets' creating a temporal collapse or collocation of times that imitates a divine perspective of all times, the "nunc stans" of God.[12] Paul G. Stanwood has argued for Crashaw's discovery of a Laudian mode of cotemporalization.[13] He, Eugene Cunnar, and Walter Davis have "shown how the poet re-enacts the liturgical worship that engenders the Word such as the Eucharistic Sacrifice and the canonical day office."[14] Eiléan Ní Chuilleanáin uses Crashaw as a consummate example of what great religious poetry can do in overpassing temporal divisions: "The encounter with the divine or the sacred is a meeting with a presence, cutting across history and tradition … That has no time for time and the ironies of time."[15]

Young's work on Crashaw and the Spanish Golden Age has also opened up for English readers Crashaw's clear affection for the Spanish poets' approaches to the subject of the Nativity, but as rich as his discussion is, the issue of time and presence only receives glancing treatment, not being central to Young's argument. I would like to move forward on the analysis of Crashaw's Nativity lyrics with Young's discussion as a helpful foundation for what I will add here.

Crashaw is as aware as Milton of the poet's ability or desire to manipulate the sequence of history. He is even more explicit than Milton will be about the poet's confrontation with the problem of eternity, as we see in the early lyric "To the Morning. Satisfaction for Sleepe." Crashaw's discussion of poetic imitation of eternity here illuminates the stance on time he takes in the later "Hymn in the Holy Nativity of Ovr Lord God" and "In the Gloriovs Epiphanie of Ovr Lord God." In "To the Morning," Crashaw complains that Apollo has withdrawn from him the patronage of his Muse and left him to seek a Muse from Morpheus in vain. Apollo has left him to the drowsy god because Crashaw has overslept and missed chapel (if the heading in the 1646 edition is genuine; the date of composition is thought to be around Easter 1634, nearly contemporaneous with Milton's Nativity Ode). Crashaw laments that, as a result, his "humble fancy finds no wings" (line 19).[16] The list of what he has been deprived of culminates in the loss of the ability to overpass time and imitate eternity:

No nimble rapture starts to Heaven and brings
Enthusiasticke flames, such as can give
Marrow to my plumpe Genius, make it live
Drest in the glorious madnesse of a Muse,
Whose feet can walke the milky way, and chuse
Her starry Throne; whose holy heats can warme
The Grave, and hold up an exalted arme
To lift me from my lazy Vrne, to climbe
Vpon the stooped shoulders of old Time;
And trace Eternity – But all is dead. (lines 20–9)

Through Aurora's intercession, Crashaw hopes for a return of these abilities to his poetic "Genius," which is able not only to walk in the heavens but to raise the dead (in this case, the sleeping Crashaw), raise him to stand on the "shoulders of old Time" and "trace Eternity." What does "trace" mean here but represent or imitate? This imitation, moreover, arises from the poet's release from the constraints of time and mortality in lines 25–7. Crashaw's use of the rhetorical figure of climax indicates that the ability to trace eternity is the highest power of the poet. In this Augustinian claim for the power of words, we see an attitude diametrically opposed to Milton's: whereas Milton asserts that "holy Song" has power over time, which it could exercise but "wisest Fate" forbids it, Crashaw admits that his laziness has prevented him from making use of the power, but that it is indeed available to him and he ought to use it.[17] He will employ it in his hymns on the Incarnation.

Although Richard Crashaw was born into the household of a Calvinist and anti-Catholic father, his stepmother had induced William Crashaw to allow the saying of morning prayer from the *Book of Common Prayer* in the household, and so from a young age, Crashaw had some familiarity with the liturgical hours he would later be obliged to recite as a beneficiatus at Loreto in Rome. Lancelot Andrewes was one of his masters at Pembroke College in Cambridge; thus we can imagine those ideas we have already seen Andrewes articulate concerning the Eucharist were familiar to Crashaw if not shared by him when he was a student. At Peterhouse under the tutelage of John Cosin (who would repudiate him when he converted to Rome), and later at Little Gidding with his friends the Ferrars, Crashaw would follow his attraction to the quasi-monastic rituals of prayer. His engagement in incensing the altar, cited together with "diverse bowings and cringeings," were condemned by Puritan investigators because they bespoke a belief in the Real (corporeal) Presence of Christ on the altar: they are the offerings of latria, due to the godhead. In his early days as a priest of the Church of England, he first became acquainted with the life and writings of Teresa of Avila. He also developed at some point in his student days a devotion to the Virgin Mary.[18] In several of his lyrics, he adopts an imitation of the perspective of the Virgin Mother.[19] This last is important if we recall that her perspective on the Incarnation is a "looking down" at the child in the manger – or in her lap – either as a nursing mother or after the deposition from the cross. Thus, even before his actual conversion, Crashaw's mind and heart were full of Roman Catholic imagery and concepts, or should we say, Anglo-Catholic ones that had derived from the Roman Church. This exposure combined with his already-confident belief in the power of words to overpass time perhaps encouraged his desire to portray Christ as corporeally present.

His great Nativity poems, "Hymn in the Holy Nativity of Ovr Lord God" and "In the Gloriovs Epiphanie of Ovr Lord God," demonstrate his continuing interest in the question of how to represent time – and Christ in and out of time – in the lyric. The poems probably date from about 1645 (perhaps 1646 or afterwards for the latter, which did not appear until the 1648 edition of Crashaw's works).[20] Crashaw amplified his use of sacrificial imagery in the later editions of 1648 and 1652 (which was posthumous and printed in Paris), amending the Nativity Hymn in significant ways after his conversion and his continued residence in Europe. The *Steps to the Temple: Sacred poems, with other delights of the Muses* was entered in the Stationer's Register on 1 June 1646, the same year in which Milton's poems had appeared (in January). Crashaw's extended description of the pagan gods in the Epiphany Hymn might reflect the newly available work or might be similarly based on Prudentius and Tasso,[21] or on Giles Fletcher, the younger's *Christs Victorie and Triumph*, published in 1610 at Cambridge. The latter was a well-known piece, which Milton had read and imitated.[22]

Crashaw's description of the sun as shamed by the greater Sun (Christ) in lines 118–24, may echo Milton's very similar conceit in the Nativity Ode (stanza VII, lines 79–84). Both poets could easily have found this oft-repeated Nativity trope in one of Augustine's sermons on the Nativity,[23] one of its earliest and most famous articulations. This image of the sun as late, as superfluous, emphasizes the subordination of earthly time to the day of Christ. Unlike Milton, Crashaw emphatically subordinates linear time to time "sub specie aeternitatis" and insists on the use of sacrificial imagery in connection with the newborn Christ Child. In this way, he identifies the day of Christ's birth and the day of his revelation to the gentiles (the Epiphany) as the day when the sun is darkened and the stars' brilliance fade – that day which is to be called "the fullness of time" according to the biblical prophet Joel (Joel 4:15) and is identified as the centre of time in the Franciscan tradition.[24] Although Crashaw is usually seen in terms of the Jesuit and baroque influences prevalent in seventeenth-century Europe, it behoves us to remember that it was the Franciscans who popularized the emphasis on the Nativity and the Passion, and the idea of the Nativity as the centre of time. Crashaw, then, is probably responding to an admixture of influences and sources, some medieval and Franciscan rather than solely Jesuit, Salesian, or indeed Counter-Reformation.[25] Because Crashaw is, more than most other poets of his age, seen in the context of more contemporary influences only, it is easy to forget that he, like Southwell, Donne, Herbert, and Milton, knew of patristic and medieval authors too.

In addition, medieval art historical sources, among them sculpture and painting, would be more familiar to the well-travelled Crashaw, Southwell, and Donne than to the young student Milton or the retired country parson, Herbert. Ever since the English Christmas edict of 1549, those church decorations and woodcuts and illuminations from books that depicted the Nativity and Epiphany, the Mass, or the crucifix were especially subjected to iconoclasm and defacing. John N. King analyses such Reformation expunging of the art historical record thus: "The loss of woodcuts for the Nativity and Epiphany … may reflect the radical Protestant conviction that artistic emphasis on those events undermines Christ's preachings, which constitute gospel truth … Reformers attacked Medieval carols and mystery plays on the same ground."[26] That Franciscan emphasis on the Nativity and the Passion, which the Continental baroque would assimilate, is what the increasing Puritanism of English art and letters would reject most definitively. In other words, the events in Christ's life that form the material for the sacramental collapse of time envisioned in many medieval Nativity lyrics and, I would argue, particularly in Southwell's, Donne's, and Crashaw's, are more and more excluded from the English artistic and literary vocabulary. Crashaw, like Southwell, often sounds more Continental than English to readers for more than just stylistic reasons.

The whole question of divine immanence in the sacramental theologies of Calvinist Anglo-Catholicism rests on a conviction that manipulation of space and time is inappropriate for God when it comes to the natural behaviour of Christ's natural body. We have seen these arguments rehearsed by leading Reformation figures in England such as Ridley and Cranmer. The laws of physics, the laws of time are absolute, and God, their creator, will not contravene them.[27] The collapse of time conveyed by the medieval norm of placing Nativity and Epiphany scenes above the altarpiece would have suggested a credulous adherence to the very arguments being made by a Weston or a Bellarmine, a throwback to the belief expressed in the Sarum Rite, that the very same corporeal body born of the Virgin in Bethlehem was present in the sacrament, even when reserved and not received.[28]

Crashaw undertakes to comment on such a concept of decorum. He emphasizes the supersession of the natural sun's authority in these two poems to say that Christ's light is the stronger of the two and, more, to say (perhaps in conscious contrast to Milton) that Christ's authority over time is greater than the natural sun's. In choosing this image, the poet removes his subject from the realm of time, where linear perspective, both spatial and temporal, must be observed. The "Day" of Christmas is not a natural day; it is the day of Christ, an "aeternall" day. In fact, Sonia Jaworska has discussed Crashaw's description of the Christ Child as "the womb of Day" in "Hymn to the Name of Jesus"; she focuses on the Christ Child as protection for the soul, because the womb is a place of shelter.[29] For my purposes, Crashaw's description indicates the submission of time to its creator.

To such a perspective, Calvinist interpretations of Peter's words in Acts 3:21 would be impossible.[30] Although Calvin is renowned for expressing the absolute power of God in contradistinction to what he saw as blasphemous hairsplitting by the schoolmen, he says himself that Christ's body cannot come down from heaven.[31] But traditionally, for Roman Catholics, Christ is the nexus of all times; he is eternal; he is omnipotent. It does not matter that he has "taken the form of a slave": his identity as Lord of time and outside of time is unchanged. Eternity is one of the central concerns of Crashaw's religious poetry, as critics such as Kerby Neill and A.R. Cirillo have remarked. Young has even asserted: "Crashaw's 'sometime' is usually eternity."[32] Both hymns, "In the Holy Nativity of Ovr Lord God" and "In the Glorious Epiphanie of Ovr Lord God" (as well as Crashaw's other poems on the Incarnation), define

Christ's light as the "master fire" whose eternity takes precedence over earthly time ruled by the sun. Crashaw's emphasis on Christ's eternity and his use of sacrificial imagery place these two poems in what I call sacramental time, as seen here in the following stanza from the Nativity Hymn:

> Welcome, all WONDERS in one sight!
> AEternity shutt in a span.
> Sommer in Winter. Day in Night.
> Heauen in earth, & GOD in MAN.
> Great little one! whose all-embracing birth
> lifts earth to heauen, stoopes heau'n to earth.

In his variation on the traditional paradoxes of the Incarnation, Crashaw writes the last major English Nativity poem to make use of sacramental space and time, which I have argued elsewhere is commonplace in medieval lyrics on the Christ Child.[33] These elements are central to his concept of the poem as a whole: the revisions he made from the original 1646 version of the poem to this just-quoted stanza from the 1648 version develop the nascent sense of the Nativity's power to collapse all things into one moment, one point.

The two changes are as follows: "Welcome to our wondring sight" becomes "Welcome, all WONDERS in one sight!"; "all-glorious birth" becomes "all-embracing birth." In the first case, Crashaw shifts the focus from the wondering of the shepherds to the wondrousness of the child.[34] Christ is all wonders. Moreover, because he is the one God, the multiplicity of wonders collapses into oneness: he is all wonders in one sight. The shepherds, and whoever may view the scene, see something small: a span, literally, the breadth of a hand. Small as this space may be, it holds within itself "AEternity," collapsing the vastness of the eternal into a "nunc stans." Crashaw further emphasizes this collapse by changing the description of Christ's birth as "all-glorious," which implies nothing about time or space, to "all-embracing." The word "all," changing its role from that of an adverb to that of a noun, now signifies the vastness of the universe and time, all people, all things. Nothing is outside the embrace of this birth: the "great little one" draws into oneness the heavens above and the earth below. Echoing the famous sixth-century Annunciation hymn "Quem terra, pontus, sidera," this image reflects the tradition of a Roman Catholic decorum; Christ's Incarnation is the intersection of the eternal with the temporal.[35] The eternal contains within itself all temporal extensions, all "time lines," but there are no extensions from the perspective of eternity. Christ's birth can only be "all-embracing" because his eternity takes precedence over the normal constraints of historical time. The pattern for this temporal collapse is the Eucharist, as it is in many medieval poems.[36] Although Crashaw does not introduce images of consumption or of the elements of the Eucharist (bread and wine), we shall later see that a further addition to the 1648 version of the Nativity Hymn does introduce the idea of sacrifice, which is characteristic of the use of sacramental time. We should remember that Crashaw, like Southwell before him, had translated Thomas Aquinas's hymns for Corpus Christi and would thus be very familiar with Aquinas's amplification of the sacrificial aspect of the Eucharist and of its import for abridgement of the laws of physics. In accord with Tridentine definitions of the sacrament, Crashaw's evocation of the sacrament through the Nativity collapses historical, linear time with regard to Christ. As I pointed out in chapter one, the Eucharist includes within it all the events of Christ's life because it is Christ; Christ as a child is not separated from Christ the adult, his birth from his Passion. His birth, in Crashaw's terms, is "all-embracing" because it is the dawn of the only day, "our aeternall Day," the day on which Christ can be both newborn Shepherd of the shepherds and the "dread lamb" – the lamb of sacrifice, the lamb of God, the lamb of the Holy City of Jerusalem. This day is the day when "HEAVEN itself lyes here below" in a nest that is both the breast of the Virgin Mary and the tomb.

The Phoenix: Intimacy and Self-Forgetfulness

Kerby Neill has discussed the significance of the Virgin Mary's place in the poem and has clearly shown that the phoenix's nest is the mother of Christ;[37] Christ is the architect of his first dwelling place. That Mary was created by Christ so he might be born from her, who becomes both his daughter and his mother, is the oft-repeated paradox Crashaw develops, making the image of the "nest" serve a dual purpose. When Tityrus challenges heaven and earth to prepare a better lodging for Jesus than the manger, the reader knows the alternative awaiting him is the tomb. However, whereas George Herbert asked that Christ might find in his soul "a better lodging than a rack or grave," Crashaw does not interiorize Christ's dwelling place as Herbert would. As Warren points out, immediately moving to the effect on oneself is antipathetic to Crashaw's concept of decorum:

> For Crashaw … this would have seemed too subjective, too self-centered, almost, one might say, too calculating an attitude. Doubtless Christ's blood was shed as a ransom for many; gratitude for benefits, however, is not piety. In Himself, as God and Man, Christ invites supreme adoration.[38]

It is this self-forgetfulness and focus on the beloved rather than the self that perhaps is what Vendler misses in Herbert's "The Starre" and Broadbent condemns in Milton's Nativity Ode. Healy puts it thus (in discussing "Hymn to the Name of Jesus"):

> Donne and Herbert may view the individual as entitled to a brief aria within the larger opera, whereas Crashaw is concerned with being a member of the chorus. For all of them, though, the opera is the same. Participation in this historical coherence is perceived as maintaining our present links with the past, but this unity of history centered on Christ also acts to suspend a temporal chronological order, joining all times together in a harmony with Christ, who is the "All-circling point. All centring sphear. / The world's one, round, Aeternall year" ("In the Glorious Epiphanie" II. 26–7)."[39]

Crashaw does not move into "applicatio" as Herbert might, or as Donne does in his 1626 sermon on the Nativity,[40] but continues to describe Christ, introducing the image of the Christ Child as phoenix:

Stanza 1

Tity. Poor WORLD (said I) what wilt thou doe
To entertain this starry STRANGER?
Is this the best thou canst bestow?
A cold, and not too cleanly, manger?
Contend, ye powres of heau'n & earth.
To fitt a bed for this huge birthe.

Stanza 2

Thyr. Proud world, said I; cease your contest
And let the MIGHTY BABE alone.
The Phaenix builds the Phaenix' nest.
Love's architecture is his own.
The BABE whose birth embraues this morn,
Made his own bed e're he was born.

These two stanzas, added by Crashaw to the Nativity Hymn in the second edition, are called by Ruth Wallerstein "the great stanzas which transmute the whole."[41] By introducing into the poem the image of the phoenix, Crashaw alludes to more than the tradition that Christ created Mary to be his mother. Wallerstein is convinced that Crashaw integrates the appearance of the legendary bird into this poem's theme and development more effectively than he has when using it in earlier poems, which can only be so if the image of the phoenix resonates throughout the poem. It does resonate, not in the theme of Christ's choice of the Virgin as his bed, but in the theme of sacrifice and rebirth. The phoenix is not a symbol of maternity, but of immolation, death, and resurrection, and had been used as such by Christians since the first century, when it was carved on Christian tombs and mentioned in the Epistle of St. Clement to the Corinthians.[42] It is thus also a symbol of hope.[43] If this image does not seem out of place at this juncture in the poem, but rather a most felicitous addition, it is because there is something familiar in the equation of the Incarnation and the Passion. The image works to unify the poem even more effectively than the first version's had done.[44] The ancient conflation of cradle and bier, of womb and tomb, is reinforced and elaborated. With the phrase "Love's architecture is his own," Crashaw combines Christ's creation of his mother and his carrying out the final acts of the redemption. When Crashaw tells us that "the Babe whose birth embraues this morn, / Made his own bed e're he was born," he means that the "mighty Babe" is the architect of both his own birth and his own rebirth; he is the planner and moulder of his own life and his own destiny. There is no need for a "wisest Fate." It is for this reason that the shepherds call the child "dread lamb." He is at once the "soft King" and the lamb of sacrifice. The phoenix's nest is at once the womb of Mary and the tomb outside Jerusalem. The image of the phoenix is also associated with myrrh and other funerary spices, so its use evokes sweet odours and underscores the ties to the gospel narrative of Christ's death and burial.[45] The "BABE whose birth embraues this morn / Made his own bed e're he was born": that bed is not only the Virgin Mary but also the place where the death and the resurrection occur.

The concurrence of all these ideas in the stanza should not surprise the reader since Crashaw also authored the famous epigram "To ovr B. LORD vpon THE choice of His sepulcher":

HOW life & death in Thee
Agree !
Thou hadst a virgin womb,
And tomb.
A IOSEPH did betroth
Them both.

Crashaw's juxtaposition of the concept of sacrifice with that of the presence of the eternal Christ Child locates his poem in Roman

Catholic tradition. Although Milton does not elaborate on his mention of the cross in the Nativity Ode, wishing to avoid colouring the manger overmuch with the tones of Golgotha, Crashaw unhesitatingly pictures the child already undergoing the Passion. In fact, the poem works from the seventh stanza onward toward a final image of the shepherds' (ergo the readers') union with the child through participation in the sacrifice.

In the "Hymn in the Holy Nativity of Ovr Lord God," Crashaw emphasizes the union between heaven and earth rather than their disunion. Kerby Neill, in fact, has argued that Crashaw revised the hymn for the later editions to make even clearer the poem's progress toward "the immolation of self in mystic union with God," "the elevation of man after his fall to a renewed union with God through the Incarnation of His Son."[46] Even the 1545 version of "A Hymn in the Nativity, sung by the Shepheards" proposes something more than a celebration. In all three editions, the Christ Child's eyes will provide the fire in which the adoring shepherds will sacrifice themselves to him, and this fire is at the same time the light of the eternal day:

Stanza 4

Tityrus. Gloomy night embrac't the place
Where The Noble Infant lay.
The BABE look't vp & shew'd his Face;
In spite of Darknes, it was DAY.
It was THY day, SWEET! & did rise
Not from the EAST, but from thine EYES.

Stanza 6

Both. We saw thee in thy baulmy Nest,
Young dawn of our aeternall DAY!
We saw thine eyes break from their EASTE
And chase the trembling shades away.
We saw thee, – & we blest the sight
We saw thee by thine own sweet light.

The reference to the sacrifice of the first-born lambs in April completes Crashaw's development of a framework of sacramental time. Although the shepherds are promising a future sacrifice of their first fruits and themselves, they already identify the Christ Child as the real sacrificial victim.

Crashaw partly accomplishes this identification by the address to Christ as the dread lamb, and he also evokes the Passion narrative by proposing to crown Christ's head. If this infant is to be crowned in April, when the first-born are sacrificed, the reader knows that it will be a crown not of flowers but of thorns. Crashaw ingeniously makes the shepherds' desire to sacrifice themselves to the baby mirror the Christ Child's not yet/already-accomplished death:

> Yet when young April's husband showrs
> Shall blesse the fruitfull Maja's bed
> We'l bring the First-born of her flowrs
> To kisse thy FEET & crown thy HEAD.
> To thee, dread lamb! whose loue must keep
> The shepheards, more than they the sheep.
>
> To THEE, meek Majesty! soft KING
> Of simple GRACES & sweet LOVES.
> Each of vs his lamb will bring
> Each his pair of sylver Doves;
> Till burnt at last in fire of Thy fair eyes,
> Our selues become our own best SACRIFICE.

Although the shepherds foresee a future sacrifice of themselves, in Crashaw's view, the Christ Child, newborn, already partakes of the sacrificial fires. It is proper to describe him in these terms. Nor can this child be praised or adequately described without reminders of his eternity. The Christ Child's eternity, in fact, becomes a matrix for the entire cosmos, so much so that the rising and setting of suns lose their significance as markers of time in both the Nativity Hymn and the later Epiphany Hymn.

Crashaw's subjugation of linear to sacramental time is both deliberate and significant. Both Ruth Wallerstein and Austin Warren noted the superseding influence of supernatural over natural light in Crashaw's series of Nativity poems ("To the Name Above Every Name," "In the Holy Nativity," "New Year's Day," and "In the Glorious Epiphanie"). A.R. Cirillo, developing their insights into his work on the Epiphany Hymn, has shown how the imagery of light and of the eternal day serve the theme of the redemption and of the coming of Christ to every believer:

> Christ has come as the dawn of a new day and becomes, on a moral level, the disinheritor of the physical sun. His supplanting of the day suggests

> not only the paradox of his birth at night (the day is born at night) but also the birth of a moral day for mankind, a day represented in Roman Catholic devotion by the presence of Christ in the monstrance, a vessel designed to resemble the radiating light of the sun around the centrally placed Eucharist ... The paradox of the Incarnation and Redemption cycles is established in its supertemporal context as the first day of Christian time.[47]

Cirillo goes on to show that this day is not merely a "first day" but a perpetual day,

> lumen de lumine, not alternating with darkness, but shining through it. For Him there is no time; His year is an eternity. In this context, the singers (the Magi as the Gentiles) are moved into the timelessness of meditation on Christ's coming into the soul ... Time yields to eternity in the sun of this mystical day.[48]

I quote from Cirillo at length because he clearly delineates the many valences of Crashaw's imagery in the Epiphany Hymn: although Cirillo's main concern is the theme of moral illumination and the rejection of materialism, he has also touched on this present chapter's theme of sacramental union with the eternal Christ Child.

When Crashaw uses the future tense to speak of that day on which the sun "from himself shall flee / For shelter to the shadow of thy TREE," he tells us that "that dark Day's clear doom shall define / Whose is the Master FIRE, which sun should shine." Proceeding to collapse time between the crucifixion and the Last Judgment, Crashaw undercuts the temporal sequence he has begun to use and melds all three events into "the supernaturall DAWN of Thy pure day," the temporal differences made indistinguishable in the light of this new sun. We can see Crashaw's identification of the baby with the adult where he describes Christ's Incarnation and death in one image: "To HIM, who by these mortall clouds has made / Thyself our sun, though thine own shade." "HIM" is God the Father; "Thyself" is Christ. The "mortall clouds" are Christ's newborn body and his death. They signify both simultaneously. As Wendy Fuller has said, "Crashaw evokes both the sorrow and the terror implicit in the Nativity."[49]

Importantly for my argument, Crashaw, unlike Milton, does not locate the justification for temporal collapse in "holy Song's" power over "fancy," but in the child himself. Christ's three advents – to men, into men, against men – all occur during his "Generall AND indifferent DAY," for, as the First King says, the child is the "All-circling point. All centring sphear. / The world's one, round, AEternall year" (lines 26–7), for which "Time is too narrow" (line 40). As St. Bernard notes in an Advent sermon,[50] the traditional three Masses celebrated on Christmas at midnight, at dawn, and in the light of day in the medieval and Renaissance Church were thought to represent these three advents all in one day.[51] Although later in the Epiphany Hymn, Crashaw has the kings refer to the eclipse of the sun on Good Friday in the future tense, the sun by the end of the poem is allowed to remain only as a shadow of Christ and has no function but to point to heaven (lines 237–54). Earthly time, governed by the sun, is definitively subordinated.

Crashaw actually divides time between Christ's birth and death conspicuously in his earlier poem "Our Lord in his circumcision to his Father" from *Steps to the Temple*, where Christ calls his blood "these first fruits of my growing death" and says his day of "dark woes" and "cradle-torments" has just begun; his death is just "new-borne" (lines 1, 11, 14, 12). Yet, although he is introducing the clarity of temporal distinctions, even here he collapses all these events, the development of Christ's death, into just one day. Cirillo shows the Nativity series' movement from the theme of Christ's advent into the world to his advent into the soul of man. Referring to transubstantiation and the reception of the sacrifice as a focal point in "To the Name Above Every Other Name," which forms part of Crashaw's Nativity group (the Feast of the Holy Name was celebrated in the first week of January because of its connection to the Circumcision),[52] Cirillo argues that Crashaw sees the three advents combined in the act of receiving communion. This physical and spiritual contact puts the communicant in the same relationship to Christ as the Magi. Infusing the illumination of the "Generall & indifferent DAY" (Epiphany Hymn, line 25) into the mind and soul of the human being, communion corresponds to the second of Bernard's three advents, which from Christ's perspective are inseparable and become so for the recipient.

Kissing the Manger

An act of reverence and affection both Southwell and Crashaw include in their Nativity poems seems at first to be a less intimate kiss than the one John Donne encourages Joseph and his soul to participate in: Crashaw's shepherds say, "We kis't the cradle of our king," perhaps in imitation of Southwell's "come kiss the manger where he lies" in "New Heaven, New Warre":

COME to your heaven you heavenly quires,
Earth hath the heaven of your desires;

Remove your dwelling to your God,
A stall is now his best abode;
Sith men their homage doe denie,
Come Angels all their fault supplie.

His chilling cold doth heate require,
Come, Seraphins in liew of fire;
This little Arke no cover hath,
Let Cherubs wings his body swath:
Come Raphaell, this Babe must eate,
Provide our little Tobie meate.

Let Gabriell be now his groome,
That first took up his earthly roome;
Let Michaell stand in his defence,
Whom love hath linck'd to feeble sence,
Let Graces rock when he doth crie,
And Angels sing his lullabie.

The same you saw in heavenly seate,
Is he that now sucks Maries teate;
Agnize your King a mortall wight,
His borrowed weede lets not your sight:
Come kisse the maunger where he lies,
That is your blisse above the skies.[53]

It is possible that in both these poems the kissing of the manger is an evocation of the priest's kissing of the altar as well as an act of devotion to the baby Jesus, since the manger was often understood to have been a hollowed-out stone trough and the baby depicted lying on it as if on an altar.[54] If Southwell and Crashaw have this parallel in mind, this act would complete the conflation of the manger of Bethlehem with the Eucharistic presence of Christ – for both Southwell and Crashaw, a real, physical presence of the ascended and glorified Jesus. "His borrowed weed lets not your sight" is a phrase that harks back to the "latens deitas" of Aquinas's Eucharistic hymn, "Adoro te devote," which both poets knew (though Southwell only translated the "Lauda Sion").[55] Crashaw translated both hymns, although he did so before his conversion to Rome, and Thomas Healy points out several elements in the translations that show Crashaw is at this point in his career still carefully preserving Laudian distinctions from Aquinas in his sacramental theology.[56] Nonetheless, it was common knowledge that several of the Fathers of the Church equated the manger with the altar.[57]

Crashaw shows that kissing the child's feet is the kings' goal in "To the Queen's Majesty," the poem accompanying the Epiphany Hymn.[58] It is equivalent to casting one's crown at the feet of the Lamb, a passage in Revelations 4:10–11 to which Crashaw refers in an image most appropriate for the Queen and her children: "The four and twenty elders fall down before him that sat on the throne, and worship him that liveth for ever and ever, and cast their crowns before the throne":

For from this day's rich seed of Diadems [11]
Does rise a radiant croppe of Royalle stemms,
A Golden harvest of crown'd heads, that meet
And crowd for kisses from the LAMB's white feet.
…
With your bright head whole groves of scepters bend [17]
Their wealthy tops; and for these feet contend.
So swore the LAMB's dread sire. And so we see't.
Crownes, and the HEADS they kisse, must court these FEET. [20]
Fix here, fair Majesty! May your Heart ne're misse
To reap new CROWNES and KINGDOMS from that kisse.[59]

In Crashaw's conceit, there are several anomalies from the image in Revelation: one is that the royal family is imagined as crowding to *receive* kisses from Christ's feet, as if any contact with the lowliest part of the Lord's body were in itself a kiss; and the other kiss, which is metaphorical rather than physical contact with the mouth, is the contact between the crowns and their physical heads. Moreover, the Queen may receive new crowns and kingdoms – clearly not earthly ones – from the kiss she gives or receives at Christ's feet. Crowns transmute and multiply from the initial reverence the three kings show to the infant Jesus.[60]

At root, however, the image remains an image of devout love and self-surrender before the infant God whom Crashaw encourages his social superiors to adore with him. That the crowns and kingdoms become crowns and kingdoms of the heart or soul is an addition to, not a subtraction from, the real, fleshly kiss the worshipper offers in the joyous, energetic poem. Crashaw rushes the lines along through the extensive use of enjambment and alliteration. Crowding, contending, courting, the Queen and her children are envisioned as avid, bustling worshippers, even shoving each other out of the way, perhaps, in their eagerness to get to the Christ Child. Perhaps Crashaw had seen grandparents (and other less rivalrous relatives) trying to get the first kiss from the first-born grandchild, or perhaps he has in mind a painting he has seen where the shepherds and kings crowd together to get closer to the manger. Crashaw might have witnessed the paraliturgical practices accompanying the placement of the Christ Child figure in the manger or on a throne that accompanied the Christmas festivities in the sixteenth and seventeenth centuries in Europe (and probably in England, too, before the Reformation). They are described here by German propagandist Naogeorgus in Barnabe Googe's 1570 English translation:

A woodden childe in clowtes is on the aultar set,
About the which both boyes and gyrles do daunce and trymly jet,
And Carrols sing in prayse of Christ, and, for to helpe them heare,
The organs aunswere every verse with sweete and solemne cheare.
The priestes do rore aloude; and round about the parentes stande
To see the sport, and with their voyce do helpe them and their hande.[61]

Crashaw seems to see nothing untoward in the bustling. Though it is no somber castigation he offers, politically Crashaw is also insisting on the subordination of earthly majesty to heavenly, although he does invoke God the Father to support his point: "So swore the LAMB's dread sire," says he, in a very Miltonic moment, punctuated by three strong stresses in a row on the last three monosyllables.

Crashaw does not just see the Christ Child as the nexus of time and the Nativity as the centre of the line of time in salvation history: he sees the kiss given to his cradle, to Christ's feet, as the moment of union between the eternal and the temporal, between God and man.[62] The heart's seal of endearment, the engagement of the whole person, soul and body, is the only appropriate response to God's descent among us:

Welcome, all WONDERS in one sight!
AEternity shutt in a span.
Sommer in Winter. Day in Night.
Heauen in earth, & GOD in MAN.
Great little one! whose all-embracing birth
lifts earth to heauen, stoopes heau'n to earth.

Yrjö Hirn commented that Crashaw's lines "'Twas once *looke up*, 'tis now *looke downe* to Heaven" were a representation in words of Mary's downward gaze upon the "child in her lap."[63] Richard Crashaw is the last major poet of the seventeenth century to look down to see a real child when he looks upon the Christ Child in his Nativity. And the time in which he sees him is *now*.

Conclusion

The Christ Child: Little Boy Lost

How sweeping was the change in the seventeenth century in England from the focus on the real human body of the Christ Child to a more exclusive focus on Christ's advent in the heart of the believer? The Christ Child, born of the Virgin Mary, laid in the manger, was no doubt a familiar object to all the seventeenth-century English poets in this study. But presenting the physical details of the Nativity beyond what the Gospel of Luke described was perilously retrograde. On both Catholic and Protestant sides, there was a reluctance to fall into the old medieval errors of depicting apocryphal versions of the Nativity as if they were historically accurate. But poets such as Southwell, Donne, and Crashaw seem to be more at ease dramatizing actual scenes with the Christ Child than are poets like Herbert and (the early) Milton.

The worry about falling into Catholic errors of reverencing relics or placing an overly carnal emphasis on "dead flesh" appears with some regularity in the Nativity poems of Church of England poets I have not covered in this study. Good examples are to be found in Francis Quarles's "Christ's Infancy" from *Divine Fancies* (1632) and Robert Herrick's "An Ode of the Birth of Our Saviour." Quarles and Herrick both seem to defer their desire to hold the Christ Child himself to the desire to touch his clothes. Of all the poets discussed in this book, Francis Quarles, father of eighteen children, imagines the most childlike child:

Hayle blessed *Virgin*, full of heavenly *Grace*,
Blest above all that sprang from humane race;
Whose Heav'n saluted *Womb* brought forth in *One*,
A blessed *Saviour*, and a blessed *Son:*
O! what a ravishment t'had beene, to see
Thy little *Saviour* perking on thy *Knee*!
To see him nuzzle in thy *Virgin* Brest;

His milke white body all unclad, undrest!
To see thy busie Fingers cloathe and wrappe
His spradling Limbs in thy indulgent *Lappe*!
To see his desprate *Eyes*, with Childish grace,
Smiling upon his smiling Mothers face!
And, when his forward strength began to bloome,
To see him *diddle* up and downe the Roome!
O, who would thinke, so sweet a *Babe* as this,
Should ere be slaine by a false-hearted *kisse*!
Had I a *Ragge*, if sure thy Body wore it,
Pardon sweet *Babe*, I thinke I should adore it:
Till then, O grant this Boone, (a boone far dearer)
The *Weed* not being, I may adore the *Wearer*.[1]

This poem by one of the most popular poets of the first half of the seventeenth century gestures at the Proleptic Passion – "O, who would think so sweet a *Babe* as this, / Should e'er be slain by a false-hearted kisse!" – and speaks to both Mary and the Christ Child ("sweet *Babe*"). But the verb tense is generally the past, when Quarles isn't venturing potentially impossible or (for a member of the Church of England) inappropriate wishes in the conditional or optative moods. With Mary mediating the desire to hold the babe, Quarles imagines the infant's little naked body nuzzled up against his mother in a pose that should strike the reader as reminiscent of many a statue and painting of the Virgin and child, but one in no wise duplicated in any of the poems we have considered. Christ's body has real, definite being but is inaccessible to the speaker. Therefore, the speaker longs for a relic, knowing that worshiping it, which he would not be able to resist doing, would require him to seek forgiveness of the divine child who would not approve of his idolatry. But, like an early modern Margery Kempe, Quarles would still do it if he were sure the relic were not fake. So it is just as well Quarles did not travel to Aachen or Dubrovnik to see the relics considered to be the swaddling clothes of the Christ Child.[2] Nonetheless, he is able to offer his adoration to the divine child – at a distance. His imagination of the flesh of the Christ Child is even more detailed in his poems based on the Canticle of Canticles, notably, in a piece in book IV statedly indebted to St. Bonaventure, poem IX on Canticles 8.1.

1

Come, come my blessed Infant, and immure thee
Within the Temple of my sacred arms;
Secure mine arms, mine arms shall then secure thee
From *Herods* fury, or the high-Priests harms;

Or if thy danger'd life sustain a losse,
My folded arms shall turn thy dying crosse.

2

But ah, what savage Tyrant can behold
The beauty of so sweet a face as this is,
And not himself be by himself controul'd,
And change his fury to a thousand kisses?
One smile of thine is worth more mines of treasure
Then there be *Myriads* in the dayes of *Cesar*.

3

O, had the *Tetrarch*, as he knew thy birth,
So known thy stock, he had not sought to paddle
In thy dear bloud; but prostrate on the earth,
Had vaild his Crown before thy royall Cradle,
And laid the Sceptre of his Glory down,
And begg'd a Heavn'ly for an Earthly Crown.

4

Illustrious Babe! how is thy handmaid grac'd
With a rich armfull! how dost thou decline
Thy Majesty, that wert so late embrac'd
In thy great Fathers arms, and now in mine!
How humbly gracious art thou, to refresh
Me with thy Spirit, and assume my flesh.

5

But must the treason of a traitours *Hail*
Abuse the sweetnesse of these ruby lips?
Shall marble-hearted cruelty assail
These Alabaster sides with knotted whips?
And must these smiling Roses entertain
The blows of scorn, and flurts of base disdain?

6

Ah! must these dainty little sprigs that twine
So fast about my neck, be pierc'd and torn

With ragged nails? and must these brows resigne
Their Crown of Glory for a crown of thorn?
Ah, must this blessed Infant tast the pain
Of deaths injurious pangs? nay, worse, be slain?

7

Sweet Babe! At what dear rates do wretched I
Commit a sinne! Lord, ev'ry sin's a dart;
And ev'ry trespasse lets a javelin flie;
And ev'ry javelin wounds thy bleeding heart:
Pardon, sweet Babe, what I have done amisse;
And seal that granted pardon with a kisse.[3]

Quarles follows up this lyric written *in persona Mariae*, which shifts into the voice of the writer himself as it discusses sin toward the end, with a meditation drawn directly from St. Bonaventure:

O sweet Jesu, I knew not that thy kisses were so sweet, nor thy society so delectable, nor thy attraction so virtuous: for when I love thee, I am clean; when I touch thee, I am chaste; when I receive thee, I am a virgin: O most sweet Jesu, thy embraces defile not but cleanse; thy attraction polluteth not, but sanctifieth: O Jesu, the fountain of universal sweetness, pardon me that I believed so late, that so much sweetness is in thy embraces.[4]

Quarles is clearly drawn to Roman Catholic devotional material, but even in the images in this poem, he defers the kisses and other physical demonstrations of affection to Mary. The final stanza spoken *in propria persona* nevertheless expresses a desire for that kiss as the seal of pardon.

Herrick also produces a Nativity lyric that has him thinking about the possibility of idolatry, "The New-yeere's Gift," in *Noble Numbers*:

Let others look for Pearle and Gold,
Tissues, or Tabbies manifold:
One onely lock of that sweet Hay
Whereon the blessed Babie lay,
Or one poor Swadling-clout, shall be
The richest New-yeers Gift to me.[5]

So instead of rich new clothes for New Year's, the speaker would prefer a relic from Christ's infancy, hay from the manger or a swaddling band. But why? Because they act as mediators between the body of Christ and the speaker. Herrick goes even further in another poem, requesting the gift of the foreskin cut from Christ at his circumcision in return for which "prettie bleeding part" the speaker will send "a bleeding heart."[6] Like Quarles, Herrick is yearning for some approximation of fleshly contact with Christ, but must be content with a non-idolatrous spiritual union in the heart. In both poets, we see awareness of their own creed's disavowal of Catholic practice in regard to precisely this question.

On the other hand, there is also some convergence among Catholics and Protestants when it comes to the ascendancy of the religion of the heart in the later seventeenth century, as Henrik Aachen argues:[7]

> In her book on the Virgin Mary in late medieval and early modern thought Donna Ellington has shown that though it affected Protestantism more thoroughly, it transformed Catholic tradition as well – leading to a certain "interiorization" of faith. Thus the transition from oral to literal religious culture had a profound influence on the mental structure of the 16th and 17th centuries, the inward Christianity more easily gaining the upper hand, as it were.[8]

Some artists made conscious attempts in their own art to promote these similarities rather than the matters that divided the different groups. For example, as part of an effort to bridge the distances between the Catholic and Lutheran musical worlds, musicians on the Continent like Michael Praetorius continued the tradition of the lullaby-type Latin carol in "En Trinitatis speculum" and other works. Thus we see in this lyric the desire to sing to the "infantulo" ("little baby"), who is "totus amabilis" ("completely lovable"), though most of the song is dedicated to the joy of the shepherds and the glory of the Trinity.

Boyd Coolman renders "totus amabilis" as "the desirable par excellence" in his book on *Knowledge, Love, and Ecstasy in the Theology of Thomas Gallus*.[9] Although Gallus himself is not a concern here, the idea of mystical or sacramental union with God is – in particular, the type of union the different poets imagine they can have, or seem to desire to have, with the Christ Child. Coolman describes the "affective *cognitio Dei*" very well for our purposes:

> Gallus's notion of the affective *cognitio Dei* via the spiritual senses seems proto-eschatological or proleptically beatific. The underlying intuition is that beatifying human "knowledge of God" must have the directness, immediacy, pleasure, smell, taste, and assimilation between knower and known that is found in physical smell, taste, and touch. Accordingly, his doctrine of the spiritual senses is not an unhappy intrusion of a platonic

> mind-body, spirit-matter dualism. Rather, it reflects the implicit awareness that in the present post-lapsarian condition *neither* physical sensation *nor* rational (conceptual, ideational, notional) knowledge, by themselves, are adequate analogues for beatifying apprehension of God. But also that such *apprehensio Dei* must eventually eschatologically entail something resembling each. That is, eternal blessedness must be an encounter of created, embodied spirit with Uncreated Spirit that is marked by the direct immediacy of physical sensing, as well being as a genuine act of spiritual intelligence.[10]

Coolman's observations about Victorine and Dionysian spirituality strike me as getting to the heart of the difference between Nativity lyrics that celebrate the flesh and babyhood of the divine Christ Child and those that see Christmas more exclusively as the great prototype of the advent of Christ into the heart of the believer. It is a difference that can be explained by the most ordinary of metaphors; there is no new mother who has seen her child in an incubator, untouchable but loved, who has not desired with all her heart to hold that baby close to her, to smell its hair, to feel the softness of its tiny hands and feet, to kiss it. The mother who cannot do this does not love her child less, but she is not as close to the baby, and the baby cannot feel her love. The embodied human being is touchable, is kissable – but the coming of the spirit of God into the heart is not. Coolman points out that, in this ecstatic theology, prolepsis between times is a characteristic. The Nativity lyric can feature this kind of prolepsis, but only if the actual child is contemplated and not just his effects. Otherwise the body is not involved.

Not having Luther's ambivalence about the relative importance of the actual event of Christmas, the Puritans in England set themselves wholeheartedly against the celebration of Christmas itself, and of course as soon as they had the power to do so, they abolished it. Ben Jonson's *Christmas His Masque* had already commented in the presence of King James I on the threat to the old country pastimes associated with the holiday and brought them back centre stage to the court in London with his majesty's approval.[11] But the Christ Child in the manger was ushered off stage for a while during the Revolution and Interregnum. We can take the words of a seventeenth-century preacher who pointed his finger at the distressing ignorance behind this exile. The anonymous "Pastor Fido," or "Faithful Shepherd," in 1652 dedicated his work on the keeping holy of the "Metropolitan Feast or the Birthday of our Saviour Jesus Christ" to his readers, dismayed at the neglect and condemnation of the feast: "Poore Pastor Fido, / Exiled a while agoe. / Grace, Mercy, Mirth, Peace, doth wish to all those / That love the Babe Jesus in his swaddling clothes."[12] In his epigraph and later in the treatise itself, he quotes John 8:56:

> Where our Savior Christ saith unto the *Pharisees, Your father Abraham rejoyced to see my day, and he saw it, and was glad*: What day was this? It was not the day of the Passion, nor of his Resurrection, nor of his Ascention into heaven, for these were to come when our Saviour spake the words, but that day was past of which he then spake; it could then be no other but the day of his coming and manifestation in the flesh ... that blessed day of his Nativity which *Abraham* by the eye of faith beheld, and saw so many years before.[13]

For Pastor Fido, the outcry against the celebration of Christmas was evidence of inattention to the true mission of the Reformation, which was to return England to the practice of the primitive Church and attentive reading of the scriptures; both provide proof that it is incumbent upon the Christian to keep the feast. But there would have been no need for his arguments if Christmas were not already imperilled. He would not address those who love the babe in swaddling clothes if he didn't know there were those who did not.

It is also worth remembering – and encouraging further study of this problem – that what typical images of the Nativity the seventeenth-century poets were acquainted with had already begun to undergo a division during this period. Poets like Southwell and Crashaw, and even Donne and Milton, who spent a good deal of time on the Continent, would have been surrounded by very different art, and more of it, in all likelihood. England itself would not have afforded many depictions in painting or sculpture of the Christ Child, having suffered one of the greatest losses of an art historical record of all the reformed countries of Europe. Iconoclasm is a physical manifestation of a rejection, as Calvin himself came to realize and deplore. On this topic, without launching into the many reasons for a peculiar culinary extinction, we can imagine the following absence as a sort of allegory of what happens in the tradition of the Nativity lyric in England. During the Puritan Interregnum, the making of mince pies along with other Christmas delicacies was forbidden by edict. After the Restoration, the mince pies returned, but the figure made of bread dough that used to crown them never came back: the baby Jesus himself.

Where did the body of the Christ Child go? It is hard to find a single poem of any stature from Milton's Nativity Ode on that describes the Christ Child as a human baby, even among the poems of the later Metaphysicals – Vaughan and Traherne among them. It will be for the hymn writers of the more enthusiastic strains of English Protestantism, the Wesleys and Isaac Watts, to create songs about the Christ Child in his Nativity until the medieval revival also revives the Nativity lyric. Since most Christians still believed Christ was the Son of God, there was a reason for the obsolescence of a once-significant subgenre and in particular of actual portrayals of Christ as a child in that subgenre. Henry Vaughan's "Christ's Nativity" will serve as one example of the Nativity lyric that the reader can now see looks back to Herrick, Herbert, and Milton, and perhaps even Crashaw, but does not portray Christ as an infant:

Awake, glad heart! get up and sing!
It is the birth-day of thy King.
Awake! awake!
The Sun doth shake
Light from his locks, and all the way
Breathing perfumes, doth spice the day.

Awake, awake! hark how th' wood rings;
Winds whisper, and the busy springs
A concert make;
Awake! awake!
Man is their high-priest, and should rise
To offer up the sacrifice.

I would I were some bird, or star,
Flutt'ring in woods, or lifted far
Above this inn
And road of sin!
Then either star or bird should be
Shining or singing still to thee.

I would I had in my best part
Fit rooms for thee! or that my heart
Were so clean as
Thy manger was!
But I am all filth, and obscene;
Yet, if thou wilt, thou canst make clean.

Sweet Jesu! will then. Let no more
This leper haunt and soil thy door!
Cure him, ease him,

O release him!
And let once more, by mystic birth,
The Lord of life be born in earth.[14]

Vaughan's "mystic birth," one of the traditional three advents of Christ, is not the only birth in this poem: he does recall the manger that came before. Vaughan even uses sacrificial language reminiscent of the language of immolation we find in Southwell and Crashaw – but man as high priest of nature? That is not the sacrifice to which the earlier poets refer. Vaughan celebrates Christ's birthday in the recurring calendar of liturgical time, not as a present event, and does not approach Jesus as a human baby. One could note that, again, Christ's mother is absent.[15] This is the pattern English Nativity poetry adopts and maintains for at least a hundred years. Traherne's "Christmas Day" works through an extended conceit of Christ as vine and the speaker as grafted plant, celebrating the greenery decking people's houses as a symbol of the re-greening of his soul; the child and his mother are never portrayed, though Traherne speaks directly to Christ throughout the poem. "To him the manger made a throne," he says: the Nativity itself is, in spite of the liturgical commemoration in which he rejoices, definitively in the past.[16]

The only other major English poet who produces a Nativity lyric of any importance before the nineteenth century is Alexander Pope, and his "Messiah" does not resemble the poems of his English Catholic forerunners so much as it does that of Milton or those of the classicists of the Continent in the period before Marino. Thus, although credal differences might account for distinctions in the portrayal of the Christ Child before the Interregnum, the drift is toward Herbert and Milton and away from Southwell and Crashaw. Although Pope was Roman Catholic, one would be hard put to discover much sacramental presence or collapse of time in his "Messiah." His project is, to the contrary, a study in literary history, even antiquarianism, and the distancing effect of archaeologizing the event of the Nativity is very noticeable in his poem. Attempting to reconcile Isaiah and Virgil's Messianic Eclogue, Pope adopts Virgil rather than the traditional English Nativity lyric in his only appeal to the "babe":

All crimes shall cease, and ancient fraud shall fail,
Returning Justice lift aloft her scale;
Peace o'er the world her olive wand extend,
And white rob'd innocence from heav'n descend.
Swift fly the years, and rise th'expected morn!
O spring to light, auspicious babe! be born. (lines 16–22)[17]

After the period covered in this study, the new accretions to the Nativity story will often hark back to the utopian vision of Virgil. Although admittedly for various reasons Pope is not a good test case for my argument, here is a Catholic whose presentation of the Christ Child does not evoke any sacramental or substantial presence or make an issue of his pre-eminence over time.[18]

A subgenre almost every major poet tried his hand at in some way in the seventeenth century thus barely draws any attention until the rebirth of the genre later in the nineteenth century. However, Georgian and Victorian medieval imitations include distinctively modern elements in their approach to representing Christ. Although one could point to other influential transformations in English society besides reformed sacramental theology, I have argued that, in itself, it was a clear and significant factor in the shifting and varied ways in which the baby Jesus was imagined poetically in the period before Cromwell. One might expect, then, that sacramental theology would figure in the representations of Jesus in the medieval revival; yet the break in the tradition was long enough at that point, I believe, to make the link between sacramentology and Christology more obscure than it was for the writers studied here. Tracing the history of the bodily representation of the Christ Child past the Puritan Revolution is a tempting task at this point, but, because it would at least double the length of this book, it must remain a project for the future, though it is worth the space here to record some preliminary observations.

Even nineteenth-century poems that look back to the medieval and early modern conventions of the Nativity lyric avoid conflation of time and physical closeness with the Christ Child. For instance, Christina Rossetti's famous "In the Bleak Midwinter" (actual title, "A Christmas Carol") brings back the mother and child, the animals at the stable, but is not sure about angels, and generally remains in the past tense:

In the bleak mid-winter,
  Frosty wind made moan,
Earth stood hard as iron,
  Water like a stone;
Snow had fallen, snow on snow,
  Snow on snow,
In the bleak mid-winter,
  Long ago.

Our God, Heaven cannot hold Him,
  Nor earth sustain;

Heaven and earth shall flee away
  When He comes to reign:
In the bleak midwinter
  A stable-place sufficed
The Lord God Almighty,
  Jesus Christ.

Enough for Him, whom cherubim
  Worship night and day,
A breastful of milk
  And a mangerful of hay;
Enough for Him whom angels
  Fall down before,
The ox and ass and camel
  Which adore.

Angels and archangels
  May have gathered there,
Cherubim and seraphim
  Throng'd the air,
But only His mother,
  In her maiden bliss,
Worshipped the Beloved
  With a kiss.

What can I give Him,
  Poor as I am?
If I were a shepherd
  I would bring a lamb,
If I were a Wise Man,
  I would do my part, –
Yet what I can I give Him,
  Give my heart.[19]

"Long ago": the Nativity assumes a mythic quality, and Mary's unique privilege of kissing the child seems a mournful reminder of an unbridgeable distance between the yearning speaker and the Jesus who will only come at the end of time to make "heaven and earth" "flee away." Also worth noting is that there is not a single writer of the seventeenth century who would have written the lines "Angels and archangels / May have gathered there." Rossetti corrects this conditional with an affirmative indicative verb in the next line, but

Christ's constant attendance by angels, to which he himself attests in the New Testament, was not a matter of doubt to any of the poets we have studied. As pious a poet as Rossetti approaches the subject of the Nativity in a way that is recognizably distinct from the medieval and early modern ancestors she is calling to mind. She is very interested in physical proximity to the child, but wards off any approachers as infringing on the sole prerogative of his mother. Later poems by Thomas Hardy ("The Oxen") and James Joyce ("Ecce Puer") could hardly be called celebrations of Christ's birth at all; they are rather testaments to the poets' painful uprooting from Christian tradition. Alfred Lord Tennyson's repeated evocations of Christmas in his poem *In Memoriam* ring in "the Christ that is to be," a new, purified Christian, an England with "sweeter manners," but almost assuredly not Christ himself. One does not expect a Nativity lyric from any poet laureate of England in these latter days. As the dreary notes of The Pogues' "Fairytale of New York" and Chloe Agnew's "We're Walking in the Air" repeat endlessly on the airwaves and in the shopping centres of England and Ireland in preparation for the Christmas holiday these days, the fact that they are being exploited by merchants to induce shoppers to buy gifts and decorations in celebration of the birth of the Son of God might well strike us as ironic, for they remind no listener of anything like that at all. What has been lost in the time intervening between us and Richard Crashaw? It is clearly the little boy in the manger himself.

But to return to the seventeenth century: in the period following the Reformation in England, the way in which a poet conceptualizes the sacramental presence of Christ predicts fairly accurately the poet's representation of the Christ Child as physically present to the speaker. This connection is because the possibility of the physical presence of Christ's body after the Ascension comes into play when the poets of the period consider both issues. The sacramentologies of Catholics and Protestants invoked the Incarnation itself more fully as a parallel of what was occurring on the altar in the liturgy when substantial Real Presence was meant, and less so or not at all when spiritual or mystic presence was meant. Whereas poets in the era before Southwell had their choice of the three advents of Christ – or any combination thereof – when it came to Christmas themes,[20] the Protestant poets of the seventeenth century were wary of attempting a mimesis of Christ's actual coming in the flesh. Sacramental or incarnational poetics are different things to the Catholic and Protestant poets. To Southwell, Crashaw, and Donne, it mattered that Christ was a real baby; his humiliation in taking on flesh and his suffering in the manger, the knowledge of the cruelty of the Passion in which he was already in some way participating was a cause for pitying and cherishing the child. The knowledge that he had been present at the creation and had already conquered death allowed for wonder and adoration. To Herbert the infancy of Christ seems not to matter at all except as a figure of his coming into the heart of the believer, and to Milton it is a moment that destroys the pagan world but does not usher in the Parousia. Henry Vaughan, Thomas Traherne, Alexander Pope (Catholic though he is), and Christina Rossetti are the heirs of this respectful yet flattened way of representing the Nativity. The dominance of the past or future tenses or of the conditional mood in these poems reinforces the conviction that the baby Jesus is not here; he cannot be seen or touched, he cannot be held or embraced.

The point of this study is not to defend the superiority of the Catholic approach over the Protestant one. Nor is it to argue that, as poems, lyrics that focus on Christ's fleshly presence are qualitatively better than ones that do not. At times, the poets herein are doing very similar things in terms of form and poetic figures regardless of their theological convictions. Moreover, on most points of belief having to do with the Christ Child, Catholics and Protestants of the time were perhaps far more united with each other than they would be with their descendants in their various confessions today, as I hope I have shown. As R.V. Young observed, the growth of interest in Protestant poetics in the field of seventeenth-century poetry has forced readers to

> take very seriously the doctrinal and theological concerns of the poets. They have, however, sometimes failed to make a sufficient distinction between poetry and versified theological polemic, with the result that comparatively minor differences between Catholic and Protestant poets have been emphasized at the expense of far more important similarities.[21]

Young's caveat is good to bear in mind when one looks, as one ought, as one inevitably does, at differences between Catholic and Protestant approaches to poetic themes in seventeenth-century religious poetry. Thus, to conclude, I observe that this study began with the question based on the Gospel of Luke, "What kind of sign is the infant wrapped in swaddling clothes and laid in a manger?" In England, the answer lay yet ahead in the years to follow in the erasure of the body of the Christ Child as a sign: "a sign which shall be contradicted" (Luke 2:34). But in the seventeenth century, the child Jesus still stood among the learned, listening and asking them questions (Luke 2:46–52). In their Nativity lyrics, the seventeenth-century English poets are doing many things, but at the core of each poem is the answer to the question Jesus would later pose to his disciples, "Who do you say that I am?" And in spite of all their meaningful differences, they all answer, "Thou art Christ, the Son of the living God."

Notes

1. Sacrament, Time, and Space in the Tudor and Stuart English Nativity Lyric

1 Ps. 112:3: "A solis ortu usque ad occasum laudabile nomen." ["From the rising of the sun, even to its setting, praiseworthy is the name of the Lord."]
2 See Gary Bouchard, *Southwell's Sphere: The Influence of England's Secret Poet* (South Bend, IN: St. Augustine's Press, 2019).
3 Paul Cefalu, *The Johannine Renaissance in Early Modern English Literature and Theology* (Oxford: Oxford University Press, 2017), 9–12 et passim.
4 Cefalu, *Johannine Renaissance*, 2. He cites Ernst Käsemann, *The Testament of Jesus: A Study of the Gospel of John in the Light of Chapter 17*, trans. G. Krodel (Minneapolis, MN: Augsburg Fortress, 1978).
5 George Walton Williams, ed., *The Complete Poetry of Richard Crashaw*, trans. George Walton Williams and Phyllis S. Bowman (Garden City, NY: Doubleday, 1970), 646.
6 Walter Davis, "The Meditative Hymnody of Richard Crashaw," *English Literary History* 50, no. 1 (Spring 1983): 126–7.
7 Thomas Lewis, *English Presbyterian Eloquence* (London: T. Bickerton, 1720), 17.
8 Henry Vaughan, "Christ's Nativity II," in *The Works of Henry Vaughan: Introduction and Texts 1646–1652; Texts 1654–1678, Letters, & Medical Marginalia; Commentaries and Bibliography*, ed. Donald R. Dickson, Alan Rudrum, and Robert Wilcher (Oxford: Oxford University Press, 2018), 107.
9 Bouchard, *Southwell's Sphere*.
10 Frank W. Brownlow, *Robert Southwell* (New York: Twayne Publishers, 1996), 155–21.
11 R.L. Greene, ed., *The Early English Carols* (Oxford: Clarendon Press, 1935); Carleton Brown, ed., *English Lyrics of the Thirteenth Century* (Oxford: Clarendon Press, 1971); Carleton Brown, ed., *Religious Lyrics of the Fourteenth Century* (Oxford: Clarendon Press, 1970).

12 Gary Kuchar, "A Greek in the Temple: Pseudo-Dionysius and Negative Theology in Richard Crashaw's 'Hymn in the Glorious Epiphany,'" *Studies in Philology* 108, no. 2 (Spring 2011): 280.

13 Andrew Louth, *The Origins of the Christian Mystical Tradition: From Plato to Denys* (Oxford: Oxford University Press, 2006), x–xi.

14 Kuchar has argued that Crashaw uses both apophatic and kataphatic language in his Epiphany hymn.

15 Caroline Walker Bynum, *Metamorphosis and Identity* (New York: Zone Books, 2001), 181.

16 See, for example, Kimberly Johnson, *Made Flesh: Sacrament and Poetics in Post-Reformation England* (Philadelphia: University of Pennsylvania Press, 2014); Ryan Netzley, *Reading, Desire, and the Eucharist in Early Modern Religious Poetry* (Toronto: University of Toronto Press, 2011); Richard Rambuss, ed., *The English Poetry of Richard Crashaw* (Minneapolis: University of Minnesota Press, 2013); Michael Martin, *The Incarnation of the Poetic Word* (Kettering, OH: Angelico Press, 2017).

17 Cefalu, *Johannine Renaissance.*

18 Johnson, *Made Flesh.* Although Johnson criticizes the examination of metaphysical poetry for its expression of confessional ideas, her study reconfirms what earlier critics opined in discussing Protestant versus Catholic poetics.

19 Ryan Netzley, *Reading.*

20 Patricia Phillippy, *Shaping Remembrance from Shakespeare to Milton* (Cambridge: Cambridge University Press, 2018), 11.

21 Gary Kuchar, "Richard Crashaw and George Herbert's *The Temple*: Mystery, Liturgy, Error," *Cithara* 57, no. 2 (2018): 65–99.

22 Hans Urs von Balthasar, *Light of the Word: Brief Reflections on the Sunday Readings* (San Francisco: Ignatius Press, 1993), 26.

23 Jonathan Gil Harris, *Untimely Matter in the Age of Shakespeare* (Philadelphia: University of Pennsylvania Press, 2008), 189.

24 Theresa M. Kenney, "'This pompe is prizèd there': Southwell's Challenge to Courtly Identities in 'New Prince, New Pompe,'" in *Precarious Identities: The Works of Fulke Greville and Robert Southwell*, ed. Vassiliki Markidou and Afroditi-Maria Panaghis (New York: Routledge, 2019), 153–71.

25 These poets thus continued a tradition dating back to patristic times of focusing more on the spiritual meaning rather than the physical description of the town. Bernard McGinn, "Bethlehem," in *Encyclopedia of the Bible and Its Reception Online*, ed. Constance Furey et al. (Berlin: De Gruyter, 2019), n.p., https://www.degruyter.com/view/db/ebr.

26 Helen Vendler, *Invisible Listeners: Lyric Intimacy in Herbert, Whitman, and Ashbery* (Princeton, NJ: Princeton University Press, 2005), 1.

27 Biblical quotations for Catholic poets (Southwell, Crashaw) are from the Douai; for Anglican poets (Donne, Herbert), from the King James Version; and for Milton, from the Geneva.
28 *The Sarum Missal, in English*, trans. and ed. A. Harford Pearson. 2nd ed. (London: The Church Press, 1884), 318. First published in 1868.
29 *The Sarum Missal, in English*, 318–19.
30 Glen Bowman, "William Tyndale's Eucharistic Theology: Lollard and Zwinglian Influences," *Anglican and Episcopal History* 66, no. 4 (December 1997): 428. This view of the issue was also Berengarius's view.
31 John Calvin, *Institutes of the Christian Religion*, trans. Henry Beveridge (Grand Rapids, MI: Eerdmans, 1989), IV, xiv, 16.
32 Calvin, *Institutes*, IV, xvii, 10.
33 Viola Larson, "John Calvin on the Sacraments: A Summary," *Theology Matters* 13, no. 4 (September/October 2007): 2.
34 Augustine, *St. Augustine: Tractates on the Gospel of John 20–54*, trans. John W. Rettig (Washington, DC: Catholic University Press, 1995), 268–9. Gerrish argues that "Calvin had no need to choose between a glorified body in heaven and an ecclesial body on earth": the body of Christ for Calvin is the mystical body of the Church, which unites both. B.A Gerrish, *Grace and Gratitude: The Eucharistic Theology of John Calvin* (Eugene, OR: Wipf and Stock, 2002), 189.
35 See Heinrich August Wilhelm Meyer, *Critical and Exegetical Handbook to the Acts of the Apostles* (Edinburgh: T & T Clark, 1883).
36 Theodore G. Tappert, trans. and ed., *The Book of Concord: The Confessions of the Evangelical Lutheran Church* (Philadelphia, PA: Mühlenberg Press, 1959), 590.
37 Calvin, *Institutes*, IV, xvii, 12.
38 John Foxe, *The Acts and Monuments of the Church; Containing the History and Sufferings of the Martyrs*, ed. M.H. Seymour (London: Scott, Webster, and Geary, 1838.
39 John Schofield, *Philip Melanchthon and the English Reformation* (Oxford: Routledge, 2017), 155.
40 "In the first place, the holy Synod teaches, and openly and simply professes, that, in the august sacrament of the holy Eucharist, after the consecration of the bread and wine, our Lord Jesus Christ, true God and man, is truly, really, and substantially contained under the species of those sensible things. For neither are these things mutually repugnant, – that our Saviour Himself always sitteth at the right hand of the Father in heaven, according to the natural mode of existing, and that, nevertheless, He be, in many other places, sacramentally present to us in his own substance, by a manner of existing, which, though we can scarcely express it in words, yet can we, by the understanding illuminated by faith, conceive, and we ought

most firmly to believe, to be possible unto God." Norman P. Tanner, SJ, ed., *Decrees of the Ecumenical Councils* (London: Sheed and Ward, 1990), 699.

41 John Hunt, *Religious Thought in England from the Reformation to the End of the Last Century: A Contribution to the History of Theology* (London: Strahan, 1873), 63. See also D.P. Walker, "The Cessation of Miracles," in *Hermeticism and the Renaissance: Intellectual History and the Occult in Early Modern Europe*, ed. Ingrid Merkel and Alan G. Debus (Washington, DC: Folger Shakespeare Library, 1988).

42 Subtlety, as Thomas Aquinas explains it (see *Summa Theologiae*, Supplement Q83, A1), is the ability to pass through spaces, which Jesus is said to have exhibited even before his death and resurrection, as in his passage through Mary's viscera in birth.

43 Thomas Aquinas, *Summa Theologiae*, III, Q1, A3.

44 See Schofield, *Philip Melanchthon*, esp. 39–40, 99, 155.

45 Roger Beckwith, "The Doctrine of the Sacraments in the Thirty-Nine Articles," *Churchman* 105, no. 1 (1991), n.p.

46 Cranmer, Thomas, *The Book of Common Prayer: The Texts of 1549, 1559, and 1662*, ed. Brian Cummings (Oxford: Oxford University Press, 2011), 681–2.

47 Ibid., 682.

48 Ibid.

49 Thomas Cranmer, *The Book of Common Prayer, 1552*, in *The Two Liturgies, A.D. 1549 and A.D. 1552*, ed. Joseph Ketley (Cambridge: The University Press, 1844).

50 See Thomas W.H. Griffith, *The Principles of Theology: An Introduction to the Thirty-Nine Articles*. (Eugene, OR: Wipf and Stock, 2005), 523–4. First published in 1930.

51 Thomas Cranmer, *A Defence of the True and Catholic Doctrine of the Sacrament of the Body and Blood of Our Saviour Christ*, in *The Work of Thomas Cranmer*, ed. G.F. Duffield (Berkshire, UK: Sutton Courtenay Press, 1965), 57.

52 Cranmer, *Defence*, 41–2.

53 Richard Hooker, *Selections from the Fifth Book of Hooker's Ecclesiastical Polity*, ed. John Keble (Oxford: J.H. Parker, 1839), 60.

54 Beckwith, "The Doctrine of the Sacraments," n.p.

55 Hooker, *Selections*, 262–3.

56 Hooker, *Selections*, 262.

57 Hooker, *Selections*, 262.

58 Hooker, *Selections*, 226. The question of which elements of the Christian faith were things indifferent or "adiaphora" was central to the Lutheran compromises of the 1500s and the Anglican and Calvinist struggles of the 1600s. Considering the manner of Christ's presence in the Eucharist as a thing indifferent definitively separates English Protestants from Catholics in this period. See "Adiaphorists," in *The Oxford Dictionary of the Christian*

Church, ed. F.L. Cross and E.A. Livingstone (Oxford: Oxford University Press, 2005).

59 Lancelot Andrewes, *The English Theological Works*, ed. J.P. Wilson and J. Bliss (Oxford: John Henry Parker, 1841–54), vol. I, 35.

60 The Gelasian Sacramentary, the second oldest extant sacramentary in the Christian world, is a source Cranmer used in constructing the *Book of Common Prayer*. Andrewes appears to be paraphrasing from the same source or from St Augustine's Sermon on the Nativity XII: "Lacta, mater, Christum, et Dominum nostrum et cibum. Lacta panem de coelo venientem, et in praesepi positum velut piorum cibaria iumentorum." Sermo 128: PL 39:1655.

61 See John S. Pendergast, "Pierre Du Moulin on the Eucharist: Protestant Sign Theory and the Grammar of Embodiment," *English Literary History* 65, no. 1 (Spring 1998): 58–73. See also Brian Douglas, *A Companion to Anglican Eucharistic Theology*, Vol. 1, *The Reformation to the 19th Century* (Leiden: Brill, 2011), 137.

62 Lancelot Andrewes, *The Private Devotions of Lancelot Andrewes (Preces Privatae)*, trans. and ed. F.E. Brightman (Gloucester, MA: Peter Smith, 1983), 123. Reprint of the 1903 edition by Methuen & Company (London).

63 Andrewes, *The English Theological Works*, vol. VIII, 13. In the *Response to Cardinal Bellarmine*, we are looking not at Andrewes's public preaching but at a work meant for educated churchmen like himself, perhaps above all for bishops and teachers.

64 Andrewes, *The English Theological Works*, vol. VIII, 262.

65 Andrewes, *The English Theological* Works, vol. VIII, 265.

66 John Donne, *Pseudo-martyr. Wherein out of certaine propositions and gradations, this conclusion is euicted. That those which are of the Romane religion in this kingdome, may and ought to take the Oath of allegiance* (London: W. Stansby for Walter Burre, 1610), B2.1.

67 George Herbert, *A Priest to the Temple, or The Country Parson*, in *The Works of George Herbert*, ed. by F.E. Hutchinson (Oxford: Clarendon Press, 1959), 259.

68 Herbert, *A Priest to the Temple*, 257–8.

69 Herbert, *A Priest to the Temple*, 258.

70 George Herbert, "The H. Communion," in *The Works of George Herbert*, ed. by F.E. Hutchinson (Oxford: Clarendon Press, 1959), 52–3. Impanation is the belief – heretical for both Catholics and Anglicans – that Christ is in the bread, which undergoes no substantial change in the confecting of the sacrament. Some claim that the eleventh-century abbot Rupert of Deutz taught impanation, but the belief was not common or ever considered orthodox.

71 Esther Gilman Richey, "Unitive Theology: George Herbert's Revision of 'The H. Communion,'" *George Herbert Journal* 35, no. 1–2 (Fall 2011 / Spring 2012): 97.

72 James M. Bromley, "Intimacy and the Body in Seventeenth Century Religious Devotion," *Early Modern Literary Studies* 11, no. 1 (May 2005): 5.1–41.
73 Milton, *On Christian Doctrine*, in *Milton: Complete Poems and Major Prose*, ed. Merritt Y. Hughes (Indianapolis, IN: Odyssey Press, 1957), 554. See John C. Ulreich Jr., "Milton on the Eucharist: Some Second Thoughts about Sacramentalism," in *Milton and the Middle Ages*, ed. John Mulryan (Lewisburg, PA: Bucknell University Press, 1987), 37–8.
74 Ulreich, "Milton on the Eucharist," 49.
75 Thomas F. Healy, *Richard Crashaw* (Leiden: Brill, 1986), 123.
76 See Kimberly Johnson, "Richard Crashaw's Indigestible Poetics," *Modern Philology* 107, no. 1 (2009): 32–51; and Ryan Netzley, "Oral Devotion: Eucharistic Theology and Richard Crashaw's Religious Lyrics," *Texas Studies in Literature and Language* 44, no. 3 (2002): 247–72. See also Robert Ellrodt, "George Herbert and Richard Crashaw: Two Versions of the Christian Paradox," in his *Seven Metaphysical Poets: A Structural Study of the Unchanging Self* (Oxford: Oxford University Press, 2000), 205–24.
77 Miri Rubin, *Mother of God: A History of the Virgin Mary* (New Haven, CT: Yale University Press, 2009); Rachel Fulton Brown, *From Judgment to Passion: Devotion to Christ and the Virgin Mary, 800–1200* (New York: Columbia University Press, 2005).
78 Bouchard, *Southwell's Sphere*.
79 Bouchard, *Southwell's Sphere*, 165.
80 St. Bernard of Clairvaux, *On the Song of Songs*, Vol. 2, *Sermons 21–46*, trans. Kilian Walsh (Kalamazoo, MI: Cistercian Publications 1976), 16–20.

2. The Christ Child on Fire: Southwell's Mighty Babe

1 This chapter is reprinted with some editorial changes from its appearance under the same title in the *English Literary Renaissance* 43, no. 3 (September 2013): 415–45.
2 The notable exceptions, aside from the poems treated in this essay, include Donne's "Immensitie Cloisterd in thy deare womb" and Crashaw's "Nativity Hymn." One could also count, to a certain extent, Milton's Nativity Ode in this small number.
3 Nine new editions followed before 1636, an unusually high number that tells us Southwell's poetry was popular, and not only among disenfranchised Catholics. One edition, *The Triumphs over Death*, contained three paeans to Southwell, which used his name openly. Louis L. Martz, *The Poetry of Meditation: A Study in English Religious Literature of the Seventeenth Century* (New Haven, CT: Yale University Press, 1954), 12. See further *The Poems of Robert Southwell, SJ*, ed. James H. McDonald and

Nancy Pollard Brown (Oxford: Oxford University Press, 1967). All further citations of Southwell's poems are from this edition, hereafter referred to as PRS.

4 For the Christ Child in Malory, see *Le Morte Darthur*, ed. Stephen H.A. Shepherd (New York: Norton, 2003), 582–3.

5 "New heaven, new warre," in PRS, 14–15.

6 George Parfitt, ed., *Ben Jonson: The Complete Poems* (New Haven, CT: Yale University Press, 1975), 465; Martz, *The Poetry of Meditation*, 83.

7 See J.J. Scarisbrick, *The Reformation and the English People* (London: Wiley-Blackwell, 1984); and Eamon Duffy, "The English Reformation after Revisionism," *Renaissance Quarterly* 59, no. 3 (Fall 2006): 720–31.

8 R.L. Greene, ed., *The Early English Carols* (Oxford: Clarendon Press, 1935); Carleton Brown, ed., *English Lyrics of the Thirteenth Century* (Oxford: Clarendon Press, 1971); Carleton Brown, ed., *Religious Lyrics of the Fourteenth Century* (Oxford: Clarendon Press, 1970).

9 Eamon Duffy, *The Stripping of the Altars: Traditional Religion in England, 1400–1580* (New Haven, CT: Yale University Press, 1992), 579–84. See, by comparison, V.A. Kolve, *The Play Called Corpus Christi* (Stanford, CA: Stanford University Press, 1966); Eleanor Prosser, *Drama and Religion in the English Mystery Plays* (Stanford, CA: Stanford University Press, 1961), 14: "The York Cycle was performed as late as 1579, and … the so-called primitive Chester plays were acted until the end of the Sixteenth century and last copied in 1607"; Lois Potter, ed., *The Revels History of Drama in English*, Vol. 1, *Medieval Drama* (London: Methuen, 1983), xlii–xliv, 25–6, 45–8. See also Leah Marcus, "The Christ Child as Sacrifice: A Medieval Tradition and the English Cycle Plays," in *The Christ Child in Medieval Culture: Alpha es et O!*, ed. Mary Dzon and Theresa M. Kenney (Toronto: Toronto University Press, 2012).

10 See John Gassner and Edward Quinn, eds., *The Reader's Encyclopedia of World Drama* (Mineola, NY: Dover, 2002), 59–61, 280–4.

11 See, for instance, Sadia Abbas, "Polemic and Paradox in Robert Southwell's Lyric Poems," *Criticism* 45, no. 4 (Fall 2003), esp. 476, and notes 3 and 4. Specifying Southwell's debt to medieval and patristic sources, this article discusses the connections between Eucharist and Nativity in Southwell. See, by comparison, Pierre Janelle, *Robert Southwell, the Writer: A Study in Religious Inspiration* (London: Sheed and Ward, 1935), 282–5 et passim.

12 Robert Southwell, *An Epistle of Comfort* (Ilkley, UK: Scholar Press, 1974), 87–8. The list, incidentally, shows that Southwell had acquired familiarity with native English saints and their writings, and perhaps English historical chronicles as well.

13 See PRS, 92, 94, 96, 99; see also Theresa M. Kenney, "The Manger as Calvary and Altar in the Middle English Nativity Lyric," in *The Christ Child*

in Medieval Culture: Alpha es et O!, ed. Mary Dzon and Theresa Kenney (Toronto: Toronto University Press, 2012), 29–65.

14 Andrew Harnack, "Robert Southwell's 'The Burning Babe' and the Typology of Christmastide," *Kentucky Philological Association Bulletin* 4 (1977): 25–9.

15 See Clifford Davidson, "Robert Southwell: Lyric Poetry, the Restoration of Images, and Martyrdom," *Ben Jonson Journal* 7, no. 1 (2000): 157–86; Belen Sy, "Robert Southwell's Poetic Self-Fashioning," *Fu Jen Studies* 34 (2001): 41–74; Scott R. Pilarz, "'To help soules': Recovering the Purpose of Southwell's Poetry and Prose," in *Discovering and (Re)covering the Seventeenth Century Religious Lyric*, ed. Eugene R. Cunnar and Jeffrey Johnson (Pittsburgh, PA: Duquesne University Press, 2001); and Scott R. Pilarz, *Robert Southwell and the Mission of Literature, 1561–1595: Writing Reconciliation* (Aldershot, UK: Ashgate, 2004).

16 PRS, 6–7.

17 See John Wycliff, *De eucharistia tractatus maior* (London: Trübner, 1892), cap. 8, 271. More important for the poets following Southwell in the ensuing decades are the discussions of Christ's body's inaccessibility in Calvin, in the Thirty-Nine Articles, and elsewhere, as discussed in chapter one.

18 PRS, 15–16.

19 V. Sethuraman, "A Reading of Robert Southwell's 'The Burning Babe,'" in *Studies in Elizabethan Literature: Festschrift to G.C. Bannerjee*, ed. Gopal Bannerjee and P.S. Sastri (New Delhi: S. Chand, 1972), 10–14. Sethuraman's brief treatment of the image does not go beyond mentioning connections this image has with love and the Passion, as well as with alchemical literature. See also Harnack, "Robert Southwell's 'The Burning Babe.'"

20 Pseudo-Gregory of Nyssa, "On the Birth of Christ," PG 46:1133–6. Yrjö Hirn, *The Sacred Shrine: A Study of the Poetry and Art of the Catholic Church* (London: Faber and Faber, 1958), 450nn38–9, 549: "The burning-bush is cited in a Mary-sermon of Bishop Proclus (d. 446). See [F. A. von] Lehner, *Die Marienverehrung* [*in den Ersten Jahrhunderten* (Stuttgart: J.G. Cotta, 1881)], p. 215. This image is used perpetually, like the enclosed garden and the sealed well, from the beginning of the fifth century in patristic literature. Cf. the index to Livius's works." Anon. hymn, "Ave virgo gravidata / Rubo Moysii signata" in Guido Maria Dreves, ed., *Analecta Hymnica Medii Aevi* (Leipzig: Fues's Verlag, 1890), 77; Hilda Graef, *Mary: A History of Doctrine and Devotion*, Vol. 1, *From the Beginnings to the Eve of the Reformation* (New York: Sheed and Ward, 1963); André Grabar, "The Virgin in a Mandorla of Light," in *Late Classical and Mediaeval Studies in Honor of Albert Mathias Friend, Jr.*, ed. Kurt Weitzmann (Princeton, NJ: Princeton University Press, 1955). For art historical evidence, see in the Getty Museum Collection, Georges Trubert, *Madonna of the Burning Bush*, French,

Provence, about 1480–90, MS. 48, FOL. 154. See also Nicholas Froment, *Moses and the Burning Bush*, French, Avignon, 1476, Triptych in Cathédrale Saint-Sauveur d'Aix. For further references, see Elizabeth Harris, "Mary in the Burning Bush: Nicolas Froment's Triptych at Aix-en-Provence," *Journal of the Warburg Institute* 1, no. 4 (April 1938), 281–6. See also Christian Hannick, "The Theotokos in Byzantine Hymnography: Typology and Allegory," in *Images of the Mother of God: Perceptions of the Theotokos in Byzantium*, ed. Maria Vassilaki (Aldershot, UK: Ashgate, 2005), 74–5.

21 Harnack, "Robert Southwell's 'The Burning Babe,'" 27.

22 *Lactantius: Divine Institutes*, trans. Anthony Bowen and Peter Garnsey (Liverpool: Liverpool University Press, 2003), bk. 7, 19:428.

23 *Catherine of Siena: The Dialogue*, trans Suzanne Noffke (New York: Paulist Press, 1980), 365–6. For the critical edition, see *Il Dialogo*, ed. Giuliana Cavallini (Siena: Edizioni Cantagalli, 1995), 585–6. St. Catherine's works were popular with the Jesuits of the late sixteenth and early seventeenth century, as an English translation of her *Vita* published in Douai in 1609 attests.

24 Carra Ferguson O'Meara, "'In the Hearth of the Virginal Womb': The Iconography of the Holocaust in Late Medieval Art." *Art Bulletin* 63 (1981): 75–89.

25 "E temo e spero, et ardo e sono un ghiaccio" ["And I fear and hope, and I burn and am an icicle"]. Bruce Wardropper, "The Religious Conversion of Profane Poetry," in *Studies in the Continental Background of Renaissance English Literature: Essays Presented to John L. Lievsay*, ed. Dale B.J. Randall and George Walton Williams (Durham, NC: Duke University Press, 1977), 211.

26 For Roger Ascham's famous disapproval of medieval books of chivalry and of Malory in particular, see *The Scholemaster Or plaine and perfite way of teaching children, to vnderstand, write and speake, the Latin tong*, ed. J.E.B. Major (Oxford, 1863 [1570]), 81: "In our forefathers tyme, whan Papistrie, as in a standing poole, covered and overflowed all England, fewe bookes were read in our tong, saving certaine bookes of Chevalrie … which … were made in Monasteries, by idle Monkes, or wanton Chanons; as one for example, Morte Arthure, the whole pleasure of which booke standeth in two speciall poyntes, in open mans slaughter, and bold bawdrye. In which book those be counted the noblest Knightes, that do kill most men without any quarell, and commit fowlest adulteries by subtlest shiftes."

27 PRS, 6–7.

28 St. Ignatius of Loyola, *The Spiritual Exercises of St. Ignatius of Loyola*, ed. Elder Mullan, SJ (New York: Cosimo Classics, 1964; reprint of the 1914 edition by P.J. Kennedy & Sons), 65–6. Mary O'Donnell, in "Quam Oblationem: The Act of Sacrifice in the Poetry of Saint Robert Southwell"

(PhD diss., University of North Carolina, 1994), argues more should be made of Southwell's knowledge of other forms of prayer such as the Mass and Liturgy of the Hours, which, unlike the *Spiritual Exercises*, he would have said every day. Her study reveals liturgical sources for the ordering of concepts, the presence of images, and the like.

29 Brian Oxley, "'Simples Are by Compounds Farre Exceld': Southwell's Longer Latin Poems and 'St. Peters Complaint,'" *Recusant History* 17, no. 4 (1985): 332.

30 Gertrud Schiller, *Iconography of Christian Art*, trans. Janet Seligman (Greenwich, CT: New York Graphic Society, 1971), 1:75.

31 Pierre Demolon et al., *L'Histoire de Douai* (Dunkerque: Westhoek-Éditions des Beffrois, 1985), 61.

32 Wycliff, *De Eucharistia tractatus maior*, cap. 8, 271.

33 See Kenney, "The Manger as Calvary and Altar," 59n7.

34 Francis Clark, *Eucharistic Sacrifice and the Reformation*, 2nd ed. (Oxford: Basil Blackwell, 1967), 266, quoting Schatzgeyer's *Tractatus de missa* (Tübingen, 1525), part II, "De sacrificio in missa seu oblatione," fol. d.2 seq. See also John Fisher, *De veritate corporis et sanguinis Christi in Eucharistia adversus Ioannem ŒOEcolampadium* (Cologne, 1527), lib. IV, cap. 29, G-H, fol. 117–18; Stephen Gardiner, *Explication and Assertion of the true Catholique Fayth touching the most blessed Sacrament of the Altar, with Confutation of a Book written against the same* (Rouen, 1551), in *Writings and Disputations of Thomas Cranmer, relative to the Sacrament of the Lord's Supper*, ed. J.E. Cox (Cambridge: The Parker Society, 1844); Thomas More, "The Answer to a Poisoned Letter," in *The Essential Thomas More*, ed. Gerard Wegemer and Stephen Smith (New Haven. CT: Yale University Press, 2020), 915–1024.

35 George Huntston Williams, "Stanislas Hosius," in *Shapers of Religious Traditions in Germany, Switzerland, and Poland, 1560–1600*, ed. Jill Raitt (New Haven, CT: Yale University Press, 1981), 161, 167.

36 Clark, *Eucharistic Sacrifice*, 269–85. Citing Clark and others, O'Donnell in "Quam Oblationem" emphasizes the presence of all aspects and times of Christ's existence in the Eucharist as an act of self-offering, not just a blood oblation, in the Fathers as well as in Southwell, *Epistle*, 49–56. I disagree with her conclusion that the Eucharist as a self-offering of Christ has a greater impact on Southwell's tendency to collapse the events of Christ's life into one than does the Eucharist as a blood oblation, but it is a point worth considering. David Aers, with a similar aim of proving the existence of less emphasis on the sacrificial aspect of Christ's self-offering, notes the same overarching of time in Langland's representation of the crucifixion in Passus 16 of the B-text: "Langland refuses to think of the Incarnation in terms which isolate the Passion from creation, from the prophetic ministry, from the resurrection, and from salvation history." David Aers,

"The Humanity of Christ: Representations in Wycliffite Texts and *Piers Plowman*," in David Aers and Lynn Staley, *The Powers of the Holy: Religion, Politics and Gender in Late Medieval English Culture* (University Park: Penn State University Press, 1996), 69.

37 *Book of Common Prayer, 1559: The Elizabethan Prayer Book*, ed. John Booty (Charlottesville: University of Virginia Press, 2005).

38 Nicholas Ridley, *The Works of Nicholas Ridley*, ed. H. Christmas (Cambridge: Parker Society, 1843), 249. See Brian Douglas's account of Bishop of London Ridley's argument against the sacrament on the altar being the same natural body Mary held in her womb. Brian Douglas, *A Companion to Anglican Eucharistic Theology*, Vol. 1, *The Reformation to the 19th Century* (Leiden: Brill, 2011), 101.

39 The *Book of Common Prayer* associated the circumcision, rather, with the circumcision of the heart: "*The Collect*. ALMYGHTIE God, whiche madeste thy blessed sonne to be circumcised, and obedyente to the law for man; Graunt us the true circumcision of thy spirite, that our hertes, and al our membres, being mortifyed from al worldly and carnal lustes, may in al thinges obey thy blessed wil; through the same thy sonne Jesus Christ our Lorde."

40 PRS, 7.

41 Southwell's translation of Aquinas's "Lauda Sion," in PRS, 24–5.

42 St. Theodore the Studite, "Sermon on the Precious and Life-Giving Cross," PG 99.691–700.

43 For a review of the debate, see Matthew Baynham, "The Naked Babe and Robert Southwell," *Notes and Queries* 50, no. 1 (March 2003): 55–6. Baynham believes that this poem is more likely the source for Shakespeare's "naked new-born Babe" in *Macbeth* rather than "The Burning Babe," which is generally cited as a possible inspiration.

44 Athanasius, "Sermon on the Incarnation of the Word," PG 25:158. See St. Athanasius, *On the Incarnation: The Treatise De Incarnatione Verbi*, trans. "A Religious of C.S.M.V." (Crestwood, NY: St. Vladimir's Seminary Press, 1998), 68. The translator points out the Egyptian provenance of the word Athanasius uses for incarnation – π μί, epidemia – a term originally used for the official entrance of a state governor into his province (14). It was also a term describing the appearances of the pagan gods. The translator renders it "advent."

45 *Piers Plowman*, B-Text, 16.102.

46 In his commentary on the line in Passus 16, which he translates as "he learned the skills of battle," A.V.C. Schmidt equates Jesus's acquisition of warrior skills with the maturation of a child Paul mentions in a non-militaristic context: "In this metaphorical account, the growing up of the human Jesus under the tutelage of Piers … is figured as the training of a young knight by a senior one, and also that of an apprentice physician

by a doctor of medicine. Compare also Gal 4:1–5." *William Langland: Piers Plowman, A New Translation of the B-Text*, trans. A.V.C. Schmidt (Oxford: Oxford University Press, 1992), 332. E. Talbot Donaldson translates the lines: "And in the womb of that wench [Mary] was he forty weeks / Till he was born a boy from her body and grew bold to fight, / And would have fought with the Fiend before the time had fully come." William Langland, *Piers Plowman: An Alliterative Verse Translation*, trans. E. Talbot Donaldson (New York: W.W. Norton, 1990), 184. The quotation from "Somer is comen" is taken from Maxwell S. Luria and Richard L. Hoffman, eds., *Middle English Lyrics* (New York: W.W. Norton, 1974), 199.

47 PRS, 14. O'Donnell provides an excellent analysis of the Warrior Babe image and its sources in "Quam Oblationem," 97–114.

48 Ephrem the Syrian, *Sermo de Domino nostro*, 3–4.9, in *Sancti Ephraem Syri Hymnes et Sermones*, ed. Thomas-Joseph Lamy, vol. 1 (Louvain, 1882), 152–8, 166–8.

49 Southwell, *Epistle*, 24–6.

50 Theresa Coletti, "Devotional Iconography in the N-Town Marian Plays," *Comparative Drama* 11, no. 1 (1977): 25–6. See also Mary Dzon, "Birgitta of Sweden and Christ's Clothing," in *The Christ Child in Medieval Culture: Alpha es et O!*, ed. Mary Dzon and Theresa M. Kenney (Toronto: University of Toronto Press, 2012), 115–44.

51 Rosemary Woolf, *The English Mystery Plays* (Berkeley: University of California Press, 1972), 267; Gail McMurray Gibson, "The Thread of Life in the Hand of the Virgin," in *Equally in God's Image: Women in the Middle Ages*, ed. Julia Bolton Holloway, Constance S. Wright, and Joan Bechtold (New York: Peter Lang, 1990), 50 ff.

52 Leo Steinberg notes an analog of this image in Homily 7, "The Annunciation," by Photius (9th c.) from *The Homilies of Photius, Patriarch of Constantinople*, trans. Cyril Mango (Cambridge, MA: Harvard University Press, 1958), 148. See Steinberg's note in a discussion of Christ's wounded body in *The Sexuality of Christ in Renaissance Art and Modern Oblivion* (New York: Pantheon Books, 1983), 375n15.

53 Southwell, *Epistle*, 134.

54 Southwell, *Epistle*, 154.

55 Southwell, *Epistle*, 133.

56 Southwell, *Epistle*, 167.

3. "Kisse Him, and with Him into Egypt Goe": John Donne and the Christ Child of "Nativitie"

1 Meditation 14 in John Donne, *The Complete Poetry and Selected Prose of John Donne*, ed. Charles M. Coffin (New York: Modern Library, 2001), 441.

2 These poems include later ones such as Donne's 1608 "Upon the Annunciation and Passion Falling Upon the Same Day." E.K. Chambers long ago pointed out the still-lively question of the difficulty of dating Donne's poems by any imagined date of his conversion in citing Donne's letter on the "Litanie," which is clearly post-conversion. *The Poems of John Donne*, ed. E.K. Chambers (London: Lawrence & Bullen, 1896), 246–7.
3 Constance Furey, *Poetic Relations: Intimacy and Faith in the English Reformation* (Chicago: University of Chicago Press, 2017), 3.
4 Furey, *Poetic Relations*, 93. See Regina Schwartz, *Sacramental Poetics at the Dawn of Secularism: When God Left the World*, ed. Mieke Bal and Het de Vries (Stanford, CA: Stanford University Press, 2008), 89, 93. See also Ryan Netzley, *Reading, Desire, and the Eucharist in Early Modern Poetry* (Toronto: University of Toronto Press, 2011), 110. Theresa DiPasquale called *La Corona* a "celebration in verse of a particularly eucharistic event: the refreshment of the soul by the blood of Christ." DiPasquale, "John Donne's Sacramental Poetics" (PhD diss., University of Virginia, 1989), 106. DiPasquale argues in her later work that Donne conceives of *La Corona* as a "sacramental offering," but a Protestant, not a Catholic one, since it is not efficacious for salvation. She notes that "Nativitie" specifically presents the command to kiss the infant Jesus as "urging and enacting a Eucharistic oneness with the divine child." Theresa DiPasquale, *Literature and Sacrament: The Sacred and the Secular in John Donne* (Pittsburgh, PA: Duquesne University Press, 1999), 61, 71.
5 Judith H. Anderson, *Translating Investments: Metaphor and the Dynamics of Cultural Change in Tudor-Stuart England* (New York: Fordham University Press, 2005), 64–73.
6 Barry Spurr also notes the speaker's desire to kiss the Child in his *See the Virgin Blest: The Virgin Mary in English Poetry* (New York: Palgrave Macmillan, 2007), 87.
7 Helen Gardner, "The Religious Poetry of John Donne," in *John Donne: A Collection of Critical Essays*, ed. Helen Gardner (Englewood Cliffs, NJ: Prentice-Hall, 1962), 123–36. Grierson assigns them a date of between 1607 and 1609 for various reasons: see, by comparison, Paul A. Parrish, *The Variorum Edition of the Poetry of John Donne: The Holy Sonnets*, vol. 7.1 (Bloomington: Indiana University Press, 2005), xci.
8 J.B. Leishman, *The Monarch of Wit: An Analytical and Comparative Study of the Poetry of John Donne* (London: Hutchinson, 1962), 257.
9 Margaret Maurer has also argued against the disprizing of *La Corona* in her "The Circular Argument of Donne's 'La Corona,'" *Studies in English Literature, 1500–1900* 22, no. 1 (1982): 51–68.
10 Jeffrey Johnson, *The Theology of John Donne* (Cambridge: D.S. Brewer, 1999), 32–6.

11 Johnson, *The Theology of John Donne*, 35. Johnson cites John Donne's "Sermon 113 before the Earl of Exeter, 1624," in *The Sermons of John Donne*, ed. George R. Potter and Evelyn Mary Simpson (Berkeley: University of California Press, 1953–62), 6:154–5.

12 Barbara K. Lewalski, *Donne's "Anniversaries" and the Poetry of Praise: The Creation of a Symbolic Mode* (Princeton, NJ: Princeton University Press, 1973), 103. However, following Eleanor McNees, Theresa DiPasquale has demonstrated that Roman Catholic liturgical elements mingle with Anglican elements in *La Corona*. DiPasquale, *Literature and Sacrament*, 71.

13 Leo the Great, *In Nativitate Domini Sermo 6*, 2–3; 5, PL 54:213–16.

14 The Virgin's womb as cloister is an ancient image, used at least as early as Pope Gregory the Great. Donne is clearly thinking about the doctrine of the Virgin birth, which since Ambrose and Augustine had been interpreted via the vision of Ezekiel that describes a closed door through which only the Holy One of Israel could pass. Sedulius's early fifth century "A solis ortus cardine," the hymn that inspired so many Nativity lyrics and well known to all the authors in this collection, uses this image, drawn directly from Ambrose: "Clausae puellae viscera / Caelestis intrat gratia: / Venter puellae baiulat / Secreta quae non noverat." Frederick Brittain, *Medieval Latin and Romance Lyric* (Cambridge: Cambridge University Press, 1951), 74. Via multitudinous translations and paraphrases, Sedulius's hymn remained a potent influence on all our poets. See Philip Schaff, *History of the Christian Church*, vol. 3, *Third Period: Nicene and Post-Nicene Christianity* (Edinburgh: T & T Clark, 1884), 417n1. See also Brian P. Dunkle, SJ, "Ambrosian Imitation in Sedulius and Prudentius," in his *Enchantment and Creed in the Hymns of Ambrose of Milan* (Oxford: Oxford University Press, 2016), 186–213.

15 Felecia Wright McDuffie comments on this image and its association with Platonic sources, but points out that "because Mary and Jesus are without sin, their bodies are not evil but simply weak … Donne describes the 'imprisonment' of Mary's womb in a positive way." McDuffie, *"To Our Bodies Turn We Then": Body as Word and Sacrament in the Works of John Donne* (New York: The Continuum International Publishing Group, 2005), 35–6. See also Anthony Bale, "God's Cell: Christ as Prisoner and Pilgrimage to the Prison of Christ," *Speculum* 91, no. 1 (2016): 1–35.

16 John Donne, *The Divine Poems*, ed. Helen Gardner (Oxford: Clarendon Press, 1978), 3. All citations of the *La Corona* sonnets are from this edition.

17 Elizabeth M.A. Hodgson, *Gender and the Sacred Self in John Donne* (Newark: University of Delaware Press, 1999), 57–9.

18 Netzley, *Reading*, 143.

19 Eiléan Ní Chuilleanáin, "Time, Place and the Congregation of Donne's Sermons," in *Literature and Learning in Medieval and Renaissance England:*

Essays presented to Fitzroy Pyle, ed. V.J. Scattergood (Dublin: Irish Academic Press 1984), 197–215. See also Bruce A. Johnson, "The Audience Shift in George Herbert's Poetry," *Studies in English Literature, 1500–1900* 35, no. 1 (Winter 1995): 89–103. Johnson's analysis of Herbert's poems shows the tripartite audience address (God, the self, the reader) to be a deliberate and conscious rhetorical strategy. Herbert's poetic debts to Donne are manifold; this approach seems to be another connection between the two poets' art. Alternatively, both might have found the rhetorical strategy in Petrarch's *Rime Sparse*.

20 John Calvin, *John Calvin's Commentaries on the Harmony of the Gospels*, vol. 1, trans. Rev. William Pringle (Edinburgh: The Calvin Translation Society, 1845), 34.

21 Helen L. Parish, *Monks, Miracles, and Magic: Reformation Representations of the Medieval Church* (Oxford: Routledge, 2005), 75.

22 Richard Hooker, *Selections from the Fifth Book of Hooker's Ecclesiastical Polity*, ed. John Keble (Oxford: J.H. Parker, 1839), 60.

23 Itrat H'usain, *The Dogmatic and Mystical Theology of John Donne* (New York: Macmillan, 1938), 17–19. H'usain cites "Sermon XI Preached in Lent, to the King, April 20, 1630 on Job 16."

24 The avoidance of intercessory prayer may be evidence of editing after composition, but it may also demonstrate that Donne is sympathetic to the reformers' doubts about intercession even well before his formal conversion.

25 John Donne, "Sermon IX Preached to the LL. upon Easter-Day, at the Communion, the king being then dangerously sick at New-Market, on Psalm 89:48. March 28, 1619." John Donne, *The Sermons of John Donne*, ed. George R. Potter and Evelyn Mary Simpson (Berkeley: University of California Press, 1953–62), 2.9:197–212. The parallel between Mary's womb and Christ's tomb was conventional, and it is possible Donne is thinking of this similarity too.

26 For those who might think this improbable, I point to Lancelot Andrewes's Christmas sermon from Christmas Day, 1614, in which he specifically uses the word "embryo" to describe the fetal stage of the Word's entrance into the world. Since Donne was in London in 1614 as a Member of Parliament, there is a chance he might have been in the congregation at Whitehall when this sermon was preached before King James. He was to be ordained priest the following year and made Royal Chaplain. English clergy of the early seventeenth century would indeed have thought of the Christ Child in the womb as being in full possession of his divinity and thus all his divine attributes. For more on this issue, see Jan M. Kozłowski, "Mary as the Ark of the Covenant in the Scene of the Visitation (Luke 1:39–56) Reconsidered," *Warszawskie Studia Teologiczne* 31 (2018): 109–16. See also

René Laurentin, *Structure et theologie de Luc I-II* (Paris: Gabalda, 1957); and Jan M. Kozłowski, "'The Fruit of Your Womb' (Luke 1:42) as 'The Lord God, Creator of Heaven and Earth' (Judith 13:18): An Intertextual Analysis." *Ephemerides Theologicae Lovanienses* 93 (2017): 339–42.

27 See Jacqueline Tasioulas, "'Heaven and Earth in Little Space': The Foetal Existence of Christ in Medieval Literature," *Medium Aevum* 76, no. 1 (2007): 24–48.

28 Donne, bafflingly, makes it "Stars." He may be referring to hermetic traditions connecting the three wise men with the three stars of Orion's Belt, which are known in Spanish as *Los Tres Reyes Magos*, or to Marsilio Ficino's treatise *De Stella Magorum*. Donne is also likely to have been thinking of the conjunction of the three planets as the "Starres": Donne owned (and autographed) a copy of Kepler's 1606 publication, *De stella nova in pede Serpentarii*, which argued that the star of Bethlehem was actually the conjunction of the planets Jupiter, Saturn, and Mars in the fiery trigon. Lastly, it is likely Donne knew Jacobus de Voragine's *Golden Legend*. Jacobus says that, the day an apparition of a boy in a star appeared to the magi, "that same day three suns appeared in the East, and gradually melded into one solar body." Jacobus de Voragine, *The Golden Legend: Readings on the Saints*, trans. William Granger Ryan, vol. 1 (Princeton, NJ: Princeton University Press, 1995), 40.

29 Evelyn Birge Vitz, "The Apocryphal and the Biblical, the Oral and the Written, in Medieval Legends of Christ's Childhood: The Old French *Evangile de l'Enfance*," in *Satura: Studies in Medieval Literature in Honour of Robert R. Raymo*, ed. Nancy M. Reale and Ruth E. Sternglantz (Donington, UK: Shaun Tyas, 2001), 124–49.

30 John Donne, *Sermons on the Psalms and the Gospels with a Selection of Prayers and Meditations*, ed. Evelyn M. Simpson (Berkeley: University of California Press, 1963). Sermon 2 on Psalm 90: 1622? (date unknown): "O satisfie us early with thy mercy, that we may rejoice and be glad all our dayes" (57).

31 "Bóg sie rodzi," Franciszek Karpiński, 1792, in *Monumenta Polonica: The First Four Centuries of Polish Poetry, A Bilingual Anthology*, ed. Bogdana Carpenter (Ann Arbor: Michigan Slavic Publications, 1989), 519.

32 Ignatius probably has in mind the *Vita Christi* of Ludolph of Saxony. I am indebted to Mary Dzon for this observation.

33 Commentators on *La Corona* have sometimes been confused at Donne's choice of events to represent, but Gardner had an inkling that liturgical and meditative structures lay behind it. Gardner, "The Religious Poetry of John Donne," 123–4.

34 St. Ignatius of Loyola, *The Spiritual Exercises of St. Ignatius*, trans. and ed. Louis J. Puhl (New York: Vintage Books, 2000), 42.

35 Felix Lope de Vega y Carpio, "Cantarcillo de la Virgen," in *Pastores de Belen: Prosas y versos divinos* (Brussels: Roger Velpio y Huberto Antonio, 1614), 185–6.

36 Joseph F. Chorpenning, *Joseph of Nazareth through the Centuries* (Philadelphia, PA: St. Joseph's University Press, 2011), 28.

37 See my discussion of this hymn in "The Manger as Calvary and Altar in the Middle English Nativity Lyric," in *The Christ Child in Medieval Culture: Alpha es et O!*, ed. Mary Dzon and Theresa M. Kenney (Toronto: University of Toronto Press, 2012), 29–65. Joseph says to the child Jesus in his arms, "David the king arose from my race / and put on a crown. Great ignominy / have I attained, for instead of a king / I am a carpenter. A crown has found me / for in my bosom is the Lord of Crowns." Ephrem the Syrian, *Ephrem the Syrian: Hymns*, ed. and trans. Kathleen McVey (New York: Paulist Press, 1989), 108.

38 Brian Patrick McGuire, "Becoming a Father and a Husband: St. Joseph in Bernard of Clairvaux and Jean Gerson," in *Joseph of Nazareth through the Centuries*, ed. Joseph F. Chorpenning (Philadelphia, PA: Saint Joseph's University Press, 2011), 49–61.

39 Bernard of Clairvaux, *Magnificat, Homilies in Praise of the Blessed Virgin Mary*, trans. Marie-Bernard Saïd and Grace Perigo (Kalamazoo, MI: Cistercian Publications, 1979). See Mary Dzon, "Joseph and the Amazing Christ Child of Late-Medieval Legend," in *Childhood in the Middle Ages and the Renaissance: The Results of a Paradigm Shift in the History of Mentality*, ed. Albrecht Classen (New York: De Gruyter, 2005), 135–57. Dzon notes that this prayer was one that Catholic priests used to recite before Mass "since they, like Joseph, were believed to hold the incarnate Christ in their hands." Dzon cites *The Raccolta, or Collection of Indulgences, Prayers and Good Works*, ed. Ambrose St. John (London: Burns & Oates, 1910), 181–2.

40 McGuire, "Becoming a Father." About this theory, McGuire is most certainly wrong, though Bernard probably did not know Ephrem's Hymn in which Joseph speaks of holding the child Jesus in his arms (see, by comparison, note 36 above). In any case, Chara Armon cites other twelfth-century authors who represent Joseph in this way. See Chara Armon, "Joseph, Stepfather of Jesus," in *Women and Gender in Medieval Europe: An Encyclopedia*, edited by Margaret Schaus (New York: Routledge, 2006), 433–5. Charles Little even points out that Joseph, in a quasi-priestly gesture, hands the swaddling clothes to Mary in the Chartres sculpture, in the Tournai Cathedral Shrine of the Virgin, and in the Brussels Hours of Jacquemart de Hesdin, all thirteenth- and fourteenth-century works. See Charles T. Little, "Joseph at Chartres: Sculpture Lost and Found," in *Arts of the Medieval Cathedrals: Studies on Architecture, Stained Glass, and Sculpture*, ed. Kathleen Nolan and Danny Sandron (Abingdon, UK: Ashgate 2015), 190.

41 It is possible that Donne also was familiar with lines from Bonaventure's *Lignum Vitae*: "Now, then, my soul, / embrace that divine manger, / press your lips upon and kiss that boy's feet. / Then, in your mind, keep the

shepherds' watch." Bonaventure, "The Tree of Life," in *Bonaventure: The Soul's Journey into God, the Tree of Life, and the Life of St. Francis*, trans. Ewert Cousins (Paulist Press, 1978), 129. He also might have known the writings of Aelred of Rievaulx, who similarly encouraged kissing the Christ Child: "Embrace that sweet crib, let love overcome your reluctance, affection drive out fear. Put your lips to those most sacred feet." Aelred of Rievaulx, *A Rule of Life for a Recluse*, trans. Mary Paul Macpherson, in *Aelred of Rievaulx: Treatises and Pastoral Prayer*, introduction by David Knowles (Kalamazoo, MI: Cistercian Publications, 1995), 2:81. See also Mary Dzon, "Out of Egypt, into England: Tales of the Good Thief for the Medieval English Audience," in *Devotional Culture in Late Medieval England and Europe: Diverse Imaginations of Christ's Life*, ed. Stephen Kelly and Ryan Perry (Turnhout: Brepols, 2014), 147–241. Bernardine of Siena (1380–1444) had said of Joseph: "Joseph, the supposed Father of our Lord Jesus Christ, and true husband of the Queen of the world and of the angels ... was chosen by the Eternal Father to be the faithful foster-parent and guardian of the most precious treasures of God, His Son and His spouse. This was the task which he so faithfully carried out. For this, the Lord said to him, 'Good and faithful servant, enter into the joy of your Lord.'" Bernardine of Siena, "Sermo 2, de S. Joseph," *Opera Omnia*, vol. 7 (Florence: Claras Aquas, 1957), 27–30. See also Brian Patrick McGuire, *Jean Gerson and the Last Medieval Reformation* (University Park, PA: Penn State University Press, 2010), 359.

42 Dzon cites Gerson's *Oeuvres complètes*, ed. Palémon Glorieux, vol. 2 (Paris: Desclée, 1960), 156.

43 Brian Patrick McGuire, "*'Shining Forth Like the Dawn'*: Jean Gerson's Sermon to the Carthusians," in *Medieval Monastic Preaching*, ed. Carolyn Muessig (Leiden: Brill, 1998), 38.

44 Albrecht Koschorke, *The Holy Family and Its Legacy: Religious Imagination from the Gospel to Star Wars* (New York: Columbia University Press, 2003), 134. He cites Gerson 7:63–99, but also mentions Bernardine of Siena and Pierre d'Ailly as influences in the growing appreciation of Joseph.

45 See Rosemary Drage Hale, "Joseph as Mother: Adaptation and Appropriation in the Construction of Male Virtue," in *Medieval Mothering*, ed. John Carmi Parsons and Bonnie Wheeler (New York: Garland Publishing, 1996), 107.

46 See John Donne, *Essayes in Divinity, Being Several Disquisitions Interwoven with Meditations and Prayers*, ed. Anthony Raspa (Montreal and Kingston: McGill-Queen's University Press, 2001), 157nn28–34.

47 John Donne, *Essayes in Divinity, Being Several Disquisitions Interwoven with Meditations and Prayers*, ed. Anthony Raspa (Montreal and Kingston: McGill-Queen's University Press, 2001), 157.

48 McGuire, *Jean Gerson*, 303. McGuire compares the two but does not claim influence.

49 Teresa of Avila, *The Life of St. Teresa of Jesus of the Order of Our Lady of Carmel*, ed. Benedict Zimmerman (New York: Benziger Brothers, 1918), 38.

50 However, an illustrated manuscript (BnF, ital. 115) of the extraordinarily popular Pseudo-Bonaventuran *Meditationes Vitae Christi* depicted Joseph holding the Christ Child in his arms: Pseudo-Bonaventure, *Meditations on the Life of Christ: An Illustrated Manuscript of the Fourteenth Century*, trans. and ed. Rosalie Green and Isa Ragusa (Paris, Bibliothèque Nationale, Ms. Ital. 115; Princeton, NJ: Princeton University Press, 1961), 22n3, 35. See, by comparison, Hildegard Erlemann, "Cum Maria et Joseph pueri Jesus convictus atque conversatio: Wunderbares und Alltägliches zur Heiligen Familie," *INTAMS Review* 10, no. 2 (2004): 251. Abb. 4: Der hl. Joseph hält das Jesuskind auf dem Arm, Italien 14. Jh., Miniatur aus den *Meditationes Vitae Christi*, Cap. X. fol. 31v., Paris, Bibliothèque Nationale, Ms. Ital. 115. Mary Dzon discusses in detail Birgitta of Sweden's vision of Joseph holding Jesus and enumerates medieval German legends about an attentive, domestic Joseph. Dzon, "Joseph and the Amazing Christ Child," 142.

51 Iohannes Molanus, *De Historia SS. Imaginum et Picturarum* (Louvain: Typis Academicis, 1776; first published in 1570).

52 Armon, "Joseph, Stepfather of Jesus," 434.

53 Chorpenning, *Joseph of Nazareth*.

54 Jean Gerson was one of the first churchmen to challenge the old stereotypes of Joseph. As Mary Dzon points out in *The Quest for the Christ Child in the Later Middle Ages*, 292n3: "Jean Gerson, Chancellor of the University of Paris in the fifteenth century, also condemned the book *De l'enfance du Sauveur*, objecting to its portrayal of Joseph as an old widower when he married the Virgin, and its 'autres erreurs et folies,' without specifying what they were; see 'Considérations sur Saint Joseph,' ed. Glorieux, pp. 76–77 … On Gerson's efforts to promote the veneration of Joseph, see McGuire, 'Becoming a Father and a Husband,' idem. Jean Gerson, 235–39; idem, 'When Jesus Did the Dishes,' Sheingorn, 'Illustrius patriarcha Joseph,' as well as Armon, 'Servus, Pater, Dominus,' pp. 256–69."

55 Very early in Christian history, Jerome himself denounced the "delirium apocryphorum." Jerome, *Liber adversus Helvidium*, PL 23:203.

56 John Donne, *Ignatius His Conclave*, 1611. Donne is referring to the apocryphal *History of Joseph the Carpenter*, thought to originate in the fifth century, which purports to be based on a letter written by Jesus himself and specifies Joseph's age at his marriage to Mary as 90 and his death as taking place at the age of 111. See Alexander Walker, trans., *The History of Joseph the Carpenter*, in *Ante-Nicene Fathers*, vol. 8, ed. Alexander Roberts, James Donaldson, and Arthur Cleveland Coxe (Buffalo, NY: Christian

Literature Publishing, 1886). Revised and edited for New Advent by Kevin Knight, http://www.newadvent.org/fathers/0805.htm. It is very strange that Donne should be familiar with the text, which was not published in Latin (translated from an Arabic original) until 1722 by Georg August Wallin. Bart D. Ehrman and Zlatko Pleše, *The Apocryphal Gospels: Texts and Translations* (Oxford: Oxford University Press, 2011): "In its present form, the History of Joseph the Carpenter is thus a compilation of various traditions concerning Mary and the 'holy family,' most likely composed in Byzantine Egypt in the late sixth or early seventh century" (158).

57 As for the Apocrypha as the Deutero-canonical books of the Bible, Donne tends to be accepting of their authority aside from the question of canonicity, as he discusses twenty years later in "A Sermon Preached at St. Paul's on Easter Day, 1627" on Hebrews 11:35: "So then, there may be good use made of an apocryphal book. It always was, and always will be impossible, for our adversaries of the Roman church, to establish that, which they have so long endeavoured, that is, to make the apocryphal books equal to the canonical." *The Sermons of John Donne*, ed. George R. Potter and Evelyn Mary Simpson (Berkeley: University of California Press, 1953–62), 7:385.

58 Gertrud Schiller attests to the rarity of images of an active or affectionate Joseph in medieval art, saying one of the most rarely depicted scenes from the infancy gospels is the dream of Joseph directing him to take the child and his mother into Egypt. Gertrud Schiller, *Iconography of Christian Art*, vol. 1, trans. Janet Seligman (Greenwich, CT: New York Graphic Society, 1971), 117. Mary Dzon has corrected this assertion in her "Joseph and the Amazing Christ-Child," 135–57; Pamela Sheingorn has also discussed portrayals of St. Joseph in medieval lore in her "Joseph the Carpenter's Failure at Familial Discipline," in *Insights and Interpretations: Studies in Celebration of the Eighty-Fifth Anniversary of the Index of Christian Art*, ed. Colum Hourihane (Princeton, NJ: Princeton University Press, 2002), 156–67.

59 R.V. Young, *Doctrine and Devotion in Seventeenth Century Poetry: Studies in Donne, Herbert, Crashaw, and Vaughan* (Cambridge: D.S. Brewer, 2000).

60 *The Sermons of John Donne*, ed. George R. Potter and Evelyn Mary Simpson (Berkeley: University of California Press, 1953–62), 6:41; P.M. Oliver, *Donne's Religious Writing: A Discourse of Feigned Devotion* (New York: Addison Wesley Longview, 1997), 103.

61 Oliver, *Donne's Religious Writing*, 103.

4. "My Saviour's Face": George Herbert's "Starre" and the Vanishing Christ Child

1 Jeanne Clayton Hunter, "'With Wings of Faith': Herbert's Communion Poems," *Journal of Religion* 62, no. 1 (1982): 57–71.

2 Esther Gilman Richey, "Unitive Theology: George Herbert's Revision of 'The H. Communion,'" *George Herbert Journal* 35, no. 1–2 (Fall 2011/Spring 2012): 97–109.
3 George Herbert, "The Starre," in F.E. Hutchinson, ed. *The Works of George Herbert* (Oxford: Clarendon Press, 1959), 74. "The Starre" does not appear in the Dr. Williams manuscript, which is in Herbert's own handwriting, but does appear in the authoritative Tanner manuscript (Bodleian MS Tanner 307), which was the source for the first printing of *The Temple* and had been in Nicholas Ferrar's possession. The last four stanzas of the poem were set to music by John Jenkins, who also composed music for several other poems by Herbert, probably shortly after the poet's death; the songs were inscribed in the Christ Church part-books after 1634; see Simon Jackson and George J. Callon, "A Newly-Identified Setting of Herbert's 'Even-song' by John Jenkins," *George Herbert Journal* 36, nos. 1–2 (Fall 2012/Spring 2013): 24. See also Vincent Duckles, "John Jenkins' Settings of Lyrics by George Herbert," *The Musical Quarterly* 48, no. 4 (October 1962): 461–75.
4 Robert Hilliard Whalen, *The Poetry of Immanence: Sacrament in Donne and Herbert* (Toronto: University of Toronto Press, 2002), 56. See also Wayne J. Hankey, "Augustinian Immediacy and Dionysian Mediation in John Colet, Edmund Spenser, Richard Hooker, and the Cardinal de Bérulle," in *Augustinus in der Neuzeit, Colloque de la Herzog August Bibliothek de Wolfenbüttel, 14–17 octobre, 1996* (Turnhout: Brepols, 1998), 125–60. Hankey's study of immediacy versus angelic mediation in Spenser is very helpful to understanding this imagery.
5 Martin Elsky, "History, Liturgy, and Point of View in Protestant Meditative Poetry," *Studies in Philology* 77, no. 1 (Winter 1980): 74.
6 See John W. Riggs, *The Lord's Supper in the Reformed Tradition: An Essay on the Mystical True Presence* (Louisville, KY: Westminster John Knox Press, 2015).
7 Helen Vendler, *The Poetry of George Herbert* (Cambridge, MA: Harvard University Press, 1975), 254.
8 Vendler, *Poetry*, 254.
9 Vendler, *Poetry*, 255.
10 Vendler, *Poetry*, 252.
11 James Boyd White, *"This Book of Starres": Learning to Read George Herbert* (Ann Arbor: University of Michigan Press, 1994), 182–3.
12 White, *"This Book of Starres,"* 189.
13 There is a tantalizing possibility that Herbert's poem is inspired by the late medieval image of the star of Bethlehem with the Christ Child's face in it, such as we see in the manuscript copy of the *Speculum humanae salvationis*. While there is no way to prove that it is, the image would make sense of

Herbert's conflation of the star with the Christ Child. See Adrian Wilson and Joseph Lancaster Wilson, eds., *A Medieval Mirror: Speculum humanae salvationis, 1324–1500* (Berkeley: University of California Press, 2002), 34.

14 Bruce A. Johnson, "The Audience Shift in Herbert's Poetry," *Studies in English Literature, 1500–1900* 35, no. 1 (Winter 1995): 90.

15 Hutchinson, *Works of George Herbert*, 233–4.

16 Helen Vendler, *Invisible Listeners: Lyric Intimacy in Herbert, Whitman, and Ashbery* (Princeton, NJ: Princeton University Press, 2005), 7.

17 James Bromley speaks at length about the issue of intimacy and the body of Christ in Herbert. See Bromley, "Intimacy and the Body in Seventeenth Century Religious Devotion," *Early Modern Literary Studies* 1, no. 1 (May 2005): 5.1–41.

18 There are notable exceptions, such as the description of Christ in Gethsemane in "The Agonie," where the speaker dwells on Christ's bloody sweat as the price of sin and his piercing on the cross as the revelation of love.

19 Rosemond Tuve, "George Herbert and Caritas," in *Essays by Rosemond Tuve*, ed. Thomas P. Roche (Princeton, NJ: Princeton University Press, 1970), 174.

20 Heather Asals, *Equivocal Predication: George Herbert's Way to God* (Toronto: University of Toronto Press, 1981), 15.

21 Nicholas of Lyre, *Bibliorum Sacrorum cum Glossa ordinaria*, facsimile reprint of editio princeps (Strassburg: A. Rusch, 1480–1), in Matthaeum cap. 2, 59–62. See also Luke 2:34–5.

22 See Yrjö Hirn, *The Sacred Shrine: A Study of the Poetry and Art of the Catholic Church* (London: Faber and Faber, 1958), 346. Psalm 18, verses 6–7 were applied to Christ's Incarnation.

23 Ficino was very well known to the neo-Platonists of the late Elizabethan period, as Andrew Hadfield notes in his biography of Edmund Spenser, also a Cambridge man (Pembroke College). Hadfield, *Edmund Spenser: A Life* (Oxford: Oxford University Press, 2012), 48, 81, 350, 447n58.

24 Mary Dzon, "Birgitta of Sweden and Christ's Clothing," in *The Christ Child in Medieval Culture: Alpha es et O!*, ed. Mary Dzon and Theresa M. Kenney (Toronto: University of Toronto Press, 2014), 124. See also Henrik Cornell, *The Iconography of the Nativity of Christ* (Uppsala: Lundquist, 1924).

25 Quoted in Dzon, "Birgitta of Sweden," 124.

26 John Donne, "Sermon 4 Preached at St. Paul's on Christmas-Day, 1626, Luke ii. 29 and 30," in John Donne, *The Sermons of John Donne*, ed. George R. Potter and Evelyn Mary Simpson (Berkeley: University of California Press, 1953–62), 7:293.

27 Patrides noted that Herbert uses "winding" here only to use it in a pejorative sense in "Jordan" ("winding stair") and, even more darkly,

in the phrase "winding sheet" in "Mortification." He suggests all the meanings unite in "A Wreath." C.A. Patrides, *The English Poems of George Herbert* (London: Dent, 1974), 23n9.

28 Ann Astell, *Eating Beauty: The Eucharist and the Spiritual Arts of the Middle Ages* (Ithaca, NY: Cornell University Press, 2006), 3.

29 Riggs, *The Lord's Supper*, 22. Riggs cites David Power, *The Eucharistic Mystery: Revitalizing the Tradition* (New York: Crossroad, 1994).

30 R.A. Durr, *On the Mystical Poetry of Henry Vaughan* (Cambridge, MA: Harvard University Press, 1962), 127.

31 See, among others, Elliott M. Simon, "Pico, Paracelsus, and Dee: The Magical Measure of Human Perfectibility," in *Gender and Scientific Discourse in Early Modern Culture*, ed. Kathleen P. Long (Abingdon, UK: Routledge, 2010), 13–40.

32 Elizabeth Clarke parallels the trinity of forces to those that make up effective rhetoric in *Theory and Theology in George Herbert's Poetry: "Divinitie, and Poesie, Met"* (Oxford: Clarendon Press, 1997), 270. "All three words are appropriate for the sort of rhetoric Herbert longs for: light, to bring wisdom: motion, to be effective: heat, to kindle love."

33 Mario A. Di Cesare, "Herbert's 'Prayer (I)' and the Gospel of John," in *"Too Rich to Clothe the Sunne": Essays on George Herbert*, ed. Claude J. Summers and Ted-Larry Pebworth (Pittsburgh, PA: University of Pittsburgh Press, 1980), 103.

34 *The Essential Aquinas: Writings on Philosophy, Religion, and Society*, ed. John Y.B. Hood. (Westport, CT: Praeger, 2002), 54.

35 Marsilio Ficino, *Platonic Theology*, trans. Michael J.B. Allen, ed. James Hankins (Cambridge, MA: Harvard University Press, 2001), 3:161.

36 Ficino, *Platonic Theology*, 3:163.

37 For the term "tripotens" in Marius Victorinus, see Ruth Majercik, "Porphyry and Gnosticism," *The Classical Quarterly* 55, no. 1 (May 2005): 291. Herbert also seems to have been influenced by Spenser's *Hymne of Heavenly Beauty*. He certainly knows Spenser, the probable source of his famous "Easter Wings" image of imping his wing. See also Wayne J. Hankey's discussion of the images of light and ascent in Spenser's poem: Hankey, "Augustinian Immediacy and Dionysian Mediation in John Colet, Edmund Spenser, Richard Hooker, and the Cardinal de Bérulle," in *Augustinus in der Neuzeit, Colloque de la Herzog August Bibliothek de Wolfenbüttel, 14–17 octobre 1996* (Turnhout: Brepols, 1998), 125–60.

38 Marguerite Rigoglioso, *The Cult of Divine Birth in Ancient Greece* (New York: Palgrave MacMillan, 2009), 158.

39 Nicholas Horsfall, "Bees in Elysium," *Vergilius* 56 (2010): 40. Horsfall cites Porphyry de Antro 18, fr.879Radt, and Scholiast on Euripides's *Hippolytus*, 73, 40.

40 Porphyry, *On the Cave of the Nymphs in the Thirteenth Book of the Odyssey: From the Greek of Porphyry*, trans. Thomas Taylor (London: John M. Watkins, 1917), section 8.
41 Curiously, bee imagery is rarely to be found in the Bible. In general, honey is associated with wisdom, moderation – and temptation. See Tova Forti, "Bee's Honey: From Realia to Metaphor in Biblical Wisdom Literature," *Vetus Testamentum* 56, no. 3 (July 2006): 327.
42 See Erwin Fahlbusch et al., eds., *Encyclopedia of Christianity*, vol. 56 (Grand Rapids, MI: Eerdmans, 2008), 263.
43 St. Anthony of Padua spoke of Christ and Christians as bees. John Mason Neale, *Mediaeval Preachers and Mediaeval Preaching* (London: J.C. Mosley, 1856), 26.
44 Hope B. Werness, *Continuum Encyclopedia of Animal Symbolism in World Art* (New York: A & C Black, 2006), 40.
45 Werness, *Continuum Encyclopedia*, 40.
46 Birgitta of Sweden, *The Revelations of St. Birgitta of Sweden*, vol. 3, *Liber Caelestis*, Books 6–7, trans. Denis Searby (Oxford: Oxford University Press, 2012).
47 Pseudo-Dionysius, *Divine Names* 588A, quoted in Majercik, "Porphyry and Gnosticism," 280–1.
48 That is not to say Pseudo-Dionysius passed by the Incarnation entirely, but the Christ Child does not appear in his meditations on it (*Divine Names* 4, 13). Pseudo-Dionysius, *The Divine Names*, in *The Complete Works*, ed. Karlfried Froehlich (Mahwah, NJ: Paulist Press, 1987), 47–132.
49 Sophie Read, *Eucharist and the Poetic Imagination in Early Modern England* (Cambridge: Cambridge University Press, 2013), 126. Read's observations regarding Henry Vaughan's "communions of light" could also well be applied to "The Starre" (174–8).
50 "Herbert's imagery here is drawn from the gospel narratives, which portray Christ as reaching out to touch individuals, or taking them by the hand (Mark 1:31, 41; 5:41; 7:32; 8:23; 9:27)." Alister McGrath, "The Alchemy of Grace: The Gospel and the Transformation of Reality in George Herbert's 'The Elixir.'" A paper given at the Literature and Theology Seminar, Oxford University, in November 2007. https://www.academia.edu/9792170/.
51 Hutchinson, *Works of George Herbert*, 65–6.
52 Harold Toliver, *George Herbert's Christian Narrative* (University Park, PA: Penn State University Press, 1993), 224.
53 See Theresa M. Kenney, "'This pompe is prizèd there': Southwell's Challenge to Courtly Identities in 'New Prince, New Pompe,'" in *Precarious Identities: The Works of Fulke Greville and Robert Southwell*, ed. Vassiliki Markidou and Afroditi-Maria Panaghis (New York: Routledge, 2020), 153–71.

54 Shall I thy woes
Number according to thy foes?
Or, since one starre show'd thy first breath,
Shall all thy death?

55 "Good Friday," in Hutchinson, *Works of George Herbert*, 38–9.

56 Richard E. Hughes, "George Herbert and the Incarnation," *Cithara* 4, no. 1 (1964): 23–4.

57 A study of the Platonizing elements in English Calvinism is outside the scope of this book. For a mention of the Herbert family's interest in this issue, see Dewey D. Wallace, *Shapers of English Calvinism 1660–1714: Variety, Persistence, and Transformation* (New York: Oxford University Press, 2011), 174.

58 Read, *Eucharist*, 205.

59 See Theresa M. Kenney, "'Sensualiter tangitur': The Christ Child 'Born a Martyr' in John Donne's Sermon for Christmas 1626." *John Donne Journal* 36 (forthcoming).

60 John Drury, *Music at Midnight: The Life and Poetry of George Herbert* (London: Penguin, 2014), 263–5. See *Pseudo-Matthaei Evangelium*, ed. Jan Gijsel, vol. 1 of *Libri de nativitate Mariae*, CCSA 9. The contraction of light is in the Protoevangelium of James (19:15) and a Latin text derived from it (J-compilation). See Ronald F. Hock, ed. and trans., *The Infancy Gospels of James and Thomas* (Santa Rosa, CA: Polebridge Press, 1995), 67.

61 Herbert does say that Christ came to an inn in another Nativity poem, "The Bag." Gene Veith emphasizes the randomness of the inn in Herbert's narrative. Veith, *Reformation Spirituality: The Religion of George Herbert* (Lewisburg, PA: Bucknell University Press, 1985), 115.

62 Richard Strier, *Love Known: Theology and Experience in George Herbert's Poetry* (Chicago: University of Chicago Press, 1983), 154–5.

63 See Theresa M. Kenney, "The Manger in the Reformation and the Counter-Reformation," in *Encyclopedia of the Bible and Its Reception Online*, ed. Constance Furey et al., vol. 7 (Berlin: De Gruyter, 2019), n.p., https://www.degruyter.com/view/db/ebr.

64 Augustine, Sermo 190, in *St. Augustine: Sermons for Christmas and Epiphany*, trans. Thomas Comerford Lawler (New York: Paulist Press, 1952), 101–6.

65 R.V. Young, *Richard Crashaw and the Spanish Golden Age* (New Haven, CT: Yale University Press, 1982), 6.

66 Strier, *Love Known*, 171n71.

67 Robert Whalen, "George Herbert's Sacramental Puritanism," *Renaissance Quarterly* 54, no. 4, part 1 (Winter 2001): 1273.

5. "Wisest Fate Says No": Milton's Nativity Ode

1 Merritt Y. Hughes, ed., *Milton: Complete Poems and Major Prose* (Indianapolis, IN: Odyssey Press, 1957), 43. All quotations from Milton are from this edition.

2 Hughes, *Milton*, 50.

3 Dayton Haskins, "Milton's Portrait of Mary as Bearer of the Word," in *Milton and the Idea of Women*, ed. Julia Walker (Urbana: University of Illinois Press, 1988), 169–84; Anton Vander Zee, "Milton's Mary: Suspending Song in the *Nativity Ode*," *Modern Philology* 108, no. 3 (February 2011): 375–99.

4 Chrysostom exerted a powerful influence over Calvin and other reformers in the age before Milton and in his own century, but here Milton does not follow him.

5 See Lowry Nelson, *Baroque Lyric Poetry* (New Haven, CT: Yale University Press, 1961), 48. See also Milton's Elegia Sexta, addressed to Diodati, which we will have occasion to consult at a later point in this argument; Hughes, *Milton*, 50–3.

6 Vander Zee, "Milton's Mary, 375–99.

7 Gordon Teskey, *The Poetry of John Milton* (Cambridge, MA: Harvard University Press, 2015), 56.

8 Ann Baynes Coiro, "'A Ball of Strife': Caroline Poetry and Royal Marriage," in *The Royal Image: Representations of Charles I*, ed. Thomas Corns (Cambridge: Cambridge University Press, 1999), 36.

9 Rosemond Tuve, *Images and Themes in Five Poems by Milton* (Cambridge, MA: Harvard University Press, 1957), 41.

10 J. Martin Evans, *The Miltonic Moment* (Lexington: University Press of Kentucky, 1998), 12.

11 Christina Fawcett, "The Orphic Singer of Milton's Nativity Ode," *Studies in English Literature 1500–1900* 49, no. 1 (Winter 2009): 105, 112.

12 Gordon Teskey, Delirious Milton: The Fate of the Poet in Modernity (Cambridge, MA: Harvard University Press, 2006).

13 Robert Milman, *The Life of Torquato Tasso*, vol. 2 (London: Henry Colburn, 1850), 297.

14 Herbert Grierson, *First Half of the Seventeenth Century* (Edinburgh: W. Blackwood and Sons, 1906), 182; John Carey, *The Complete Shorter Poems of John Milton* (New York: Columbia University Press, 1967), 101–15.

15 Blossom Feinstein, "On the Hymns of John Milton and Gian Francesco Pico," *Comparative Literature* 20, no. 3 (Summer 1968): 245–53.

16 Jacopo Torriti, Santa Maria Maggiore, 1296.

17 Southwell, Donne, Crashaw, and others use the present tense or an admixture of tenses to create the same effect in their poems on the Nativity and elsewhere.

18 Lowry Nelson, "Góngora and Milton: Toward a Definition of the Baroque," *Comparative Literature* 6, no. 1 (Winter 1954): 53–63.

19 Blossom Feinstein, "On the Hymns of John Milton and Gian Francesco Pico," *Comparative Literature* 20, no. 3 (Summer 1968): 253.

20 See Theresa M. Kenney, "The Manger as Calvary and Altar in the Middle English Nativity Lyric," in *The Christ Child in Medieval Culture: Alpha es et O!*, ed. Mary Dzon and Theresa Kenney (Toronto: University of Toronto Press, 2012), 29–65.

21 Edward W. Tayler, *Milton's Poetry: Its Development in Time* (Pittsburgh, PA: Duquesne University Press, 1979), 35. For further development of this view, see Don Cameron Allen, *The Harmonious Vision: Studies in Milton's Poetry* (Baltimore: Johns Hopkins University Press, 1970), 26–8; Gregory F. Goekjian, "Deference and Silence: Milton's Nativity Ode," *Milton Studies* 21 (1985): 119–35; Ralph Waterbury Condee, *Structure in Milton's Poetry: From the Foundation to the Pinnacles* (University Park: Pennsylvania State University Press, 1974), 53–4; Nelson, *Baroque Lyric Poetry*, 48–51.

22 Tayler, *Milton's Poetry*, 35. For development of the implications of such conflation, see Roger Lass, "Poem as Sacrament: Transcendence of Time in the Advent Sequence from the Exeter Book," *Annuale Mediaevale* 7 (1966): 3–15. See also Katherine Bache Trower, "Temporal Tensions in the *Visio of Piers Plowman*," *Medieval Studies* 35 (1973): 389–412.

23 Nelson, *Baroque Lyric Poetry*, 48.

24 Erich Auerbach, "Figura," in *Scenes from the Drama of European Literature*, trans. Ralph Manheim (New York: Meridian Books, 1959), 29; Goekjian, "Deference and Silence," 123–6; Condee, *Structure in Milton's Poetry*, 51–4.

25 Mother Mary Christopher Pecheux, "The Image of the Sun in Milton's Nativity Ode." *Huntington Library Quarterly* 28, no. 4 (1975): 315–33. See also Tuve, *Images and Themes*, 41.

26 L.C. Martin, ed., *The Poems English, Latin, and Greek of Richard Crashaw* (Oxford: Clarendon Press, 1927), 183–4. All quotations of Crashaw's works are from this edition.

27 See Kenney, "The Manger as Calvary and Altar," 29–65.

28 Michael Bauman convincingly argues this point in *Milton's Arianism* (Frankfurt am Main: Verlag Peter Lang, 1987). See also J.H. Hanford, "The Youth of Milton," in *Studies in Shakespeare, Milton, and Donne* (New York: Haskell House, 1964), 122–4.

29 Marcus Aurelius C. Prudentius, "Corde natus ex parentis," *Liber Cathemerinon*, Hymnus 9, in *Prudentius*, vol. 1, trans. H.J. Thompson. Loeb Classical Library. (Cambridge, MA: Harvard University Press, 1962), 76–85; Ambrose, "Veni, redemptor gentium," in *Analecta Hymnica Medii Aevi* (Leipzig: Fues's Verlag, 1890), 13–14.

30 Hughes, *Milton*, 956.

31 Beverly Sherry, "Milton's 'Mystic Nativity,'" *Milton Quarterly* 17, no. 4 (1983): 108–16.

32 The traditional division between a circular pagan conception of time and a linear Judeo-Christian one is overly simplified but useful in this context

given Milton's references to Virgil. For a discussion of different modes of time, see Kenney, "The Manger as Calvary and Altar," 32–7. See also Gerhard Jaritz and Gerson Moreno-Riaño, eds., *Time and Eternity: The Medieval Discourse* (Turnhout: Brepols, 2003).

33 Stanley Fish, *How Milton Works* (Cambridge, MA: Harvard University Press, 2001), vii, 2 et passim.

34 Walter Clyde Curry, *Milton's Ontology, Cosmogony, and Physics* (Lexington: University Press of Kentucky, 2015), 45. The passage in Milton is to be found in Hughes, *Milton*, 905.

35 Tim Hegedus, *Early Christianity and Ancient Astrology* (New York: Peter Lang, 2007), 116. Hegedus cites Epiphanius of Salamis, *Panarion*, Books II and III, trans. Frank Williams (Leiden: Brill, 1987), 16.2.2–3.

36 George Walton Williams, ed., *The Complete Poetry of Richard Crashaw*, trans. George Walton Williams and Phyllis S. Bowman (Garden City, NY: Doubleday, 1970), 292–3. The English translation by Williams and Bowman follows:

> We are wretched from Excess and we vanish after a time.
> The fates scrutinize us and judge our works.
> We are the natural disposition of fate, the ambition of sins;
> The seal and purpose of death are we.

Clearly, the fates are not synonymous with God in Crashaw's nevertheless Christian poem.

37 Barbara Lewalski, *Protestant Poetics and the Seventeenth-Century Religious Lyric* (Princeton, NJ: Princeton University Press, 1979), 258–9.

38 Simona Cohen, *Transformations of Time and Temporality in Medieval and Renaissance Art* (Leiden: Brill, 2014), 41. Cohen cites the major authorities on the subject including Arnaldo Momigliano, "Time in Ancient Historiography," *History and Theory* 6 (1966): 1–23; and Henri-Charles Puech, "Gnosis and Time," in *Man and Time: Papers from the Eranos Yearbooks*, ed. Joseph Campbell (Princeton, NJ: Princeton University Press, 1973), 38–84.

39 Jonathon Goldberg, "Hesper-Vesper: Aspects of Venus in a Seventeenth-Century Trope," *Studies in English Literature 1500–1900* 15, no. 1 (Winter 1975): 44.

40 Ibid.

41 See, by comparison, Patrick J. Cullen, "Imitation and Metamorphosis: The Golden Age Eclogue in Spenser, Milton, and Marvell," *PMLA* 84, no. 6 (October 1969): 1559–70.

42 Pietro Siniscalco, "Tempo," *Dizionario patristico e di Antichità Cristiane*, 2 vols. (Roma: Marietti, Institutum Patristicum Augustinianum, 1984), 2:3361. Siniscalco 3361 and Gilles Quispel, "Time and History in Patristic Christianity," in *Man and Time: Papers from the Eranos Yearbooks*, ed. Joseph

Campbell (Princeton, NJ: Princeton University, 1973), 86–7, both write with reference to Oscar Cullmann, *Christus und die Zeit* (Zurich: Zollikon, 1946), in particular page 35.

43 "If ... the Word had become man in Jesus Christ, it was clear that this event could not but be one and have universal, cosmic implications and repercussions." J. Dupuis, "The Uniqueness of Jesus Christ in the Early Christian Tradition," Religious Pluralism, *Jeevadhara* 47 (September/October 1978): 398–408. See esp. 406–7.

44 *Man and Time: Papers from the Eranos Yearbooks*, ed. Joseph Campbell (Princeton, NJ: Princeton University Press, 1973), 130–1; Albert Schweitzer, *The Quest of the Historical Jesus: a Critical Study of Its Progress from Reimarus to Wrede*, trans W. Montgomery (New York: Macmillan, 1948); Martin Werner, *The Formation of Christian Dogma*, trans. S.G.F. Brandon (New York: A & C Black, 1957).

45 See, by comparison, J. Martin Evans on Milton's use of Virgil's eclogue in "The Poetry of Absence" in *The Miltonic Moment*, 51. Describing Milton's picture of this Golden Age, Evans asserts: "In place of the new Jerusalem Milton shows us an abandoned leper-house" (36).

46 Alison Shell, *Catholicism, Controversy, and the English Literary Imagination, 1558–1660* (Cambridge: Cambridge University Press, 1999), 67.

47 Wayne J. Hankey, "Augustinian Immediacy and Dionysian Mediation in John Colet, Edmund Spenser, Richard Hooker, and the Cardinal de Bérulle," *Augustinus in der Neuzeit, Colloque de la Herzog August Bibliothek de Wolfenbüttel, 14–17 octobre 1996* (Turnhout: Brepols, 1998), 125–60.

48 Sherry, "Milton's 'Mystic Nativity,'" 108–16.

49 Sherry, "Milton's 'Mystic Nativity.'"

50 Guy Jobin, "Instituer l'évidement? Heuristique kénotique et positivité éthique," *Laval théologique et philosophique* 67, no. 1 (2011): 75. See also Edward T. Oakes, SJ, "Kenotic Christology: Thomasius, Gess, Mackintosh," in his *Infinity Dwindled to Infancy: A Catholic and Evangelical Christology* (Grand Rapids, MI: Eerdmans, 2011), 319–30, esp. 321.

51 Hilton Kelliher, "Crashaw at Cambridge," in *New Perspectives on the Life and Art of Richard Crashaw*, ed. John R. Roberts (Columbia: University of Missouri Press, 1990), 212.

52 Theodore G. Tappert, trans. and ed., *The Book of Concord: The Confessions of the Evangelical Lutheran Church* (Philadelphia, PA: Mühlenberg Press, 1959), 590.

53 John Calvin, *Institutes of the Christian Religion*, trans. Henry Beveridge (Grand Rapids, MI: Eerdmans, 1957), IV, xvii, 12.

54 *The Geneva Bible: The Annotated 1602 New Testament Edition*, ed. Gerald T. Sheppard (Cleveland: The Pilgrim Press, 1989), 99.

55 Michael Lieb, "Milton and the Kenotic Theology: Its Literary Bearing." *English Literary History* 37, no. 3 (September 1970): 344, citing Augustine.

56 John Milton, "Elegia Sexta," lines 81–3, in Hughes, *Milton*, 52. Broadbent notes that the crying Christ Child of Prudentius is not present in the Nativity Ode. J.B. Broadbent, "The Nativity Ode," in *The Living Milton: Essays by Various Hands*, ed. Frank Kermode (London: Routledge, 2014), 15.
57 Peter Dronke, *Forms and Imaginings: From Antiquity to the Fifteenth Century* (Roma: Edizioni di Storia e Letteratura, 2007), 72–4. Milton's vacillation between crying and smiling is interesting: the ostensibly more formal and classical form of the Elegy to Diodati features a more human baby to whom, at the same time, Milton refers as our God.
58 Dronke, *Forms and Imaginings*, 72. Dronke's translation from Latin is in Italian; the English translations are mine.
59 Dronke, *Forms and Imaginings*, 73.
60 Leo Steinberg, *The Sexuality of Christ in Renaissance Art and in Modern Oblivion* (New York: Pantheon Books, 1983). See also John Pope-Hennessy, *The Virgin with the Laughing Child* (H.M. Stationery Office, 1949), 73.
61 See Kenney, "The Manger as Calvary and Altar," 29–65.
62 See Broadbent's more acerbic denunciation of this passage's effect on the anti-incarnational qualities of the Nativity Ode. Broadbent, "The Nativity Ode," 21. Broadbent's excellent study covers many of Milton's scriptural sources, which is one reason I have not dwelt much on them here.
63 Condee, *Structure in Milton's Poetry*, 52.
64 John Milton, *Poems of Mr. John Milton, Both English and Latin* (London: Humphrey Moseley, 1645), 20–2. (Facsimile of this edition is available online, and here's an index of the actual pages: https://babel.hathitrust.org/cgi/pt?id=mdp.39015029507046&view=1up&seq=43&q1=Circumcision.

6. "We Kis't the Cradle of Our King": Affection, Awe, and Abridging the Laws of Time in Crashaw

1 See Maureen Sabine, *Feminine Engendered Faith: The Poetry of John Donne and Richard Crashaw* (Basingstoke, UK: Palgrave Macmillan, 1992).
2 Quevedo's "Reconocimiento propio, y ruego piedoso antes de comulgar" speaks of his heart as a "pesebre [manger] acompañado / De brutos apetitos, que en mi io sento." The poet equates the coming of the child Jesus into the sinful human heart with the reception of the Eucharist. Lope de Vega's "Cantarcillo de la Virgen" (1614), Luis de Góngora's "De un solo Clavel ceñida" (1617), and Tarquinio Merula's "Canzonetta spirituale sopra alla nanna" (Venice, 1636) are some of the most famous of these types of learned poems (rather than carols), but my study confines itself to England – its unique historical situation and unique flourishing of the subgenre among its educated religious poets. One expects to and does find more focus on the manger and Christmas itself in Luther and in Lutheran

countries than in Calvinist or Zwinglian ones. See Theresa M. Kenney, "The Manger in the Early Modern Period," in *Encyclopedia of the Bible and Its Reception Online*, vol. 17, ed. Constance Furey et al. (Berlin: De Gruyter, 2019), n.p., https://www.degruyter.com/view/db/ebr.

3 See Alison Shell, *Catholicism, Controversy, and the English Literary Imagination, 1558–1660* (Cambridge: Cambridge University Press, 1999); Sabine, *Feminine Engendered Faith*; and Kimberly Johnson, *Made Flesh: Sacraments and Poetics in Post-Reformation England* (Philadelphia: University of Pennsylvania Press, 2014).

4 Helen C. White, "Richard Crashaw, 'Poet and Saint,'" in her *The Metaphysical Poets: A Study in Religious Experience* (New York: Macmillan, 1936), 233.

5 Richard Rambuss, "Crashaw and the Metaphysical Shudder; Or, How to Do Things with Tears," *Structures of Feeling in Seventeenth-Century Cultural Expression*, ed. Susan McClary (Toronto: University of Toronto Press, 2013), 257.

6 R.V. Young, *Richard Crashaw and the Spanish Golden Age* (New Haven, CT: Yale University Press, 1982), 2–3.

7 Young, *Richard Crashaw*, 51–68.

8 The "Sursum corda" comes from the Catholic Mass originally; Calvinists retained it.

9 Hilton Kelliher, "Crashaw at Cambridge," in *New Perspectives on the Life and Art of Richard Crashaw*, ed. John R. Roberts (Columbia: University of Missouri Press, 1990), 183–92.

10 Austin Warren, *Richard Crashaw: A Study in Baroque Sensibility* (Ann Arbor: University of Michigan Press, 1967), 210–11n2. See also Young, *Richard Crashaw*, 11.

11 Itrat H'usain, *The Mystical Element in the Metaphysical Poets of the Seventeenth Century* (New York: Biblo & Tannen Publishers, 1948), 159–92.

12 Augustine, *Confessions*, 10.14. In *Eighty-Three Different Questions*, Augustine says: "In God's sight, [nothing exists] as past or future, but everything is now." In the *City of God*, he also says: "God comprehends all these in a stable and eternal present … Nor is there any difference between his present, past, and future knowledge. His knowledge is not like ours which has three tenses." *Eighty-Three Different Questions*, trans. David L. Mosher (Washington DC: Catholic University of America Press, 1982).

13 Paul G. Stanwood, "Time and Liturgy in Donne, Crashaw, and T S. Eliot," *Mosaic* 12 (1979): 94–5. Walter Davis also noted that Crashaw enacted the Jesuit poet Strada's understanding of a poet as "medius inter Deum et homines." Davis, "The Meditative Hymnody," *English Literary History* 50, no. 1 (Spring 1983): 107. See also Eugene Cunnar, *Essays on Richard Crashaw*, ed. Robert M. Cooper (Lewiston, NY: Edwin Mellen Press, 1979).

14 Sabine, *Feminine Engendered Faith*, 211.

15 Eiléan Ní Chuilleanáin, "Poetry and Mystery," *Religion & Literature* 45, no. 3 (Autumn 2013): 187. She discusses Donne and Herbert as well in developing this observation, but Crashaw is her supreme example of the ways in which poetry can speak of the direct encounter with the divine.
16 L.C. Martin, ed., *The Poems English, Latin, and Greek of Richard Crashaw* (Oxford: Clarendon Press, 1927), 183–4. All quotations of Crashaw's works are from this edition.
17 Crashaw's desire for eternity to break through into time is also something he expresses in his "On Hope, By way of Question and Answer, betweene A. Cowley, and R. Crashaw," an answer poem in which Crashaw took the optimistic and Cowley the pessimistic side: "Fair Hope! our earlier Heaven! By Thee / Young Time is taster to Eternity." Helen Gardner, *The Metaphysical Poets* (Oxford: Oxford University Press, 1957), 196.
18 Sabine, *Feminine Engendered Faith*, 150 et passim.
19 Sabine's discussion of "On the Blessed Virgin's Bashfulnesse" is helpful in understanding the role of Crashaw's imagination of Mary in directing his gaze to Christ; Sabine, *Feminine Engendered Faith*, 149.
20 Although Wallerstein dates the Nativity Hymn earlier, to 1631, L.C. Martin argues that there is no evidence for such a supposition. Ruth Wallerstein, *Richard Crashaw: A Study in Style and Poetic Development*, University of Wisconsin Studies in Language and Literature 37 (Madison: University of Wisconsin Press, 1935), 52. Martin, *The Poems*, xlvii.
21 Giles Fletcher, *Christs Victorie and Triumph*, in *Poetical Works of Giles and Phineas Fletcher*, ed. F.S. Boas (Cambridge: Cambridge University Press, 1908–9); Prudentius, *Apotheosis*, in *Prudentius*, trans. H.J. Thompson, Loeb Classical Library (Cambridge, MA: Harvard University Press, 1949), 1:153–5; Torquato Tasso, "Per il presepio di nostro signore nella cappella di sisto v in Santa Maria Maggiore," in *Opere*, vol. 2 (Milan: Rizzoli Editore, 1963), 4. See, by comparison, Herbert Grierson, *First Half of the Seventeenth Century* (Edinburgh: W. Blackwood and Sons, 1906), 2; John Carey, *The Complete Shorter Poems of John Milton* (New York: Columbia University Press, 1967), 98.
22 He had amplified the line "The cursed oracles were strucken dumb" to lines 173–236 of the Nativity Ode, the sixty-three–line set piece often seen as destructive to the unity of the poem but commended for its elegiac tone.
23 "This day is sacred, not because of the visible sun, but because of the Birth of Him who is the invisible Creator of the sun. He chose this day to be born on, as he chose the Mother he was to be born from, and he made both the day and the Mother." Augustine, "Sermon 190 on the Nativity of Our Lord," PL 38, 1019.
24 The author of the *Meditationes Vitae Christi* says that the day of the Nativity is called "the fullness of time" in the tradition of the concept of time schematized by Bonaventure (1221–74). Pseudo-Bonaventure, *Meditations on the Life of Christ: An Illustrated Manuscript of the Fourteenth Century,*

trans. and ed. Isa Ragusa and Rosalie B. Green (Princeton, NJ: Princeton University Press, 1961), 20–1. See also Joseph Ratzinger, *The Theology of History in St. Bonaventure* (Chicago: Franciscan Herald Press, 1971), 142–3.

25 The Franciscan tradition has its own influence on the Counter-Reformation saints. Francis de Sales is well aware of many of the details of Francis of Assisi's devotional life and his suffering of the stigmata, as can be seen in his 1616 *Treatise on the Love of God*, which also recounts a young knight's pilgrimage to the place of the Nativity in Bethlehem: "And one could not say how many tears there he shed, contemplating those which the Son of God, little infant of the Virgin, had watered that holy stable, kissing and kissing again a hundred times that sacred earth, and licking the dust on which the sacred infancy of the divine Babe had been received." Francis de Sales, *Treatise on the Love of God*, trans. Henry Benedict Mackey (New York: Cosimo Classics, 2007), 315. The knight eventually dies of a broken heart on Mt. Olivet. If Crashaw read this piece by Francis de Sales as well, he would have been able to remember the example just quoted of devotion in Bethlehem.

26 John N. King, *English Reformation Literature: The Tudor Origins of the Protestant Tradition* (Princeton, NJ: Princeton University Press, 1982), 1–49.

27 John Calvin, *Institutes of the Christian Religion*, trans. Henry Beveridge, vol. 4 (Grand Rapids, MI: Eerdmans, 1957), IV, xvii, 12.

28 See Theresa M. Kenney, "The Manger in the Reformation and Counter-Reformation," in *Encyclopedia of the Bible and Its Reception Online*, vol. 17, ed. Constance Furey et al. (Berlin: De Gruyter, 2019), n.p., https://www.degruyter.com/view/db/ebr; and André Grabar, *Christian Iconography: A Study of Its Origins* (Princeton, NJ: Princeton University Press, 1968).

29 Sonia Jaworska, "'Eternity Shut in a Span': The Word Being Born and Giving Birth in the Poetry of Richard Crashaw," in *Poetic Revelations. Word Made Flesh Made Word: The Power of the Word III*, ed. Mark S. Burrows, Jean Ward, and Małgorzata Grzegorzewska (London: Routledge, 2017), 61.

30 Calvin was convinced that Jesus had to remain in heaven until the Second Coming; Lutherans argued that the scriptures also speak of the Father inhabiting the heavens without implying that he is restricted from being omnipresent. See Heinrich August Wilhelm Meyer, *Critical and Exegetical Handbook to the Acts of the Apostles* (Edinburgh: T & T Clark, 1883). Crashaw clearly believes that Christ's Incarnation does not restrict his accessibility to modern worshippers.

31 See David Steinmetz, "Calvin and the Absolute Power of God," *Journal of Medieval and Renaissance Studies* 18, no. 1 (Spring 1988): 65–79.

32 Young, *Richard Crashaw*, 8. Kerby Neill, "Structure and Symbol in Crashaw's 'Hymn in the Nativity,'" *PMLA* 63, no. 1 (1948): 112; A.R. Cirillo, "Crashaw's 'Epiphany Hymn': The Dawn of Christian Time," *Studies in Philology* 67, no. 1 (January 1970): 67–88.

33 See Kenney, "The Manger as Calvary and Altar in the Middle English Nativity Lyric," in *The Christ Child in Medieval Culture: Alpha es et O!*, ed. Mary Dzon and Theresa Kenney (Toronto: University of Toronto Press, 2012), 29–65.

34 Mary Dzon has pointed out to me that, in Birgitta of Sweden's famous vision, Mary proclaims: "Welcome."

35 Guido Maria Dreves and Clemens Blume, *Ein Jahrtausend Lateinischer Hymnendichtung*. Erster Teil (Leipzig: Fues's Verlag, 1890), 50:86–7. Richard Zoozmann, *Laudate Dominum. Lobet den Herrn* (München, 1928), S. 69ff.

36 See Kenney, "The Manger as Calvary and Altar," 29–65.

37 Neill, "Structure and Symbol," 112–13.

38 Warren, *Richard Crashaw*, 130.

39 Thomas F. Healy, "Crashaw and the Sense of History," in *New Perspectives on the Life and Art of Richard Crashaw*, ed. John R. Roberts (Columbia: University of Missouri Press, 1990), 64.

40 Theresa M. Kenney, "'Sensualiter tangitur': The Christ Child 'Born a Martyr' in John Donne's Sermon for Christmas 1626." *John Donne Journal* 36 (forthcoming).

41 Wallerstein, *Richard Crashaw*, 40.

42 Crashaw probably knows the image from Ovid, Lactantius, or Chaucer (*Book of the Duchess*, lines 981–4). Geoffrey Chaucer, *The Book of the Duchess*, in *Chaucer's Major Poetry*, ed. Albert C Baugh (Englewood, NJ: Prentice-Hall, 1963), 20. But Crashaw could have gotten it from Pliny or St. Clement or, indeed, any number of contemporary sources. See N.F. Blake, ed., *The Phoenix* (Manchester: Manchester University Press, 1968); Madonna Gauding, *The Signs and Symbols Bible: The Definitive Guide to the World of Symbols* (New York: Sterling, 2009); Roelof van den Broek, *The Myth of the Phoenix According to Classical and Early Christian Traditions* (Leiden: Brill, 1971); John Spencer Hill, "The Phoenix," *Religion & Literature* 16, no. 2 (Summer 1984): 61–6; Misako Himuro, "The Phoenix in the *First Epistle of Clement to the Corinthians*," *Renaissance Studies* 12, no. 4 (December 1998): 523–44. The reference is in any case a learned one: it is most unlikely that any of our poets ever saw an image of a phoenix, at least in an English church; Arthur H. Collins claims that, except in Hereford Cathedral, no identifiable image of a phoenix is to be found in English churches. Collins, *Symbolism of Animals and Birds Represented in English Church Architecture* (New York: McBride, Nast, 1913), 50–1.

43 Erwin Fahlbusch et al., *Encyclopedia of Christianity*, vol. 56 (Grand Rapids, MI: Eerdmans, 2008), 263.

44 Robert Herrick designates the unfortunate Charles I as the phoenix in a Christmas poem sung before the king in Whitehall in a case of rather dreadful historical irony. Robert Herrick, "Another New-yeeres Gift, or

Song for the Circumcision," *The Complete Poetry of Robert Herrick*, ed. Tom Cain and Ruth Connolly (Oxford: Oxford University Press, 2013), 1:349–50.

45 See Françoise Lecocq, "L'œuf du phénix. Myrrhe, encens et cannelle dans le mythe du phénix," *L'animal et le savoir, de l'Antiquité à la Renaissance*, *Schedae* 17, no. 2 (2009): 73–106.

46 Neill, "Structure and Symbol," 112.

47 Cirillo, "Crashaw's 'Epiphany Hymn,'" 67–88.

48 Cirillo, "Crashaw's 'Epiphany Hymn,'" 77, 79; Neill, "Structure and Symbol," 106.

49 Wendy Fuller, "Paradox Lost: Pope's Auspicious Babe and the Death of a Renaissance Tradition," unpublished paper delivered at the Renaissance Society of America: Southern California Conference on 17 April 1982.

50 St. Bernard of Clairvaux, *Sermo 5, In Adventu Domini*, 1–3, in *Sancti Bernardi Opera*, ed. J. Leclercq and H. Rochais, vol. 4 (Rome: Editiones Cisterciences, 1966), 188–90. See also Rob Faesen, "The Three Births of Christ and the Christmas Liturgy in the Temple of Our Soul, the Evangelical Pearl, and the Arnhem Mystical Sermons," *Ons Geestelijk Erf* 81, no. 1 (2010): 121–37; and Klaus Reinhardt, "L'idée de naissance de Dieu dans l'âme chez Nicolas de Cues et l'influence d'Eckhart," in *La naissance de Dieu dans l'âme chez Eckhart et Nicolas de Cues*, ed. Marie-Anne Vannier (Paris: Cerf, 2006), 85–99.

51 Amédée Gastoué, *Noël* (Paris: Bloud, 1907).

52 Cirillo, "Crashaw's 'Epiphany Hymn,'" 70.

53 Robert Southwell, *The Poems of Robert Southwell, SJ*, ed. James Harold McDonald and Nancy Pollard Brown (Oxford: Clarendon Press, 1967), 13–14.

54 See Peter Keller, *Die Wiege des Christuskindes: ein Haushaltsgerät in Kunst und Kult* (Worms: Wernersche Verlagsgesellschaft, 1998).

55 See Anne Sweeney's discussion of the translation and its relation to Southwell's "performing word" in Sweeney, *Robert Southwell: Snow in Arcadia: Redrawing the English Landscape, 1586–95* (Manchester: Manchester University Press, 2006), 241–5.

56 See Thomas F. Healy, *Richard Crashaw* (Leiden: Brill, 1986), 123–6. The oldest altar stone existing in the Christian world is the stone of the Chapel of Mary in the Coptic Church of Al Muharraq in Egypt, thought to be the Christ Child's bed during the early part of the Holy Family's sojourn in that country. See "The Manger: Ritual Law and Soteriology," in J. Duncan M. Derrett, *Studies in the New Testament*, vol. 2, *Midrash in Action and as a Literary Device* (Leiden: Brill, 1978), 48–53. See, by comparison, "Il significato della mangiatoio" in the same volume, 54–9.

57 Kissing holy objects is a rite well understood by Catholics and Orthodox Christians – and even uneducated ones probably do not think, as a pagan

would, that a god or saint resides in the object – but the resemblance to pagan worship of created things rather than the Creator makes the ritual anathema to Protestants of most denominations. For instance, when Crashaw became the curate of the Holy House of Loreto in the last year of his life, he was taking care of what is believed to be the actual house of the Holy Family, and it was venerated with kisses by so famous a saint – and hero of Crashaw's – as Francis de Sales. See Warren, *Richard Crashaw*, 59–60. Warren cites Godfrey E. Phillips, *Loreto and the Holy House: Its History Drawn from Authentic Sources* (London: R. & T. Washbourne, 1917), 159–63. Kissing the altar is a rite the Roman Catholic priest performs at the beginning of Mass, and authors even as late as Prosper Guéranger (1805–75) equated kissing the altar with kissing the manger. See John Saward, *Cradle of Redeeming Love: The Theology of the Christmas Mystery* (San Francisco: Ignatius Press, 2002), introduction. He cites Dom Prosper Guéranger's *The Liturgical Year: Advent*, vol. 1, trans. Dom Laurence Shepherd (Dublin: O'Toole and Son, 1870).

58 George Walton Williams, ed., *The Complete Poetry of Richard Crashaw*, trans. George Walton Williams and Phyllis S. Bowman (Garden City, NY: Doubleday, 1970), 47.

59 Williams points out that just a few months after the publication of this poem, the King was executed, and the Queen and her children were dispossessed of the crowns to which Crashaw refers herein (*The Complete Poetry*, 47n23). Crashaw's royalism has often been noted, but it is instructive to see that he values crowns mainly for their ability to be thrown before the feet of Christ.

60 In another distinction from more radical Reformed opinion, Crashaw merely accepts without question the identification of the Magi as kings and their number as three, whereas Calvin, in his commentary on Luke, had scoffed at these very extra-biblical traditions. See *Calvin's New Testament Commentaries*, vol. 2, *A Harmony of the Gospels: Matthew, Mark, and Luke*, trans. T.H.L. Parker (Grand Rapids, MI: Eerdmans, 1995). Popular literature had already introduced this difference between Reformed and Roman Catholic interpretations of the Magi in Barnabe Googe's translation of Thomas Naogeorgus's *The popish kingdome, or reigne of Antichrist* in 1570: "The wise mens day here followeth, who out from Persia farre, / Brought gifts and presents unto Christ, conducted by a starre. / The Papistes do belieeve that these were kings, and so them call, / And do affirme that of the same there were but three in all." Thomas Naogeorgus, *The popish kingdome, or reigne of Antichrist, written in Latine verse by Thomas Naogeorgus, and englyshed by Barnabe Googe*, trans. Barnabe Googe (London: Henrie Denham, 1570); ed. Robert Charles Hope (London: Chiswick Press, 1880), 47.

61 Naogeorgus, *The popish kingdome*, 45. This book was dedicated to Philip of Hesse by its German author and to Elizabeth by Googe. Naogeorgus is of course describing German customs, but similar ones prevailed in England. Many of the Christmas customs of England remained in place even after the Interregnum, but it is interesting to note that the Christ Child himself disappears from them, by and large. As I comment in the conclusion, the pastry constructions of the Christ Child in the manger that used to appear on the tops of the manger/tomb-shaped mince pies of the early modern period were prohibited under Cromwell and did not return after the Restoration. The connection of the Christ Child with food was probably too offensively Catholic.

62 The prayer before Communion of the Liturgy of St. John Chrysostom conflates the images of fire and sacrifice with the kiss that is the reception of the Eucharist: "Let the fiery coal of Your most pure Body and Your most precious Blood bring me sanctification, enlightenment and strengthening of my lowly soul and body." Chrysostom, an author well known to all the poets in this study, and much cited in John Donne's sermons, for instance, returns to this idea elsewhere, not just in the Divine Liturgy. Cranmer had studied the Liturgy of St. John Chrysostom in preparing the *Book of Common Prayer*, and Chrysostom's writings on the Eucharist were central to his and Ridley's disputations on the Eucharist. It is tempting to imagine Crashaw had read the same, but with different effect.

63 Yrjö Hirn, *The Sacred Shrine: A Study of the Poetry and Art of the Catholic Church* (London: Faber and Faber, 1958), 374, 537–8n57.

Conclusion: The Christ Child: Little Boy Lost

1 Francis Quarles, *Francis Quarles' Divine Fancies: A Critical Edition*, ed. William T. Liston (New York: Routledge, 1992), 9. See also Joseph E. Illick, "Child-Rearing in Seventeenth Century England and America," in *The History of Childhood*, ed. Lloyd deMause (Lanham, MD: Rowman & Littlefield, 1995), 339n54. Illick is discussing approaches to God and paternal attitudes toward children. Quarles is thoroughly Anglican in his wholehearted acceptance of the Thirty-Nine Articles and Laudian in his practices. Here, in the *Divine Fancies*, he is adamant about the importance of bodily gesture at the Lord's Supper:

> You'l take it *sitting*: Pray; and no man know it;
> You'l doe, and yet you will not seeme to doe it:
> You'l bow your *Heart*, although you bend no *Knee*;
> Tis like your *Selfe*; You seeme, not What you bee. (186)

2 See Ante Dračevac, *La Cathédrale de Dubrovnik*, trans. Françoise Kveder (Zagreb: Privredni Vjesnik, 1988), 50; and Sophie Oosterwijk, "The Swaddling-Clothes of Christ: A Medieval Relic on Display," *Medieval Life* 13 (2000): 25–30.

3 Francis Quarles, *Emblemes by Francis Quarles* (Cambridge: Printed by R.D. for Francis Eglesfield ..., 1643; Ann Arbor, MI: Early English Books Online Text Creation Partnership), 221–2. http://name.umdl.umich.edu/A56969.0001.001. The influence of Giambattista Marino is also noteworthy here.

4 Quarles, *Emblemes*, 223.

5 Robert Herrick, *The Complete Poetry of Robert Herrick*, ed. Tom Cain and Ruth Connolly (Oxford: Oxford University Press, 2013), 1:339.

6 Herrick, "To his Saviour: A New-Yeers gift," in *The Complete Poetry*, 1:360.

7 Henrik V. Aachen, "Human Heart and Sacred Heart: Reigning in Religious Individualism. The Heart Figures in 17th Century Devotional Piety and the Emergence of the Cult of the Sacred Heart." In *Categories of Sacredness in Europe, 1500–1800*, ed. Arne Bugge Amundsen and Henning Laugerud, 131–58 Conference of the Norwegian Institute in Rome 2001 (Oslo: Universitet i Oslo, 2015).

8 Aachen, "Human Heart and Sacred Heart." Aachen cites Donna Spivey Ellington, *From Sacred Body to Angelic Soul. Understanding Mary in late Medieval and Early Modern Europe* (Washington, DC: Catholic University of America Press, 2001), 19 et passim. Ellington herself refers her reader to Ted A. Campbell's entire book, *The Religion of the Heart: A Study of European Religious Life in the Seventeenth and Eighteenth Centuries* (Eugene, OR: Wipf and Stock, 2000).

9 Boyd Taylor Coolman, *Eternally Spiralling into God: Knowledge, Love, and Ecstasy in the Theology of Thomas Gallus* (Oxford: Oxford University Press, 2017), 252.

10 Coolman, *Eternally Spiralling into God*, 252.

11 Leah Marcus, *The Politics of Mirth: Jonson, Herrick, Milton, Marvell, and the Defense of Old Holiday Pastimes* (Chicago: University of Chicago Press, 1986), 76–85.

12 Pastor Fido (pseud.), "Festorum Metropolis: The Metropolitan Feast of the Birthday of our Saviour Jesus Christ, Annually to be kept holy, by them that call upon him in all Nations, Proved by Scriptures, the practice of the Church, Primitive and Reformed; the Testimonies of the Fathers, and Moderne Divines; strong Reasons, grounded on the Word of God; confirming Miracles, etc." (London: Matthew Simmons, 16 August 1652), n.p. [prefatory material].

13 Pastor Fido, "Festorum Metropolis," 7.

14 Henry Vaughan, *Henry Vaughan: The Complete Poems*, ed. Alan Rudrum (New Haven, CT: Yale University Press, 1976), 372.

15 The presence or absence of Mary is an important factor in Nativity lyrics, but the present study has had to bow to limits of time and space and exclude discussion of her role, aside from a point or two concerning her part in Milton's Nativity Ode.

16 Thomas Traherne, "On Christmas-Day," in *Poems of Felicity*, ed. by H.I. Bell (Oxford: Oxford University Press, 1910), 49–50.

17 Alexander Pope, *The Complete Poetical Works of Alexander Pope*, ed. Henry R. Boynton (Boston: Houghton Mifflin, 1903), 84.

18 Among the reasons to which I refer is the pronounced deist quality of much of Pope's religious work, such as the "Universal Prayer." There is also the issue of the reluctance of Catholic poets to advertise their allegiances publicly before Catholic emancipation; however, Pope was a Freemason, so attention to his sacramental vision is perhaps beside the point.

19 Christina Rossetti, *Complete Poems of Christina Rossetti: A Variorum Edition*, vol. 1, ed. R.W. Crump (Baton Rouge, LA: Louisiana State University Press, 1979), 216–17.

20 Guides to meditation that would be read once again by Victorian authors, such as Thomas à Kempis's *Imitation of Christ*, featured sermons on both the mystic presence of Christ in the soul and participation in the joy of witnessing the actual Nativity of Christ.

21 R.V. Young, *Doctrine and Devotion in Seventeenth-Century Poetry* (Cambridge: D.S. Brewer, 2000), 219.

Bibliography

Bibliographic abbreviations: CCCM = *Corpus Christianorum, Continuatio Mediaevalis;* CCSA = *Corpus Christianorum, Series Apocryphorum;* CCSL = *Corpus Christianorum, Series Latina;* CPL = *Clavis Patrum Latinorum;* PG = *Patrologia Graeca,* ed. J.-P. Migne, 161 vols. (Paris, 1857–66); PL = *Patrologia Latina,* ed. J.-P. Migne, 221 vols. (Paris, 1844–64).

Aachen, Henrik V. "Human Heart and Sacred Heart: Reigning in Religious Individualism. The Heart Figures in 17th Century Devotional Piety and the Emergence of the Cult of the Sacred Heart." In *Categories of Sacredness in Europe, 1500–1800,* edited by Arne Bugge Amundsen and Henning Laugerud, 131–58. Conference of the Norwegian Institute in Rome 2001. Oslo: Universitet i Oslo, 2015. https://enid.w.uib.no/library/texts/human-heart-and-sacred-heart-reining-in-religious-individualism-the-heart-figure-in-17th-century-devotional-piety-and-the-emergence-of-the-cult-of-the-sacred-heart/.

Abbas, Sadia. "Polemic and Paradox in Robert Southwell's Lyric Poems." *Criticism* 45, no. 4 (Fall 2003): 453–82.

Adams, Marilyn McCord. *Some Later Medieval Theories of the Eucharist: Thomas Aquinas, Giles of Rome, Duns Scotus, and William Ockham.* Oxford: Oxford University Press, 2010.

Aelred of Rievaulx. *A Rule of Life for a Recluse.* Translated by Mary Paul Macpherson. In *Aelred of Rievaulx: Treatises and Pastoral Prayer.* Introduction by David Knowles. Vol. 2. Kalamazoo, MI: Cistercian Publications, 1995.

Aers, David. "The Humanity of Christ: Representations in Wycliffite Texts and *Piers Plowman.*" In *The Powers of the Holy: Religion, Politics and Gender in Late Medieval English Culture,* by David Aers and Lynn Staley, 43–76. University Park, PA: Penn State University Press, 1996.

à Lapide, Cornelius Cornelii, SJ. *The Great Commentary of Cornelius à Lapide.* Translated and edited by Thomas W. Mossman. Edinburgh: J. Grant, 1908.

Allen, Don Cameron. *The Harmonious Vision: Studies in Milton's Poetry*. Baltimore: Johns Hopkins University Press, 1970.

Allison, Dale C. *Studies in Matthew: Interpretation Past and Present*. Grand Rapids, MI: Baker Academic, 2005.

Ambrose, St. *Expositio Evangelii secundam Lucam*. Edited by M. Adriaen. CCSL 14. Turnhout: Brepols, 1957.

– *Expositio in evangelium secundum Lucam comprehensa*. PL 15 coll. 1527D–1850D.

– *De incarnationis dominicae sacramento*. CPL 152. PL 16:817–83.

– "Veni, redemptor gentium," in *Analecta Hymnica Medii Aevi*, 13–14. Leipzig: Fues's Verlag, 1890.

Anderson, Judith H. *Translating Investments: Metaphor and the Dynamics of Cultural Change in Tudor-Stuart England*. New York: Fordham University Press, 2005.

Andrewes, Lancelot. *The English Theological Works*. Edited by J.P. Wilson and J. Bliss. Vol. 1. Oxford: John Henry Parker, 1841–54.

– *The Private Devotions of Lancelot Andrewes* (*Preces Privatae*). Translated and edited by F.E. Brightman. Gloucester, MA: Peter Smith, 1983. Reprint of the 1903 edition by Methuen & Company (London).

– *The Works of Lancelot Andrewes*. Vol. 8, *Response to Cardinal Bellarmine*. New York: AMS Press, 1967.

Anselm, St. *Libri sancti Anselmi "Cur Deus homo": prima forma inedita*. Vol. 3 of *Analecta Gregoriana*, edited by Eugenius Druwé, SJ. Rome: Gregorianum, 1933.

Apocrypha Hiberniae, Vol. I, *Evangelia Infantiae*. Edited by Martin McNamara, et al. Turnhout: Brepols, 2001.

Aquinas, St. Thomas. *The Childhood of Christ*. Edited by Roland Potter. Cambridge: Cambridge University Press, 2006.

– *Commentary on Aristotle's De Anima*. Translated by Kenelm Foster, OP, and Sylvester Humphries, OP. New Haven, CT: Yale University Press, 1951.

– *The Essential Aquinas: Writings on Philosophy, Religion, and Society*. Edited by John Y.B. Hood. Westport, CT: Praeger, 2002.

– *De unione Verbi incarnati*. Translated and edited by Roger W. Nutt. Dallas Medieval Texts and Translations, vol. 21. Leuven: Peeters, 2015.

Areford, David. "Christ Child Creator." In *Quid est sacramentum? Visual Representations of Sacred Mysteries in Early Modern Europe, 1400–1700*, edited by Walter S. Mellon, Elizabeth Carson Paston, and Lee Palmer Wandel, 456–93. Leiden: Brill, 2019.

Aristotle. *On the Generation of Animals*. Translated by A.L. Peck. Cambridge, MA: Harvard University Press, 1942.

– *On the Heavens*. Translated by W.K.C. Guthrie. Cambridge, MA: Harvard University Press, 1939.

– *The Physics: Vols. 1–2*. Translated by Philip H. Wicksteed and Francis Macdonald Cornford. Cambridge, MA: Harvard University Press, 1929.

Armon, Chara. "Joseph, Stepfather of Jesus." In *Women and Gender in Medieval Europe: An Encyclopedia*, edited by Margaret Schaus, 433–5. New York: Routledge, 2006.

Asals, Heather. *Equivocal Predication: George Herbert's Way to God*. Toronto: University of Toronto Press, 1981.

Ascham, Roger. *The Scholemaster Or plaine and perfite way of teaching children, to vnderstand, write and speake, the Latin tong*. Edited by J E.B. Major. Oxford: Oxford University Press, 1863. First published in 1570 by John Daye (London).

Astell, Ann. *Eating Beauty: The Eucharist and the Spiritual Arts of the Middle Ages*. Ithaca, NY: Cornell University Press, 2006.

Athanasius, St. *On the Incarnation: The Treatise De Incarnatione Verbi*. Translated by "A Religious of C.S.M.V." Crestwood, NY: St. Vladimir Seminary Press, 1998.

– "Λόγος περὶ τῆς ἐνανθρωπήσεως τοῦ Λόγου" ["Oratio de Incarnatione Verbi"]. PG 25:158.

Auerbach, Erich. "Figura." In *Scenes from the Drama of European Literature*. Translated by Ralph Manheim. New York: Meridian Books, 1959.

Augustine, St. *City of God against the Pagans*. Translated by Henry Bettenson. London: Penguin, 2003. Reprint.

– *Confessiones*. PL 32:649–868.

– *Eighty-Three Different Questions*. Translated by David L. Mosher. Washington DC: Catholic University of America Press, 1982.

– "In Psalmum 87 Enarratio." PL 37:1110–20.

– *Sermons* 336.5. PL 38.1:475.

– *St. Augustine: Sermons for Christmas and Epiphany*. Translated by Thomas Comerford Lawlor. New York: Paulist Press, 1952.

– *St. Augustine: Tractates on the Gospel of John 20–54*. Translated by John W. Rettig. Washington, DC: Catholic University Press, 1995.

Bale, Anthony. "God's Cell: Christ as Prisoner and Pilgrimage to the Prison of Christ." *Speculum* 91, no. 1 (2016): 1–35.

Barker, Arthur. "The Pattern of Milton's Nativity Ode." *University of Toronto Quarterly* 10, no. 2 (1941): 167–81.

Bauman, Michael. *Milton's Arianism*. Frankfurt am Main: Verlag Peter Lang, 1987.

Baynham, Matthew. "The Naked Babe and Robert Southwell." *Notes and Queries* 50, no. 1 (March 2003): 55–6.

Beckwith, Carl. "Suffering without Pain: The Scandal of Hilary of Poitiers' Christology." In *In the Shadow of the Incarnation: Essays on Jesus Christ in the Early Church in Honor of Brian E. Daley, S.J.*, edited by Peter Martens, 71–96. Notre Dame, IN: University of Notre Dame Press, 2008.

Beckwith, Roger. "The Doctrine of the Sacraments in the Thirty-Nine Articles." *Churchman* 105, no. 1 (1991): n.p.

Bede the Venerable, St. *Complete Works of Bede*. Translated and edited by J.A. Giles. London: Wittiger, 1843. CCSL 120.276.

Begheyn, Paul J., SJ. "The Collection of Copper Plates by the Wierix Family in the Jesuit Church 'De Krijtberg' in Amsterdam." *Quærendo* 31, no. 3 (2001): 192–204.

Benet, William Rose. *The Reader's Encyclopedia*. New York: Thomas Y. Crowell, 1965.

Berkouwer, G.C. *Studies in Dogmatics: The Sacraments*. Grand Rapids, MI: W.B. Eerdmans, 2013.

Bernardine of Siena, St. "Sermo 2, de S. Joseph." In *Opera Omnia*, vol. 7, 27–30. Florence: Claras Aquas, 1957.

Bernard of Clairvaux, St. *Magnificat, Homilies in Praise of the Blessed Virgin Mary*. Translated by Marie-Bernard Saïd and Grace Perigo. Kalamazoo, MI: Cistercian Publications, 1979.

– *On the Song of Songs*. Vol. 2, *Sermons 21–46*. Translated by Kilian Walsh, OCSO. Kalamazoo, MI: Cistercian Publications 1976.

– *Sancti Bernardi Opera*. Edited by J. Leclercq and H. Rochais. Vol. 4. Rome: Editiones Cistercienses, 1966.

– *Sermons for the Seasons and Principal Festivals of the Year*. Vol. 1. Translated by Ailbe John Luddy. Westminster, MD: Carroll Press, 1950.

Birgitta of Sweden. *The Revelations of St. Birgitta of Sweden*. Vol. 3, *Liber Caelestis*, Books 6–7. Translated by Denis Searby. Oxford: Oxford University Press, 2012.

Blake, N.F., ed. *The Phoenix*. Manchester: Manchester University Press, 1968.

Bloch, Chana. *Spelling the Word: George Herbert and the Bible*. Berkeley: University of California Press, 1985.

Blunt, Anthony. "The Council of Trent and Religious Art." In *Artistic Theory in Italy 1450–1600*, 103–36. Oxford: Clarendon Press, 1970.

Blunt, John Henry, ed. *An Annotated Book of Common Prayer*. New York: Longmans, 1907.

Bonaventure, St. *Bonaventure: The Soul's Journey into God, the Tree of Life, and the Life of St. Francis*. Translated by Ewert Cousins. New York: Paulist Press, 1978.

– *Bringing Forth Christ: Five Feasts of the Boy Jesus*. Translated by Eric Doyle, OFM. Oxford: SLG Press, 1984.

– *Holiness of Life Being St. Bonaventure's De Perfectione Vitae ad Sorores*. Translated by Laurence Costello, OFM. Edited by Fr Wilfrid, OFM. Potosi, WI: St. Athanasius Press, 2014. Reprint of the 1928 edition by B. Herder (St. Louis, MO).

– *On the Life of Our Lord and Savior Jesus Christ*. New York: P.J. Kenedy, 1881.

– "On the Perfection of Life" ["De perfectione vitae ad sorores"]. In *Works of St. Bonaventure: Writings on the Spiritual Life*. Vol. 10. Edited by F. Edward Coughlin, 139–95. St. Bonaventure, NY: Franciscan Institute Publications, 2006.

– *Vitis mystica: A Treatise on the Passion of Our Lord (Ascribed to St. Bernard).* Translated by W.R.B. Brownlow. London: R. Washbourne, 1873.

Book of Common Prayer, 1559: The Elizabethan Prayer Book. Edited by John E. Booty. Charlottesville: University of Virginia Press, 2005.

Booty, John E. *John Jewel as Apologist of the Church of England.* London: SPCK, 1963.

Bosio, Antonio. *Roma Sotterranea, opera postuma di Antonio Bosio Romano, antiquario ecclesiastico singolare de' suoi tempi. Compita, disposta, et accresciuta dal M. R. P. Giovanni Severani da S. Severino*. Rome, 1632.

Bouchard, Gary. *Southwell's Sphere: The Influence of England's Secret Poet*. South Bend, IN: St. Augustine's Press, 2019.

– "Who Knows Not Colin's Clout? Assessing the Impact of Southwell's Literary Success upon Spenser." *LATCH* 3 (2010): 151–63.

Bowman, Glen. "William Tyndale's Eucharistic Theology: Lollard and Zwinglian Influences." *Anglican and Episcopal History* 66, no. 4 (December 1997): 422–34.

Brandt, K. Weil-Garris. "Michelangelo's Pietà for the Cappella del Rè di Francia." In *Michelangelo: Selected Scholarship in English*, edited by W.E. Wallace, 217–59. Hamden, CT: Garland Press, 1995.

Bray Gerald, "Scripture and Tradition in Reformation Thought." *Evangelical Review of Theology* 19, no. 2 (April 1995): 157–66.

Brittain, Frederick. *Medieval Latin and Romance Lyric*. Cambridge: Cambridge University Press, 1951.

Broadbent, J.B. "The Nativity Ode." In *The Living Milton: Essays by Various Hands*, edited by Frank Kermode, 12–31. London: Routledge, 2014.

Bromley, James M. "Intimacy and the Body in Seventeenth Century Religious Devotion." *Early Modern Literary Studies* 11, no. 1 (May 2005): 5.1–41.

Brooks, Peter Newman. *Thomas Cranmer's Doctrine of the Eucharist*. London: Macmillan, 1965.

Broussolle, J.C. *Le Christ de la Légende Dorée*. Paris: Maison de la Bonne Presse, 1903.

Brown, Carleton, ed. *English Lyrics of the Thirteenth Century*. Oxford: Clarendon Press, 1971.

– ed. *Religious Lyrics of the Fourteenth Century*. Oxford: Clarendon Press, 1970.

Brown, Rachel Fulton. *From Judgment to Passion: Devotion to Christ and the Virgin Mary, 800–1200*. New York: Columbia University Press, 2002.

Brownlow, Frank W. *Robert Southwell*. New York: Twayne Publishers, 1996.

Bunter, William B, ed. *A Milton Encyclopedia*. Lewisburg, PA: Bucknell University Press, 1978.

Bynum, Caroline Walker. *Christian Materiality: An Essay on Religion in Late Medieval Europe*. New York: Zone Books, 2011.

– *Holy Feast, Holy Fast*. Berkeley: University of California Press, 1987.

– *Metamorphosis and Identity*. New York: Zone Books, 2001.

– *Wonderful Blood: Theology and Practice in Late Medieval Northern Germany and Beyond*. Philadelphia: University of Pennsylvania Press, 2007.

Calvin, John. *Calvin's New Testament Commentaries*. Vol. 2, *A Harmony of the Gospels: Matthew, Mark, and Luke*. Translated by T.H.L. Parker. Grand Rapids, MI: Eerdmans, 1995.

– *De Externis Mediis ad Salutem*. In *Corpus Reformatum*. Edited by Gulielmus Baum. Vo1. 30, 1066–7. Brunsvigae: C.A. Schwetschke et Filium, 1864.

– *La forme des prières et chants écclesiastiques*. Strasbourg, 1545, and Geneva, 1542.

– *Institutes of the Christian Religion*. Translated by Henry Beveridge. Grand Rapids, MI: Eerdmans, 1957.

– *John Calvin's Commentaries on the Harmony of the Gospels*. Vol. 1. Translated by Rev. William Pringle. Edinburgh: The Calvin Translation Society, 1845.

Campbell, Ted. *The Religion of the Heart: A Study of European Religious Life in the Seventeenth and Eighteenth Centuries*. Eugene, OR: Wipf and Stock, 2000.

Cardwell, Edward, ed. *The Two Books of Common Prayer, Set Forth by the Authority of Parliament in the Reign of King Edward the Sixth*. Oxford: Oxford University Press, 1841.

Carey, John. *The Complete Shorter Poems of John Milton*. New York: Columbia University Press, 1967.

Catherine of Siena, St. *Catherine of Siena: The Dialogue*. Translated by Suzanne Noffke. New York: Paulist Press, 1980.

– *Il Dialogo*. Edited by Giuliana Cavallini. Siena: Edizioni Cantagalli, 1995.

Cefalu, Paul. *The Johannine Renaissance in Early Modern English Literature and Theology*. Oxford: Oxford University Press, 2017.

Chambers, A.B. "The Meaning of the 'Temple' in John Donne's *La Corona* Sonnets." *The Journal of English and Germanic Philology* 59, no. 2 (April 1960): 212–17.

– *Transfigured Rites in Seventeenth-Century English Poetry*. Columbia: University of Missouri Press, 1992.

Chaucer, Geoffrey. *The Book of the Duchess*. In *Chaucer's Major Poetry*. Edited by Albert C Baugh. Englewood, NJ: Prentice-Hall, 1963.

Cheetham, Francis. *English Medieval Alabasters with a Catalogue of the Collection in the Victoria and Albert*. Woodbridge, UK: Boydell & Brewer, 2005. Reprint of 1984 edition by Phaidon Press (London).

Chorpenning, Joseph F., OSFS. *Joseph of Nazareth through the Centuries*. Philadelphia, PA: St. Joseph's University Press, 2011.

Chrysostom, John. "12th Homily on the Statutes." In *St. Chrysostom: On the Priesthood; Ascetic Treatises; Select Homilies and Letters; Homilies on the Statutes,* translated by W.R.W. Stephens and edited by Philip Schaff, 471–80. New York: Scribner 1903.

Cirillo, A.R. "Crashaw's 'Epiphany Hymn': The Dawn of Christian Time." *Studies in Philology* 67, no. 1 (January 1970): 67–88.

Clark, Francis. *Eucharistic Sacrifice and the Reformation*. 2nd ed. Oxford: Basil Blackwell, 1967.

Clarke, Elizabeth. *Theory and Theology in George Herbert's Poetry: "Divinitie, and Poesie, Met."* Oxford: Clarendon Press, 1997.

Classen, Albrecht. *Childhood in the Middle Ages and the Renaissance: The Results of a Paradigm Shift in the History of Mentality*. Berlin: Walter de Gruyter, 2005.

Clement, St. "St. Clement: Epistle to the Corinthians." In *The Ante-Nicene Fathers*, vol. 1, edited by Alexander Roberts, Sir James Donaldson, and Arthur Cleveland Coxe, 1–22. Grand Rapids, MI: Eerdmans, 1950, 2007. Reprint of the 1885 edition by Christian Literature Publishing (New York).

Cohen, Simona. *Transformations of Time and Temporality in Medieval and Renaissance Art*. Leiden: Brill, 2014.

Coiro, Ann Baynes. "'A Ball of Strife': Caroline Poetry and Royal Marriage." In *The Royal Image: Representations of Charles I*, edited by Thomas Corns, 26–46. Cambridge: Cambridge University Press, 1999.

Coletti, Theresa. "Devotional Iconography in the N-Town Marian Plays." *Comparative Drama* 11, no. 1 (1977): 22–44.

Collins, Arthur H. *Symbolism of Animals and Birds Represented in English Church Architecture*. New York: McBride, Nast, 1913.

Condee, Ralph Waterbury. *Structure in John Milton's Poetry: From the Foundation to the Pinnacles*. University Park: Pennsylvania State University Press, 1974.

Coolman, Boyd Taylor. *Eternally Spiralling into God: Knowledge, Love, and Ecstasy in the Theology of Thomas Gallus*. Oxford: Oxford University Press 2017.

Cornell, Henrik. *The Iconography of the Nativity of Christ*. Uppsala: Lundquist, 1924.

Corns, Thomas N. "On the Morning of Christ's Nativity," "The Nativity," "The Circumcision," and "The Passion." In *A Companion to Milton*, edited by Thomas N. Corns, 215–31. Malden, MA: Blackwell, 2001.

Cousins, Anthony D. *The Catholic Religious Poets from Southwell to Crashaw: A Critical History*. Fakenham, UK: Sheed and Ward, 1991.

Cousins, Anthony D., and R.J. Webb. "Donne's Annunciation." *Explicator* 65, no. 3 (2010): 136–7.

Cranmer, Thomas. *The Book of Common Prayer: The Texts of 1549, 1559, and 1662*. Edited by Brian Cummings. Oxford: Oxford University Press, 2011.

– *The Book of Common Prayer, 1552*. In *The Two Liturgies, A.D. 1549 and A.D. 1552*, edited by Joseph Ketley, 9–158. Cambridge: The University Press, 1844.

– *A Defence of the True and Catholic Doctrine of the Sacrament of the Body and Blood of Our Saviour Christ*. In *The Work of Thomas Cranmer*, edited by G.F. Duffield, 45–231. Berkshire, UK: Sutton Courtenay Press, 1965.

– *Writings and Disputations of Thomas Cranmer, Relative to the Sacrament of the Lord's Supper*. Edited by J.E. Cox. Cambridge: The Parker Society, 1844.

Cullen, Patrick. "Imitation and Metamorphosis: The Golden Age Eclogues in Spenser, Milton, and Marvell." *PMLA* 84, no. 6 (Oct 1969): 1559–70.

Cullmann, Oscar. *Christus und die Zeit*. Zurich: Zollikon, 1946.

Cunnar, Eugene. *Essays on Richard Crashaw*. Edited by Robert M. Cooper. Lewiston, NY: Edwin Mellen Press, 1979.

Curry, Walter Clyde. *Milton's Ontology, Cosmogony, and Physics*. Lexington: University Press of Kentucky, 2015.

Daly, Peter, ed. *The English Emblem and the Continental Tradition*. New York: AMS Press, 1988.

– "Southwell's 'Burning Babe' and the Emblematic Practice." *Wascana Review* 3 (1968): 29–44.

David, Zdenêk V. *Finding the Middle Way: The Utraquists' Liberal Challenge to Rome and Luther*. Washington, DC: Woodrow Wilson Center Press, 2003.

Davidson, Clifford. "Robert Southwell: Lyric Poetry, the Restoration of Images, and Martyrdom." *Ben Jonson Journal* 7, no. 1 (2000): 157–86.

Davies, H. Neville. "Laid Artfully Together: Stanzaic Design in Milton's 'On the Morning of Christ's Nativity.'" In *Fair Forms: Essays in English Literature from Spenser to Jane Austen*, edited by Maren-Sofie Røstvig, 85–118. Totowa, NJ: Rowman & Littlefield, 1975.

Davis, Raymond, trans. *The Book of Pontiffs*. Liverpool: Liverpool University Press, 2000.

Davis, Walter. "The Meditative Hymnody of Richard Crashaw." *English Literary History* 50, no. 1 (Spring 1983): 107–29.

Davisson, Darrell D. *The Epiphany Altarpiece by Gentile da Fabriano: Liturgical, Patristic, and Apocryphal Sources*. Tehachapi, CA: Lupin Hill House, 2016.

De Bérulle, P. Pierre. *Discours de l'estat et des grandeurs de Jésus*. Paris: Niffre Fils, 1866. First published 1623.

Debongnie, Pierre. "The Confessions of Jeanne Frey." In *Satan*, edited by Bruno de Jésus-Marie, OCD, and translated by Malachy Carroll et al., 223–61. New York: Sheed and Ward, 1952.

Deckard, Michael Funk, and Péter Losonczi, eds. *Philosophy Begins in Wonder: An Introduction to Early Modern Philosophy, Theology, and Science*. Cambridge: James Clarke, 2011.

Decrees of the Ecumenical Councils. Edited by Norman P. Tanner, SJ. London: Sheed and Ward, 1990.

De Lubac, Henri. *Medieval Exegesis*. Grand Rapids, MI: Wm. B. Eerdmans, 1998.

Demolon, Pierre, et al. *L'Histoire de Douai*. Dunkerque: Westhoek-Éditions des Beffrois, 1985.

Denvir, Bernard, ed. *Art Treasures of Italy*. New York: Galahad Books, 1980.

Denzinger, Heinrich. *Enchiridion Symbolorum: Compendium of Creeds, Definitions, and Declarations on Matters of Faith and Morals*. Edited by Peter Hünermann. 43rd ed. San Francisco: Ignatius Press, 2012.

Derrett, J. Duncan M. *Studies in the New Testament*. Vol. 2, *Midrash in Action and as a Literary Device*. Leiden: Brill, 1978.

Derrida, Jacques. "Plato's Pharmacy." In *Dissemination*, translated by Barbara Johnson, 67–122. Chicago: University of Chicago Press, 1981.

De Sales, Francis. *Treatise on the Love of God*. Translated by Henry Benedict Mackey. New York: Cosimo Classics, 2007.

Deshman, Robert. *The Benedictional of Aethelwold*. Princeton, NJ: Princeton University Press, 1995.

Despres, Denise L. "Adolescence and Interiority in Aelred's Lives of Christ." In *Devotional Culture in Late Medieval England and Europe: Diverse Imaginations of Christ's Life*, edited by Ryan Perry and Stephen Kelly, 107–25. Turnhout: Brepols, 2014.

DiPasquale, Theresa. "John Donne's Sacramental Poetics." PhD diss., University of Virginia, 1989.

– *Literature and Sacrament: The Sacred and the Secular in John Donne*. Pittsburgh, PA: Duquesne University Press, 1999.

Dix, Dom Gregory, OSB. *The Shape of the Liturgy*. London: Dacre Press, 1945.

Doherty, M.J. "Salvation History, Poetic Form, and the Logic of Time in Milton's Nativity Ode." *Milton Studies* 25 (1989): 21–42.

Donne, John. *The Complete Poetry and Selected Prose of John Donne*. Edited by Charles M. Coffin. New York: Modern Library, 2001.

– *The Divine Poems*. Edited by Helen Gardner. Oxford: Clarendon Press, 1978.

– *Essayes in Divinity, Being Several Disquisitions Interwoven with Meditations and Prayers*. Edited by Anthony Raspa. Montreal and Kingston: McGill-Queen's University Press, 2001.

– *Ignatius His Conclave*. Edited by Timothy Stafford Healy. Oxford: Clarendon Press, 1969.

– *The Oxford Edition of the Sermons of John Donne*. Vol. 1, *Sermons Preached at the Jacobean Courts, 1615–19*, edited by Peter McCullough. Oxford: Oxford University Press, 2015.

– *The Poems of John Donne*. Vol. 1. Edited by E.K. Chambers. London: Lawrence & Bullen, 1896.

– *Pseudo-martyr*. Edited by Anthony Raspa. Montreal and Kingston: McGill-Queen's University Press, 1993.

– *Pseudo-martyr. Wherein out of certaine propositions and gradations, this conclusion is euicted. That those which are of the Romane religion in this kingdome, may and ought to take the Oath of allegiance*. London: W. Stansby for Walter Burre, 1610.
– *The Sermons of John Donne*. Edited by George R. Potter and Evelyn Mary Simpson. 10 vols. Berkeley: University of California Press, 1953–62.
– *Sermons on the Psalms and the Gospels with a Selection of Prayers and Meditations*. Edited by Evelyn M. Simpson. Berkeley: University of California Press, 1963.
– *The Works of John Donne, D.D.* 6 vols. London: John W. Parker, 1839.
[*Douai-Rheims Bible*.] *The Holy Bible, translated from the Latin vulgate: Diligently compared with the Hebrew, Greek, and other editions in Divers languages. The Old Testament, first published by the English College at Doway, A.D. 1609. And the New Testament. First published by the English College at Rhemes, A.D. 1582. With annotations, references, and an historical and chronological index*. Dublin: Hugh Fitzpatrick for Richard Cross, 1791.
Douglas, Brian. *A Companion to Anglican Eucharistic Theology*. Vol. 1, *The Reformation to the 19th Century*. Leiden: Brill, 2011.
Dračevac, Ante. *La Cathédrale de Dubrovnik*. Translated by Françoise Kveder. Zagreb: Privredni Vjesnik, 1988.
Dreves, Guido Maria, ed. *Analecta Hymnica Medii Aevi*. Leipzig: Fues's Verlag, 1890.
Dreves, Guido Maria, and Clemens Blume. *Ein Jahrtausend Lateinischer Hymnendichtung*. Erster Teil. Leipzig: Fues's Verlag, 1890.
Dronke, Peter. *Forms and Imaginings: From Antiquity to the Fifteenth Century*. Roma: Edizioni di Storia e Letteratura, 2007.
Drury, John. *Music at Midnight: The Life and Poetry of George Herbert*. London: Penguin, 2014.
Duckles, Vincent. "John Jenkins' Settings of Lyrics by George Herbert." *The Musical Quarterly* 48, no. 4 (October 1962): 461–75.
Duffy, Eamon. "The English Reformation after Revisionism." *Renaissance Quarterly* 59, no. 3 (Fall 2006): 720–31.
– *The Stripping of the Altars: Traditional Religion in England, 1400–1580*. New Haven, CT: Yale University Press, 1992.
Dunkle, Brian P., SJ. *Enchantment and Creed in the Hymns of Ambrose of Milan*. Oxford: Oxford University Press, 2016.
Dupuis, J. "The Uniqueness of Jesus Christ in the Early Christian Tradition." Religious Pluralism. *Jeevadhara* 47 (September/October 1978): 398–408.
Durr, R.A. *On the Mystical Poetry of Henry Vaughan*. Cambridge, MA: Harvard University Press, 1962.
Dzon, Mary. "Birgitta of Sweden and Christ's Clothing." In *The Christ Child in Medieval Culture: Alpha es et O!*, edited by Mary Dzon and Theresa M. Kenney, 115–44. Toronto: University of Toronto Press, 2012.

– "Cecily Neville and the Apocryphal *Infantia salvatoris* in the Middle Ages." *Mediaeval Studies* 71 (2009): 235–300.

– "Joseph and the Amazing Christ-Child of Late-Medieval Legend." In *Childhood in the Middle Ages and the Renaissance: The Results of a Paradigm Shift in the History of Mentality*, edited by Albrecht Classen, 135–57. New York: De Gruyter, 2005.

– "Out of Egypt into England: Tales of the Good Thief for Medieval English Audiences." In *Devotional Culture in Late Medieval England and Europe: Diverse Imaginations of Christ's Life*, edited by S. Kelly and R. Perry, 147–241. Turnhout: Brepols, 2014.

– *The Quest for the Christ Child in the Later Middle Ages*. Philadelphia: University of Pennsylvania Press, 2017.

– "Wanton Boys in Middle English Texts and the Christ Child in Minneapolis, University of Minnesota, MS Z822 N81." In *Medieval Lifecycles: Continuities and Change*, edited by Karen Smyth and Isabelle Cochelin, 81–145. Turnhout: Brepols, 2013.

Dzon, Mary, and Theresa Kenney, eds. *The Christ Child in Medieval Culture: Alpha es et O!* Toronto: University of Toronto Press, 2012.

Ehrman, Bart, and Zlatko Pleše. *The Apocryphal Gospels: Texts and Translations*. Oxford: Oxford University Press, 2011.

Eliot, Thomas Stearns. *For Lancelot Andrewes: Essays on Style and Order*. London: Faber & Gwyer, 1928.

Ellington, Donna Spivey. *From Sacred Body to Angelic Soul: Understanding Mary in Late Medieval and Early Modern Europe*. Washington, DC: Catholic University of America Press, 2001.

Elliott, J.K. *A Synopsis of the Apocryphal Nativity and Infancy Narratives*. Leiden: Brill, 2006.

Ellrodt, Robert. *Seven Metaphysical Poets: A Structural Study of the Unchanging Self*. Oxford: Oxford University Press, 2000.

Elsky, Martin. "History, Liturgy, and Point of View in Protestant Meditative Poetry." *Studies in Philology* 77, no. 1 (Winter 1980): 67–83.

Elton, G.R. *Reformation Europe, 1517–1559*. 2nd ed. Oxford: Blackwell, 1963.

Entzminger, Robert L. "The Epiphanies in Milton's Nativity Ode." *Renaissance Papers* 25 (1981): 21–31.

Ephrem the Syrian. *Ephrem the Syrian: Hymns*. Edited and translated by Kathleen McVey. New York: Paulist Press, 1989.

– *Sermo de Domino nostro*. In *Sancti Ephraem Syri, Hymni et Sermones*. Edited by Thomas-Joseph Lamy. Vol. 1. Mechlinae: H. Dessain, 1882.

Euler, Carrie. "Huldrych Zwingli and Heinrich Bullinger." In *A Companion to the Eucharist in the Reformation*, edited by Lee Palmer Wandel, 57–74. Leiden: Brill, 2014.

Evans, J. Martin. *The Miltonic Moment*. Lexington: University Press of Kentucky, 1998.

– "A Poem of Absences." *Milton Quarterly* 27, no. 1 (1993): 31–5.

Faesen, Rob. "The Three Births of Christ and the Christmas Liturgy in the Temple of Our Soul, the Evangelical Pearl, and the Arnhem Mystical Sermons." *Ons Geestelijk Erf* 81, no. 1 (2010): 121–37.

Fahlbusch, Erwin, et al., eds. *Encyclopedia of Christianity*. Vol. 56. Grand Rapids, MI: Eerdmans, 2008.

Fawcett, Christina. "The Orphic Singer of Milton's Nativity Ode." *Studies in English Literature 1500–1900* 49, no. 1 (Winter 2009): 105–20.

Feinstein, Blossom. "On the Hymns of John Milton and Gian Francesco Pico." *Comparative Literature* 20, no. 3 (Summer 1968): 245–53.

Ficino, Marsilio. *Platonic Theology*. 6 vols. Translated by Michael J.B. Allen. Edited by James Hankins. Cambridge, MA: Harvard University Press, 2001.

– "De stella magorum." In *Opera*, edited by M. Sancipriano and P.O. Kristeller, 572–4. Turin, 1959. Reprint of the 1576 edition (Basel).

Finney, Paul Corby. *The Invisible God: The Earliest Christians on Art*. New York: Oxford University Press, 1994.

– ed. *Seeing Beyond the Word*. Grand Rapids, MI: Eerdmans, 1999.

Fish, Stanley. *How Milton Works*. Cambridge, MA: Harvard University Press, 2001.

– *The Living Temple: George Herbert and Catechizing*. Berkeley: University of California Press, 1978.

Fisher, St. John. *De veritate corporis et sanguinis Christi in Eucharistia adversus Ioannem ŒOEcolampadium*. Cologne, 1527.

Fletcher, Giles. *Christs Victorie and Triumph*. In *Poetical Works of Giles and Phineas Fletcher*, edited by F.S. Boas. Cambridge: Cambridge University Press, 1908–9.

Fontijn-Harris, Claire. "The Virgin's Voice: Representations of Mary in Seventeenth-Century Italian Song." In *Maternal Measures: Figuring Caregiving in the Early Modern Period*, edited by Naomi J. Miller and Naomi Yavneh, 135–62. Aldershot, UK: Ashgate, 2000.

Forti, Tova. "Bee's Honey: From Realia to Metaphor in Biblical Wisdom Literature." *Vetus Testamentum* 56, no. 3 (July 2006): 327–41.

Foxe, John. *The Acts and Monuments of the Church; Containing the History and Sufferings of the Martyrs*. Edited by M.H. Seymour. London: Scott, Webster, and Geary, 1838.

Freeman, Rosemary. *English Emblem Books*. London: Chatto & Windus, 1948.

Fuller, Wendy. "Paradox Lost: Pope's Auspicious Babe and the Death of a Renaissance Tradition." Unpublished paper delivered at the Renaissance Society of America: Southern California Conference, 17 April 1982.

Furey, Constance. *Poetic Relations: Intimacy and Faith in the English Reformation*. Chicago: University of Chicago Press, 2017.

Gardiner, Stephen. *Explication and Assertion of the true Catholique Fayth touching the most blessed Sacrament of the Altar, with Confutation of a Book written against the same*. Rouen, 1551.

Gardner, Helen. *The Metaphysical Poets*. Oxford: Oxford University Press, 1957.
– "The Religious Poetry of John Donne." In *John Donne: A Collection of Critical Essays*, edited by Helen Gardner, 123–36. Englewood Cliffs, NJ: Prentice-Hall, 1962.
Gassner, John, and Edward Quinn, eds. *The Reader's Encyclopedia of World Drama*. Mineola, NY: Dover Publications, 2002.
Gastoué, Amédée. *Noël*. Paris: Bloud, 1907.
Gauding, Madonna. *The Signs and Symbols Bible: The Definitive Guide to the World of Symbols*. New York: Sterling, 2009.
Gavrilyuk, Paul. *The Suffering of the Impassible God: The Dialectics of Patristic Thought*. Oxford: Oxford University Press, 2004.
The Geneva Bible: The Annotated 1602 New Testament Edition. Edited by Gerald T. Sheppard. Cleveland: The Pilgrim Press, 1989.
Gerrish, B.A. *Grace and Gratitude: The Eucharistic Theology of John Calvin*. Eugene, OR: Wipf and Stock, 2002.
Gerson, Jean. "Considérations sur Saint Joseph." In *Oeuvres complètes*, vol. 5, edited by Msgr. Palémon Glorieux, 376–98. Paris: Desclée, 1966.
Gertsman, Elina. "Signs of Death: The Sacrificial Christ Child in Late Medieval Art." In *The Christ Child in Medieval Culture*, edited by Mary Dzon and Theresa M. Kenney, 66–91. Toronto: University of Toronto Press, 2012.
Gibson, Gail McMurray. "The Thread of Life in the Hand of the Virgin." In *Equally in God's Image: Women in the Middle Ages*, edited by Julia Bolton Holloway, Constance S. Wright, and Joan Bechtold, 46–54. New York: Peter Lang, 1990.
Girard, René. *The Scapegoat*. Baltimore: Johns Hopkins University Press, 1986.
Goekjian, Gregory F. "Deference and Silence: Milton's Nativity Ode." *Milton Studies* 21 (1985): 119–35.
Goldberg, Jonathon. "Hesper-Vesper: Aspects of Venus in a Seventeenth-Century Trope." *Studies in English Literature 1500–1900* 15, no. 1 (Winter 1975): 37–55.
Gondreau, Paul. *The Passions of Christ's Soul in the Theology of St. Thomas Aquinas*. Scranton, PA: University of Scranton Press, 2009.
Goodblatt, Chanita. *The Christian Hebraism of John Donne: Written with the Fingers of Man's Hand*. Pittsburgh, PA: Duquesne University Press, 2010.
Göser, Artur. *Kirche und Lied: Der Hymnus "Veni redemptor gentium" bei Müntzer und Luther*. Würzburg: Königshausen & Neumann, 1995.
Goulder, M.D., and M.L. Sanderson. "St. Luke's Genesis." *Journal of Theological Studies* 8, no. 1 (1957): 12–30.
Grabar, André. *Christian Iconography: A Study of Its Origins*. Princeton, NJ: Princeton University Press, 1968.

– "The Virgin in a Mandorla of Light." In *Late Classical and Mediaeval Studies in Honor of Albert Mathias Friend, Jr.*, edited by Kurt Weitzman, 305–11. Princeton, NJ: Princeton University Press, 1955.

Graef, Hilda. *Mary: A History of Doctrine and Devotion*. Vol. 1, *From the Beginnings to the Eve of the Reformation*. New York: Sheed and Ward, 1963.

Grant, Patrick. "Augustinian Spirituality and the Holy Sonnets of John Donne." *ELH* 38, no. 4 (1971): 542–61.

Greene, R.L., ed. *The Early English Carols*. Oxford: Clarendon Press, 1935.

Grierson, Herbert. *First Half of the Seventeenth Century*. Edinburgh: W. Blackwood and Sons, 1906.

– *The Works of John Donne*. Oxford: Oxford University Press, 1931.

Griffith, Thomas W.H. *The Principles of Theology: An Introduction to the Thirty-Nine Articles*. Eugene, OR: Wipf and Stock, 2005. First published in 1930.

Guéranger, Dom Prosper. *The Liturgical Year: Advent*. Vol. 1. Translated by Dom Laurence Shepherd. Dublin: O'Toole and Son, 1870.

Hadfield, Andrew. *Edmund Spenser: A Life*. Oxford: Oxford University Press, 2012.

Hale, Rosemary Drage. "Imitatio Mariae: Motherhood Motifs in Devotional Memoirs." *Mystics Quarterly* 16, no. 4 (December 1990): 193–203.

– "Joseph as Mother: Adaptation and Appropriation in the Construction of Male Virtue." In *Medieval Mothering*, edited by John Carmi Parsons and Bonnie Wheeler, 101–16. New York: Garland Publishing, 1996.

Hamburger, Jeffrey F. *Nuns as Artists: The Visual Culture of a Medieval Convent*. Berkeley: University of California Press, 1997.

Hanford, J.H. "The Youth of Milton." In *Studies in Shakespeare, Milton, and Donne*, 89–163. New York: Haskell House, 1964.

Hankey, Wayne J. "Augustinian Immediacy and Dionysian Mediation in John Colet, Edmund Spenser, Richard Hooker, and the Cardinal de Bérulle." In *Augustinus in der Neuzeit, Colloque de la Herzog August Bibliothek de Wolfenbüttel, 14–17 octobre 1996*, 125–60 (Turnhout: Brepols, 1998).

Hannick, Christian. "The Theotokos in Byzantine Hymnography: Typology and Allegory." In *Images of the Mother of God: Perceptions of the Theotokos in Byzantium*, edited by Maria Vassilaki, 69–76. Aldershot, UK: Ashgate Publishing, 2005.

Harnack, Andrew. "Both Protestant and Catholic: George Herbert and 'To all Angels and Saints.'" *George Herbert Journal* 11, no. 1 (Fall 1987): 23–39.

– "Robert Southwell's 'The Burning Babe' and the Typology of Christmastide." *Kentucky Philological Association Bulletin* 4 (1977): 25–9.

Harris, Elizabeth. "Mary in the Burning Bush: Nicolas Froment's Triptych at Aix-en-Provence." *Journal of the Warburg Institute* 1, no. 4 (April 1938): 281–6.

Harris, Jonathan Gil. *Untimely Matter in the Time of Shakespeare*. Philadelphia: University of Pennsylvania Press, 2008.

Haskins, Dayton. "Milton's Portrait of Mary as Bearer of the Word." In *Milton and the Idea of Women*, edited by Julia Walker, 169–84. Urbana: University of Illinois Press, 1988.

Healy, Thomas F. "Crashaw and the Sense of History." In *New Perspectives on the Life and Art of Richard Crashaw*, edited by John R. Roberts, 49–65. Columbia: University of Missouri Press, 1990.

– *Richard Crashaw*. Leiden: Brill, 1986.

Hegedus, Tim. *Early Christianity and Ancient Astrology*. New York: Peter Lang, 2007.

Henry, H.T. "Ambrosian." In *The Catholic Encyclopedia*, edited by Charles George Herbermann et al. Vol. 1. New York: The Universal Knowledge Foundation, 1913.

Herbert, George. *The Latin Poetry of George Herbert: A Bilingual Edition*. Translated by Mark McCloskey and Paul R. Murphy. Athens, OH: Irvington Publishers, 1965.

– *The Works of George Herbert*. Edited by F.E. Hutchinson. Oxford: Clarendon Press, 1959.

Herrick, Robert. *The Complete Poetry of Robert Herrick*. Vol. 1. Edited by Tom Cain and Ruth Connolly. Oxford: Oxford University Press, 2013.

Hildegard of Bingen. "Ein unveröffentlichtes Hildegard-Fragment (Codex Berolin. Lat. Qu. 674)." Edited by Heinrich Schipperges. *Sudhoffs Archiv für Geschichte der Medizin* 40 (1956): 41–77.

Hill, John Spencer. "The Phoenix." *Religion & Literature* 16, no. 2 (Summer 1984): 61–6.

Himuro, Misako. "The Phoenix in the *First Epistle of Clement to the Corinthians*." *Renaissance Studies* 12, no. 4 (December 1998): 523–44.

Hirn, Yrjö. *The Sacred Shrine: A Study of the Poetry and Art of the Catholic Church*. London: Faber and Faber, 1958. Reprint of the 1912 first English edition by Macmillan (London).

Hock, Ronald F., ed. and trans. *The Infancy Gospels of James and Thomas*. With Introduction, Notes, and Original Text Featuring the New Scholars Version Translation. Santa Rosa, CA: Polebridge Press, 1995.

Hodgson, Elizabeth M.A. *Gender and the Sacred Self in John Donne*. Newark: University of Delaware Press, 1999.

Hollander, Robert, and Jean Hollander, trans. and eds. *Dante's Paradiso*. New York: Harcourt, 2006.

Hooker, Richard. *Selections from the Fifth Book of Hooker's Ecclesiastical Polity*. Edited by John Keble. Oxford: J.H. Parker, 1839.

Hopper, Stanley Romaine, R. Melvin Keiser, and Tony Stoneburner. *The Way of Transfiguration: Religious Imagination as Theopoiesis*. Louisville, KY: Westminster/John Knox Press, 1992.

Horsfall, Nicholas. "Bees in Elysium." *Vergilius* 56 (2010): 39–45.

Howard, W. Scott. "Companions with Time: Milton, Tasso, and Renaissance Dialogue." *The Comparatist* 28 (May 2004): 5–28.

Hughes, Merritt Y., ed. *Milton: Complete Poems and Major Prose*. Indianapolis, IN: Odyssey Press, 1957.

– *A Variorum Commentary on the Poems of John Milton*. Vol. 1. New York: Columbia University Press, 1972.

Hughes, Richard E. "George Herbert and the Incarnation." *Cithara* 4, no. 1 (1964): 22–32.

Hunt, John. *Religious Thought in England from the Reformation to the End of the Last Century: A Contribution to the History of Theology*. London: Strahan, 1873.

Hunter, Jeanne Clayton. "'With Wings of Faith': Herbert's Communion Poems." *Journal of Religion* 62, no. 1 (1982): 57–71.

Hunter, William Bridges. "Milton on the Incarnation." In *Bright Essence: Studies in Milton's Theology*, 131–48. Salt Lake City: University of Utah Press, 1971.

– *Milton's English Poetry: Being Entries from a Milton Encyclopedia*. Lewisburg, PA: Bucknell University Press, 1986.

H'usain, Itrat. *The Dogmatic and Mystical Theology of John Donne*. New York: Macmillan, 1938.

– *The Mystical Element in the Metaphysical Poets of the Seventeenth Century*. New York: Biblo & Tannen Publishers, 1948.

Ignatius of Loyola, St. *The Spiritual Exercises of St. Ignatius*. Translated and edited by Louis J. Puhl. New York: Vintage Books, 2000.

– *The Spiritual Exercises of St. Ignatius of Loyola*. Edited by Elder Mullan, SJ. New York: Cosimo Classics, 1964. Reprint of the 1914 edition by P.J. Kennedy & Sons (New York).

Illick, Joseph E. "Child-Rearing in Seventeenth Century England and America." In *The History of Childhood*, edited by Lloyd deMause, 303–50. Lanham, MD: Rowman & Littlefield, 1995.

Isidore of Seville. "*Etymologiae* 12.8." In J.P. Migne PL 82. Taken from Faustinus Arévalo, *Isidori Hispalensis opera omnia*. 7 vols. Rome, 1797–1803.

Jackson, Simon, and George J. Callon. "A Newly-Identified Setting of Herbert's 'Even-song' by John Jenkins." *George Herbert Journal* 36, nos. 1–2 (Fall 2012/Spring 2013): 23–43.

Jacobs, Laurence H. "'Unexpressive Notes': The Decorum of Milton's Nativity Ode." *Essays in Literature* 1, no. 2 (1974): 166–77.

Jacobus de Voragine. *The Golden Legend: Readings on the Saints*. Translated by William Granger Ryan. 2 vols. Princeton, NJ: Princeton University Press, 1995.

Janelle, Pierre. *Robert Southwell the Writer: A Study in Religious Inspiration*. London: Sheed and Ward, 1935.

Jaritz, Gerhard, and Gerson Moreno-Riaño, eds. *Time and Eternity: The Medieval Discourse*. Turnhout: Brepols, 2003.

Jaworska, Sonia. "'Eternity Shut in a Span': The Word Being Born and Giving Birth in the Poetry of Richard Crashaw." In *Poetic Revelations. Word Made Flesh Made Word: The Power of the Word III*. Edited by Mark S. Burrows, Jean Ward, and Małgorzata Grzegorzewska, 54–68. London: Routledge, 2017.

Jeffrey, David L. *A Dictionary of Biblical Tradition in English Literature*. Grand Rapids, MI: W.B. Eerdmans, 1992.

Jewel, John. *A Defence of tbe Apologie of tbe Churche of Englande, conteininge an Answeare to a certaine Booke lately set foorthe by M. Hardinge, and Entituled, A Confutation of &c*. London, 1567.

Jobin, Guy. "Instituer l'évidement? Heuristique kénotique et positivité éthique." *Laval théologique et philosophique* 67, no. 1 (2011): 69–86.

John Damascene. *On the Holy Icons*. Translated by David Anderson. Crestwood, NY: St. Vladimir's Seminary Press, 1980.

– *Three Treatises on the Divine Images*. Translated and edited by Andrew Louth. Crestwood, NY: St. Vladimir Seminary Press, 2003.

Johnson, Aaron P. "Philosophy, Hellenicity, Law: Porphyry on Origen, Again." *The Journal of Hellenistic Studies* 132 (2012): 55–69.

Johnson, Bruce A. "The Audience Shift in Herbert's Poetry." *Studies in English Literature, 1500–1900* 35, no. 1 (Winter 1995): 89–103.

Johnson, Jeffrey. *The Theology of John Donne*. Cambridge: D.S. Brewer, 1999.

Johnson, Kimberly. *Made Flesh: Sacrament and Poetics in Post-Reformation England*. Philadelphia: University of Pennsylvania Press, 2014.

– "Richard Crashaw's Indigestible Poetics." *Modern Philology* 107, no. 1 (2009): 32–51.

Juan de la Cruz, San. *Obras Completas*. Edited by Lucinio Ruano de la Iglésia. Madrid: Biblioteca de Autores Cristianos, 1982.

Junod, Eric, and Jean-Daniel Kaestli, eds., "Acta Iohannis." In CCSA. Turnhout: Brepols, 1983.

Just, Arthur A., and Thomas C. Oden, eds. *Luke*. Downers Grove, IL: Intervarsity Press, 2003.

Karampetsos, E.D. *Dante and Byzantium*. Boston: Somerset Hall Press, 2009.

Karpiński, Franciszek. "Bóg się rodzi" (1792). In *Monumenta Polonica: The First Four Centuries of Polish Poetry, A Bilingual Anthology*, edited by Bogdana Carpenter, 519. Ann Arbor: Michigan Slavic Publications, 1989.

Karris, Robert J. *Commentary on the Gospel of John by Bonaventure*. Vol. 8, part 2. St. Bonaventure, NY: Franciscan Institute, 2007.

Keller, Peter. *Die Wiege des Christuskinde: ein Haushaltsgerät in Kunst und Kult*. Worms: Wernersche Verlagsgesellschaft, 1998.

Kelley, Thomas Forrest. *The Exultet in Southern Italy*. Oxford: Oxford University Press, 1996.

Kelliher, Hilton. "Crashaw at Cambridge." In *New Perspectives on the Life and Art of Richard Crashaw*, edited by John R. Roberts, 180–214. Columbia: University of Missouri Press, 1990.

Kenney, Theresa M. "The Manger as Calvary and Altar in the Middle English Nativity Lyric." In *The Christ Child in Medieval Culture: Alpha es et O!*, edited by Mary Dzon and Theresa Kenney, 29–65. Toronto: University of Toronto Press, 2012.

– "The Manger in the Reformation and Counter-Reformation." In *Encyclopedia of the Bible and Its Reception Online*, edited by Constance Furey et al. Volume 17, n.p. Berlin: De Gruyter, 2019. https://www.degruyter.com/view/db/ebr.

– "'Sensualiter tangitur': The Christ Child 'Born a Martyr' in John Donne's Sermon for Christmas 1626." *John Donne Journal* 36 (forthcoming).

– "'This pompe is prizèd there': Southwell's Challenge to Courtly Identities in 'New Prince, New Pompe.'" In *Precarious Identities: The Works of Fulke Greville and Robert Southwell*, edited by Vassiliki Markidou and Afroditi-Maria Panaghis, 153–71. New York: Routledge, 2019.

Kerrigan, William. *The Prophetic Milton*. Charlottesville: University Press of Virginia, 1974.

Kessler, Herbert L. *Seeing Medieval Art: Rethinking the Middle Ages*. Peterborough, ON: Broadview Press, 2004.

Kieckhefer, Richard. "Ihesus ist unser! The Christ Child in the German Sister Books." In *The Christ Child in Medieval Culture: Alpha es et O!*, edited by Mary Dzon and Theresa M. Kenney, 167–98. Toronto: University of Toronto Press, 2012.

King, John W. *English Reformation Literature: The Tudor Origins of the Protestant Tradition*. Princeton, NJ: Princeton University Press, 1982.

Kingsley, Lawrence W. "Mythic Dialectic in the Nativity Ode." *Milton Studies* 4 (1972): 163–75.

Kolve, V.A. *The Play Called Corpus Christi*. Stanford, CA: Stanford University Press, 1966.

Kolvenbach, Peter-Hans, SJ. "Do Not Hide the Hidden Life of Christ." *Centrum Ignatianum Spiritualitatis* 24, no. 3 (1993): 11–25.

Koschorke, Albrecht. *The Holy Family and Its Legacy: Religious Imagination from the Gospel to Star Wars*. New York: Columbia University Press, 2003.

Kozłowski, Jan M. "'The Fruit of Your Womb' (Luke 1:42) as 'The Lord God, Creator of Heaven and Earth' (Judith 13:18): An Intertextual Analysis." *Ephemerides Theologicae Lovanienses* 93 (2017): 339–42.

– "Mary as the Ark of the Covenant in the Scene of the Visitation (Luke 1:39–56) Reconsidered." *Warszawskie Studia Teologiczne* 31 (2018): 109–16.

Kuchar, Gary. "A Greek in the Temple: Pseudo-Dionysius and Negative Theology in Richard Crashaw's 'Hymn in the Glorious Epiphany.'" *Studies in Philology* 108, no. 2 (2011): 261–98.

– *The Poetry of Religious Sorrow in Early Modern England*. Cambridge: Cambridge University Press, 2008.

– "Richard Crashaw and George Herbert's *The Temple*: Mystery, Liturgy and Error," *Cithara* 57, no. 2 (2018): 65–99.

Lactantius. *Lactantius: Divine Institutes*. Translated by Anthony Bowen and Peter Garnsey. Liverpool: Liverpool University Press, 2003.

Langland, William. *Piers Plowman: An Alliterative Verse Translation*. Translated by E. Talbot Donaldson. New York: W.W. Norton, 1990.

– *William Langland: Piers Plowman, A New Translation of the B-Text*. Translated by A.V.C. Schmidt. Oxford: Oxford University Press, 1992.

Larson, Viola. "John Calvin on the Sacraments: A Summary." *Theology Matters* 13, no. 4 (September–October 2007): 1–12.

Lass, Roger. "Poem as Sacrament: Transcendence of Time in the Advent Sequence from the Exeter Book." *Annuale Mediaevale* 7 (1966): 3–15.

Laud, William. *A Relation of the Conference between William Laud, Lord Archbishop of Canterbury, and Mr. Fisher the Jesuit*. London: Thomas Bassett, Thomas Dring, 1686.

Laurentin, René. *Structure et théologie de Luc I-II*. Paris: Gabalda, 1957.

Lecocq, Françoise. "L'œuf du phénix. Myrrhe, encens et cannelle dans le mythe du phénix." *L'animal et le savoir, de l'Antiquité à la Renaissance, Schedae* 17, no. 2 (2009): 73–106.

Leishman, J.B. *The Monarch of Wit: An Analytical and Comparative Study of the Poetry of John Donne*. London: Hutchinson, 1962.

Leo the Great, St. *In Nativitate Domini Sermo* 6, 2–3; 5, PL 54: 213–16.

Lewalski, Barbara K. *Donne's "Anniversaries" and the Poetry of Praise: The Creation of a Symbolic Mode*. Princeton, NJ: Princeton University Press, 1973.

– "How Radical Was the Young Milton?" In *Milton and Heresy*, edited by Stephen B. Dobranski and John P. Rumrich, 49–72. Cambridge: Cambridge University Press, 2009.

– *Protestant Poetics and the Seventeenth-Century Religious Lyric*. Princeton, NJ: Princeton University Press, 1979.

Lewis, C.S. *English Literature of the Sixteenth Century Excluding Drama*. Oxford: Clarendon Press, 1962.

Lewis, Thomas. *English Presbyterian Eloquence*. London: T. Bickerton, 1720.

Lieb, Michael. "Milton and the Kenotic Theology: Its Literary Bearing." *English Literary History* 37, no. 3 (September 1970): 342–60.

Little, Charles T. "Joseph at Chartres: Sculpture Lost and Found." In *Arts of the Medieval Cathedrals: Studies on Architecture, Stained Glass, and Sculpture*, edited by Kathleen Nolan and Danny Sandron, 179–96. Abingdon, UK: Ashgate 2015.

Lope de Vega y Carpio, Félix. "Cantarcillo de la Virgen." In *Nine Centuries of Spanish Literature: A Dual Language Anthology*, edited by Seymour Resnick and Jeanne Pasmantier, 250–2. New York: Dover, 2012.

– "Cantarcillo de la Virgen." In *Pastores de Belen: Prosas y versos divinos*. Brussels: Roger Velpio y Huberto Antonio, 1614.

Louth, Andrew. *The Origins of the Christian Mystical Tradition: From Plato to Denys*. Oxford: Oxford University Press, 2006.

Love, Nicholas. *The Mirrour of the Blessed Lyf of Jesu Christ*. Edited by Lawrence F. Powell. Oxford: Clarendon Press, 1908.

– *Nicholas Love, The Mirror of the Blessed Life of Jesus Christ: A Full Critical Edition*. Edited by Michael G. Sargent. Exeter, UK: University of Exeter Press, 2005.

Lumpkin, Ben Gray. "Fate in *Paradise Lost*." *Studies in Philology* 44, no. 1 (January 1947): 56–68.

Luria, Maxwell S., and Richard L. Hoffman, eds. *Middle English Lyrics*. New York: W.W. Norton, 1974.

Luther, Martin. *Luther at the Manger: Christmas Sermons on Isaiah 9:6*. Translated by Nathaniel Biebert. Milwaukee, WI: Northwestern Publishing House, 2017.

– *Luther's Works*. Vol. 35, *Prefaces to the Old Testament*. Edited by Diane Jacobson. Minneapolis, MI: Fortress Press, 1961.

– *The Sermons of Martin Luther*. Volume 1. Edited by Pastor Gregory L. Jackson. N.p: CreateSpace, 2017.

Luzvic, Stephanus. Translated by Henry Hawkins. *The Devout Hart or Royal Throne of the Pacifical Solomon*. Rouen: John Cousturier, 1634.

MacCulloch, Diarmaid. *The Reformation*. New York: Viking, 2003.

– *Thomas Cranmer: A Life*. New Haven, CT: Yale University Press, 1996.

Maclaren, I.S. "Milton's Nativity Ode: The Function of Poetry and Structures of Response in 1629." *Milton Studies* 15 (1981): 181–200.

MacLehose, William. "The Holy Tooth: Dentition, Childhood Development, and the Cult of the Christ Child." In *The Christ Child in Medieval Culture: Alpha es et O!*, edited by Mary Dzon and Theresa M. Kenney, 200–23. Toronto: University of Toronto Press, 2012.

Madigan, Kevin. *The Passions of Christ in High-Medieval Thought*. Oxford: Oxford University Press, 2007.

Maher, Michael W., SJ. *Devotion, the Society of Jesus, and the Idea of Saint Joseph*. Philadelphia, PA: St. Joseph's University Press, 2000.

Majercik, Ruth. "Porphyry and Gnosticism." *The Classical Quarterly* 55, no. 1 (May 2005): 277–92.

Mâle, Émile. *L'Art religieux après le Concile de Trente: Étude sur l'iconographie de la fin du XVIe, du XVIIe et du XVIIIe siècles en Italie, en France, en Espagne et en Flandres*. Paris: Librairie Armand Colin, 1932.

– *L'Art religieux du XIIIe siècle en France: Étude sur les origines de l'iconographie du Moyen Age*. Paris: Librairie Armand Colin, 1948.

Malory, Thomas. *Le Morte Darthur*. Edited by Stephan H. A. Shepherd. New York: W.W. Norton, 2003.

Manganiello, Stephen C. *The Concise Encyclopedia of the Revolutions and Wars of England, Scotland, and Ireland, 1639–1660*. Oxford: Scarecrow Press, 2004.

Marcus, Leah. *Childhood and Cultural Despair: A Theme and Variations in Seventeenth-Century Literature*. Pittsburgh, PA: University of Pittsburgh Press, 1978.

– "The Christ Child as Sacrifice: A Medieval Tradition and the English Cycle Plays." In *The Christ Child in Medieval Culture: Alpha es et O!*, edited by Mary Dzon and Theresa M. Kenney, 3–28. Toronto: University of Toronto Press, 2012.

– *The Politics of Mirth: Jonson, Herrick, Milton, Marvell, and the Defense of Old Holiday Pastimes*. Chicago: University of Chicago Press, 1986.

Marotti, Arthur F. *John Donne, Coterie Poet*. Madison: University of Wisconsin Press, 1986.

Martin, L.C., ed. *The Poems English, Latin, and Greek of Richard Crashaw*. Oxford: Clarendon Press, 1927.

Martin, Michael. *The Incarnation of the Poetic Word*. Kettering, OH: Angelico Press, 2017.

– *Literature and the Encounter with God in Post-Reformation England*. Farnham, UK: Ashgate, 2014.

Martz, Louis L. *The Poetry of Meditation: A Study in English Religious Literature of the Seventeenth Century*. New Haven, CT: Yale University Press, 1954.

Maurer, Margaret. "The Circular Argument of Donne's 'La Corona.'" *Studies in English Literature, 1500–1900* 22, no. 1 (1982): 51–68.

McDuffie, Felicia Wright. *"To Our Bodies Turn We Then": Body as Word and Sacrament in the Works of John Donne*. New York: The Continuum International Publishing Group, 2005.

McGinn, Bernard. "Bethlehem." In *Encyclopedia of the Bible and Its Reception Online*, edited by Constance Furey et al., n.p. Berlin: De Gruyter, 2019. https://www.degruyter.com/view/db/ebr.

McGrath, Alister. "The Alchemy of Grace: The Gospel and the Transformation of Reality in George Herbert's 'The Elixir.'" A paper given at the Literature and Theology Seminar, Oxford University, November 2007. https://www.academia.edu/9792170/.

McGuire, Brian Patrick. "Becoming a Father and a Husband: St. Joseph in Bernard of Clairvaux and Jean Gerson." In *Joseph of Nazareth through the Centuries*, edited by Joseph F. Chorpenning, OSFS, 49–61. Philadelphia, PA: St. Joseph's University Press, 2011.

– *Jean Gerson and the Last Medieval Reformation*. University Park, PA: Penn State University Press, 2010.

– "'*Shining Forth Like the Dawn*': Jean Gerson's Sermon to the Carthusians." In *Medieval Monastic Preaching*, edited by Carolyn Muessig, 37–52. Leiden: Brill, 1998.

McIlroy, Claire Elizabeth. *The English Prose Treatises of Richard Rolle*. Cambridge: D.S. Brewer, 2004.

McNamee, M.B. "An Additional Eucharistic Allusion in van der Weyden's Columba Triptych." *Studies in Iconography* 2 (1976): 107–13.

McNees, Eleanor J. *Eucharistic Poetry: The Search for Presence in the Writings of John Donne, Gerard Manley Hopkins, Dylan Thomas, and Geoffrey Hill.* Lewisburg, PA: Bucknell University Press, 1992.

Meier, T.K. "Milton's Nativity Ode: Sectarian Discord." *Modern Language Review* 65 (1970): 7–10.

Meijering, E.P., ed. *Hilary of Poitiers on the Trinity: De trinitate 1:1–19, 2, 3.* Leiden: Brill, 1982.

Meyer, Heinrich August Wilhelm. *Critical and Exegetical Handbook to the Acts of the Apostles*. Edinburgh: T & T Clark, 1883.

Meynell, Wilfred, ed. *The Works of Francis Thompson*. London: Burns and Oates, 1913.

Miles, Clement. *Christmas Customs and Traditions: Their History and Significance.* New York: Dover Publications, 1976. Reprint of the 1912 edition by T. Fisher Unwin (London).

Milman, Robert. *The Life of Torquato Tasso*. Vol. 2. London: Henry Colburn, 1850.

Milton, John. "On the Morning of Christ's Nativity." In *Milton: Complete Poems and Major Prose*, edited by Merritt Y. Hughes, 42–9. Indianapolis, IN: Odyssey Press, 1957.

– *Paradise Regained*. In *Milton: Complete Poems and Major Prose*, edited by Merritt Hughes, 483–530. Indianapolis, IN: Odyssey Press, 1957.

– *Poems of Mr. John Milton, Both English and Latin.* London: Humphrey Moseley, 1645.

Minnis, Alistair. "Affection and Imagination in 'The Cloud of Unknowing' and Hilton's 'Scale of Perfection.'" *Traditio* 39 (1983): 323–66.

Molanus, Iohannes. *De Picturis et Imaginibus Sacris, Liber unus, tractans de vitandis circa eas abusibus ac de earundem significationibus*. Louvain, 1570. Subsequent editions all appeared under the title *De Historia Sanctarum Imaginum et Picturarum.*

Moore-Keish, Martha L. *Do This in Remembrance of Me: A Ritual Approach to Reformed Eucharistic Theology*. Grand Rapids, MI: Eerdmans, 2008.

More, St. Thomas. "The Answer to a Poisoned Letter." In *The Essential Thomas More*, edited by Gerard Wegemer and Stephen Smith, 915–1014. New Haven, CT: Yale University Press, 2020.

Morris, David B. "Drama and Stasis in Milton's 'Ode on the Morning of Christ's Nativity.'" *Studies in Philology* 68 (1971): 207–22.

Mueller, William R. *John Donne: Preacher*. Princeton, NJ: Princeton University Press, 1962.

Mulryan, John, ed. *Milton and the Middle Ages.* Lewisburg, PA: Bucknell University Press, 1982.

Naogeorgus, Thomas. *The popish kingdome, or reigne of Antichrist, written in Latine verse by Thomas Naogeorgus, and englyshed by Barnabe Googe*. Translated by Barnabe Googe. London: Henrie Denham, 1570. Edited by Robert Charles Hope. London: Chiswick Press, 1880.

Neale, John Mason. *Mediaeval Preachers and Mediaeval Preaching: A Series of Extracts, Translated from the Sermons of the Middle Ages, Chronologically Arranged; with Notes and an Introduction*. London: J.C. Mosley, 1856.

Neill, Kerby. "Structure and Symbol in Crashaw's 'Hymn in the Nativity.'" *PMLA* 63, no. 1 (1948): 101–13.

Nelson, Lowry. *Baroque Lyric Poetry*. New Haven, CT: Yale University Press, 1961.

– "Góngora and Milton: Toward a Definition of the Baroque." *Comparative Literature* 6, no. 1 (Winter 1954): 53–63.

Netzley, Ryan. "Oral Devotion: Eucharistic Theology and Richard Crashaw's Religious Lyrics." *Texas Studies in Literature and Language* 44, no. 3 (2002): 247–72.

– *Reading, Desire, and the Eucharist in Early Modern Religious Poetry*. Toronto: University of Toronto Press, 2011.

Neunheuser, Burkhard. "Il Sangue di Cristo, effuso alla Croce e nell'Eucaristia, secondo le miniature di libri liturgici del primo medio evo." *Studia Anselmiana* 4, no. 3 (1984); 1419–33.

Nicholas of Lyre. *Bibliorum Sacrorum cum Glossa ordinaria*. Facsimile reprint of editio princeps. Strassburg: A. Rusch, 1480–1.

– *Postillae perpetuae in Vetus ac Novum Testamentum*. 5 vols. Rome, 1471–2. Bâle edition, 1506.

Ní Chuilleanáin, Eiléan. "Poetry and Mystery." *Religion & Literature* 45, no. 3 (Autumn 2013): 187.

– "Time, Place and the Congregation of Donne's Sermons." In *Literature and Learning in Medieval and Renaissance England: Essays Presented to Fitzroy Pyle*, edited by V.J. Scattergood, 197–215. Dublin: Irish Academic Press, 1984.

Nilgen, Ursula. "The Epiphany and the Eucharist: On the Interpretation of Eucharistic Motifs in Mediaeval Epiphany Scenes." *Art Bulletin* 49 (December 1967): 311–16.

Notker Balbulus. *Liber sequentiarum* (or *hymnorum*). PL 131:1003–26.

Nuttal, A.D. *The Alternative Trinity: Gnostic Heresy in Marlowe, Milton, and Blake*. Oxford: Clarendon Press, 1998.

Oakes, Edward T., SJ. *Infinity Dwindled to Infancy: A Catholic and Evangelical Christology*. Grand Rapids, MI: Eerdmans, 2011.

O'Connell, Patrick F. "'La Corona': Donne's Ars Poetica Sacra." In *The Eagle and the Dove: Reassessing John Donne*, edited by Claude J. Summers and Ted-Larry Pebworth, 119–30. Columbia: University of Missouri Press, 1986.

Ó Cuív, Brian, ed. "Edition of the Latin Infancy Gospels (J Compilation): Arundel and Hereford Forms." In CCSA, vol. 14, 671–957. Turnhout: Brepols, 2001.

O'Donnell, Mary. "Quam Oblationem: The Act of Sacrifice in the Poetry of Saint Robert Southwell." PhD diss., University of North Carolina, 1994. https://libres.uncg.edu/ir/uncg/f/O'Donnell_uncg_9520540.pdf.

Oliver, P.M. *Donne's Religious Writing: A Discourse of Feigned Devotion*. New York: Addison Wesley Longview, 1997.

O'Meara, Carra Ferguson. "'In the Hearth of the Virginal Womb': The Iconography of the Holocaust in Late Medieval Art." *Art Bulletin* 63 (1981): 75–89.

Oosterwijk, Sophie. "The Swaddling-Clothes of Christ: A Medieval Relic on Display." *Medieval Life* 13 (2000): 25–30.

Osborne, Lawrence James. "Changes in Milton's Theology from the 'Nativity Ode' Through 'Of True Religion.'" PhD diss., Stanford University, 1951.

Osgood, Charles G. "*Paradise Lost* 9: 506; Nativity Hymn 133–153." *American Journal of Philology* 41, no. 1 (1920): 76–80.

Ossa-Richardson, Anthony. *The Devil's Tabernacle: The Pagan Oracles in Christian Thought*. Princeton, NJ: Princeton University Press, 2013.

Oxford Dictionary of the Christian Church. Edited by F.L. Cross and E.A. Livingstone. Oxford: Oxford University Press, 2005.

Oxley, Brian. "'Simples Are by Compounds Farre Exceld': Southwell's Longer Latin Poems and 'St. Peters Complaint.'" *Recusant History* 17, no. 3 (1985): 330–40.

Parfitt, George, ed. *Ben Jonson: The Complete Poems*. New Haven, CT: Yale University Press, 1975.

Parish, Helen L. *Monks, Miracles, and Magic: Reformation Representations of the Medieval Church*. Oxford: Routledge, 2005.

Parrish, Paul A. *The Variorum Edition of the Poetry of John Donne: The Holy Sonnets*. Vol. 7.1. Bloomington: Indiana University Press, 2005.

Pastor Fido (pseud.) "Festorum Metropolis: The Metropolitan Feast of the Birthday of our Saviour Jesus Christ, Annually to be kept holy, by them that call upon him in all Nations, Proved by Scriptures, the practice of the Church, Primitive and Reformed; the Testimonies of the Fathers, and Moderne Divines; strong Reasons, grounded on the Word of God; confirming Miracles, etc." London: Matthew Simmons, 16 August 1652.

Patrides, C.A. *The English Poems of George Herbert*. London: Dent, 1974.

Patterson, Annabel. "Milton's Heroic Sonnets." In *A Concise Companion to Milton*, edited by Angelica Duran, 78–94. Malden, MA: John Wiley and Sons, Blackwell Publishing, 2007.

Pecheux, Mother Mary Christopher. "The Image of the Sun in Milton's 'Nativity Ode.'" *Huntingdon Library Quarterly* 38, no. 4 (1975): 315–33.

Pedrojetta, G. "*Marino e la meraviglia*." In *Interpretazione e meraviglia*, XIV Colloquio sulla interpretazione, a cura di G. Galli, 95–105. Pisa: Giardini, 1994.

Pendergast, John S. "Pierre Du Moulin on the Eucharist: Protestant Sign Theory and the Grammar of Embodiment." *English Literary History* 65, no. 1 (Spring 1998): 47–68.

Peter Lombard. *Commentarium in psalmos davidicos*. PL 191: 817–18.

Pezzini, Domenico. *The Translation of Hymns and Other Religious Texts in the Middle Ages: Tracts and Rules, Hymns and Saints' Lives*. Bern: Peter Lang, 2008.

Phillippy, Patricia. *Shaping Remembrance from Shakespeare to Milton*. Cambridge: Cambridge University Press, 2018.

Phillips, Godfrey E. *Loreto and the Holy House: Its History Drawn from Authentic Sources*. London: R. & T. Washbourne, 1917.

Phillips, John. *The Reformation of Images: Destruction of Art in England, 1535–1660*. Berkeley: University of California Press, 1973.

Photius. *The Homilies of Photius, Patriarch of Constantinople*. Translated by Cyril Mango. Cambridge, MA: Harvard University Press, 1958.

Pilarz, Scott R. *Robert Southwell and the Mission of Literature, 1561–1595: Writing Reconciliation*. Aldershot, UK: Ashgate, 2004.

– "'To help soules': Recovering the Purpose of Southwell's Poetry and Prose." In *Discovering and (Re)covering the Seventeenth Century Religious Lyric*, edited by Eugene R. Cunnar and Jeffrey Johnson, 41–61. Pittsburgh, PA: Duquesne University Press, 2001.

Pliny. *Natural History*. Vol. 2, *Books 3–7*, translated by H. Rackham. Cambridge, MA: Harvard University Press, 1942.

Pope, Alexander. *The Complete Poetical Works of Alexander Pope*. Edited by Henry R. Boynton. Boston: Houghton Mifflin, 1903.

Pope-Hennessy, John. *The Virgin with the Laughing Child*. London: H.M. Stationery Office, 1949.

Porphyry. *On the Cave of the Nymphs in the Thirteenth Book of the Odyssey: From the Greek of Porphyry*. Translated by Thomas Taylor. London: John M. Watkins, 1917.

Potter, Lois, ed. *The Revels History of Drama in English*. Vol. 1, *Medieval Drama*. London: Methuen, 1983.

Praz, Mario. *Studies in Seventeenth-Century Imagery*. Rome: Edizioni di Storia e Letteratura, 1964 and 1974.

Preston, Claire. *Bee*. London: Reaktion Books, 2006.

Prosser, Eleanor. *Drama and Religion in the English Mystery Plays*. Stanford, CA: Stanford University Press, 1961.

Prudentius, Marcus Aurelius C. *Apotheosis*. In *Prudentius*, translated by H.J. Thompson, vol. 1, 116–99. Loeb Classical Library. Cambridge, MA: Harvard University Press, 1949. Reprint 1962. All quotations are from the 1962 edition.

– "Corde natus ex parentis." *Liber Cathemerinon*, Hymnus 9. In *Prudentius*, translated by H.J. Thompson, vol. 1, 76–8. Loeb Classical Library.

Cambridge, MA: Harvard University Press, 1942. Reprint 1962. All quotations are from the 1962 edition.

Pseudo-Bonaventure. *Meditaciones Vite Christi*. Edited by Mary Stallings-Taney. CCCM 153. Turnhout: Brepols, 1997.

– *Meditations on the Life of Christ*. Translated by Francis Taney, Ann Miller, and Mary Stallings-Taney. Asheville, NC: Pegasus Press, 2000.

– *Meditations on the Life of Christ: An Illustrated Manuscript of the Fourteenth Century*. Translated and edited by Isa Ragusa and Rosalie B. Green. Princeton, NJ: Princeton University Press, 1961.

Pseudo-Dionysius. *The Divine Names*. In *The Complete Works*, edited by Karlfried Froehlich, 47–132. Mahwah, NJ: Paulist Press, 1987.

Pseudo-Gregory of Nyssa. "On the Birth of Christ." PG 46:1127–50.

Pseudo-Matthaei Evangelium. Edited by Jan Gijsel. Vol. 1 of *Libri de nativitate Mariae*. CCSA, 9.

Puech, Henri-Charles. "Gnosis and Time." In *Man and Time: Papers from the Eranos Yearbooks*, edited by Joseph Campbell, 38–84. Princeton, NJ: Princeton University Press, 1973. First published in 1957.

Quarles, Francis. *The Complete Works in Prose and Verse of Francis Quarles*. Edited by Alexander Grosart. 3 vols. Blackburn, UK: Printed for Private Circulation, 1881.

– *Emblemes by Francis Quarles*. Cambridge: Printed by R.D. for Francis Eglesfield ..., 1643; Ann Arbor, MI: Early English Books Online Text Creation Partnership, 2011. http://name.umdl.umich.edu/A56969.0001.001.

– *Francis Quarles' Divine Fancies: A Critical Edition*, edited by William T. Liston. New York: Routledge, 1992.

Quinn, Dennis. "John Donne's Principles of Biblical Exegesis." *Journal of English and German Philology* 61, no. 2 (1962): 313–29.

Quint, David. "Expectation and Prematurity in Milton's 'Nativity Ode.'" *Modern Philology* 97, no. 2 (November 1999): 195–219.

Quispel, Gilles. "Time and History in Patristic Christianity." In *Man and Time: Papers from the Eranos Yearbooks*, edited by Joseph Campbell, 85–107. Princeton, NJ: Princeton University, 1973. First published in 1957.

Rajan, Balachandra. "In Order Serviceable." *Modern Language Review* 63, no. 1 (1968): 13–22.

Rambuss, Richard. "Crashaw and the Metaphysical Shudder; Or, How to Do Things with Tears." In *Structures of Feeling in Seventeenth-Century Cultural Expression*, edited by Susan McClary, 253–71. Toronto: University of Toronto Press, 2013.

– ed. *The English Poetry of Richard Crashaw*. Minneapolis: University of Minnesota Press, 2013.

Randall, Randy C. "The Reformation and the Visual Arts." Master's thesis. Reformed Theological Seminary, December 2007. https://rts.edu/wp-content/uploads/2019/05/Randall-Reformation_and_Visual_Arts.pdf.

Ransome, Hilda. *The Sacred Bee in Ancient Times and Folklore*. Mineola, NY: Dover, 2004. Reprint of 1937 edition by George Allen & Unwin (London).

Ratzinger, Joseph. *The Theology of History in St. Bonaventure*. Chicago: Franciscan Herald Press, 1971.

Read, Sophie. *Eucharist and the Poetic Imagination in Early Modern England*. Cambridge: Cambridge University Press, 2013.

Reinhardt, Klaus. "L'idée de naissance de Dieu dans l'âme chez Nicolas de Cues et l'influence d'Eckhart." In *La naissance de Dieu dans l'âme chez Eckhart et Nicolas de Cues*, edited by Marie-Anne Vannier, 85–99. Paris: Cerf, 2006.

Richey, Esther Gilman. "Unitive Theology: George Herbert's Revision of 'The H. Communion.'" *George Herbert Journal* 35, no. 1–2 (Fall 2011/ Spring 2012): 97–109.

Ridley, Nicholas. *The Works of Nicholas Ridley*. Edited by H. Christmas. Cambridge: Parker Society, 1843.

Riggs, John W. *The Lord's Supper in the Reformed Tradition: An Essay on the Mystical True Presence*. Louisville, KY: Westminster John Knox Press, 2015.

Rigoglioso, Marguerite. *The Cult of Divine Birth in Ancient Greece*. New York: Palgrave MacMillan, 2009.

Rittgers, Ronald K. *The Reformation of Suffering: Pastoral Theology and Lay Piety in Late Medieval and Early Modern Germany*. Oxford: Oxford University Press, 2012.

Robertson, Jean. "Robert Southwell's 'New Heaven, New Warre.'" *Huntington Library Quarterly* 45, no. 1 (1982): 82–4.

Robinson, Matthew. "Christ as the Central Metaphysical Principle in St. Augustine's Theory of Time: *Confessions*, Book 11." In *Studia Patristica*. Vol. 43, *Augustine, Other Latin Writers*, edited by Frances Margaret Young and P. Parvis, 227–32. Louvain: Peeters, 2006.

Romano, J.R. "Heaven's Youngest Teemed Star." *Milton Quarterly* 15, no. 3 (1981): 80–8.

Ross, Malcolm. *Poetry and Dogma: The Transfiguration of Eucharistic Symbols in Seventeenth Century English Poetry*. New Brunswick, NJ: Rutgers University Press, 1954.

Rossetti, Christina. *Complete Poems of Christina Rossetti: A Variorum Edition*. Vol. 1. Edited by R.W. Crump. Baton Rouge, LA: Louisiana State University Press, 1979.

Rubin, Miri. *Corpus Christi: The Eucharist in Late Medieval Culture*. Cambridge: Cambridge University Press, 1991.

– *Mother of God: A History of the Virgin Mary*. New Haven, CT: Yale University Press, 2009.

Ryley, George. *Mr. Herbert's Temple and the Church Militant Explained and Improved (Bodleian MS Rawl. D. 199)*. Edited by Maureen Boyd and Cedric C. Brown. London: Pickering, 1987.

Sabine, Maureen. *Feminine Engendered Faith: The Poetry of John Donne and Richard Crashaw*. Basingstoke, UK: Palgrave Macmillan, 1992.

Safer, Elaine. "On the Morning of Christ's Nativity." In *Milton's English Poetry: Being Entries from A Milton Encyclopedia*, edited by William B. Hunter and John T. Shawcross, 91–101. Lewisburg, PA: Bucknell University Press, 1986.

Sánchez, Reuben. "'The Sad Prophet Jeremiah' as an Icon of Renaissance Melancholy." In *Typology and Iconography in Donne, Herbert, and Milton: Fashioning the Self after Jeremiah*, 1–24. New York: Palgrave Macmillan, 2014.

The Sarum Missal, Edited from Three Early Manuscripts. Edited by John Wickham Legg. Oxford: Clarendon Press, 1916.

The Sarum Missal, in English. Translated and edited by A. Harford Pearson. 2nd ed. London: The Church Press, 1884. First published in 1868.

Saward, John. *Cradle of Redeeming Love: The Theology of the Christmas Mystery*. San Francisco: Ignatius Press, 2002.

Scarisbrick, J.J. *The Reformation and the English People*. London: Wiley-Blackwell, 1984.

Schaff, Philip. *History of the Christian Church*. Vol. 3, *Third Period: Nicene and Post-Nicene Christianity*. Edinburgh: T & T Clark, 1884.

Schatzgeyer, Kasper. *Tractatus de missa*. Tübingen, 1525.

Schiller, Gertrud. *Iconography of Christian Art*. Vol. 1. Translated by Janet Seligman. Greenwich, CT: New York Graphic Society, 1971.

Schlegel, Ursula. "The Christ Child as Devotional Image in Medieval Italian Sculpture: A Contribution to Ambrogio Lorenzetti Studies." *The Art Bulletin* 52, no. 1 (March 1970): 1–10.

Schofield, John. *Philip Melanchthon and the English Reformation*. Oxford: Routledge, 2017.

Schwartz, Regina. "Real Hunger: Milton's Version of the Eucharist." *Religion and Literature* 31, no. 3 (Autumn 1999): 1–17.

– *Sacramental Poetics at the Dawn of Secularism: When God Left the World*. Cultural Memory in the Present series. Edited by Mieke Bal and Het de Vries. Stanford, CA: Stanford University Press, 2008.

Schweitzer, Albert. *The Quest of the Historical Jesus: A Critical Study of Its Progress from Reimarus to Wrede*. Translated by W. Montgomery. New York: Macmillan, 1948.

Selden, Raman. "John Donne's 'Incarnational Conviction.'" *Critical Quarterly* 17, no. 1 (March 1975): 55–73.

Sellers, R.V. *The Council of Chalcedon: A Historical and Doctrinal Survey*. London: SPCK, 1961.

Serra, Aristide. *Sapienza e contemplazione di Maria secondo Luca 2, 19.51b*. Rome: Edizioni Marianum, 1982.

Sethuraman, V. "A Reading of Robert Southwell's 'The Burning Babe.'" In *Studies in Elizabethan Literature: Festschrift to G.C. Bannerjee*, edited by Gopal Bannerjee and P.S. Sastri, 10–14. New Delhi: S. Chand., 1972.

Shakespeare, William. *Hamlet*. The Riverside Shakespeare series. Edited by G. Blakemore Evans. New York: Houghton Mifflin, 1974.

Shawcross, John T. *John Milton: The Self and the World*. Lexington: University Press of Kentucky, 2015.

Sheingorn, Pamela. "Joseph the Carpenter's Failure at Familial Discipline." In *Insights and Interpretations: Studies in Celebration of the Eighty-Fifth Anniversary of the Index of Christian Art*, edited by Colum Hourihane, 156–67. Princeton, NJ: Princeton University Press, 2002.

– "Reshapings of the Childhood Miracles of Jesus." In *The Christ Child in Medieval Culture: Alpha es et O!*, edited by Mary Dzon and Theresa M. Kenney, 254–92. Toronto: University of Toronto Press, 2012.

Shell, Alison. *Catholicism, Controversy, and the English Literary Imagination, 1558–1660*. Cambridge: Cambridge University Press, 1999.

Sherry, Beverley. "Milton's 'Mystic Nativity.'" *Milton Quarterly* 17, no. 4 (1983): 108–16.

Shullenberger, William. "Christ as Metaphor: Figural Instruction in Milton's Nativity Ode." *Notre Dame English Journal* 14, no. 1 (1981): 41–58.

Simon, Elliott M. "Pico, Paracelsus, and Dee: The Magical Measure of Human Perfectibility." In *Gender and Scientific Discourse in Early Modern Culture*, edited by Kathleen P. Long, 13–40. Abingdon, UK: Routledge, 2010.

Simplicius. *Simplicius: On Aristotle On the Heavens* 2.1–9. Translated by Ian Mueller. London: Bloomsbury, 2014.

Simpson, E.M. *A Study of the Prose Works of John Donne*. Oxford: Clarendon Press, 1948.

Siniscalco, Pietro. "Time." In *Encyclopedia of Ancient Christianity*, edited by Angelo Di Berardino, translated by Adrian Walford, vol. 2, 839–40. New York: Oxford University Press, 1992.

– "Tempo." In *Dizionario patristico e di Antichità Cristiane*, edited by Angelo Di Berardino, vol. 2, 3361. Roma: Marietti, Institutum Patristicum Augustinianum, 1984.

Skouen, Tina. "The Rhetoric of Passion in Donne's Holy Sonnets." *Rhetorica: A Journal of the History of Rhetoric* 27, no. 2 (Spring 2009): 159–88.

Sloane, Thomas O. "Dr. Donne and the Image of Christ." *Rhetorica: A Journal of the History of Rhetoric* 24, no. 2 (Spring 2006): 187–216.

Smith, George W., Jr. "Milton's Method of Mistakes in the Nativity Ode." *Studies in English Literature* 18, no. 1 (1978): 107–23.

Somon, Matthieu. "The Ineffability of Incarnation in Le Brun's *Silence* or *Sleep of the Child*." In *Image and Incarnation: The Early Modern Doctrine of the Pictorial Image*, edited by Walter Mellon and Lee Palmer Wandel, 137–57. Leiden: Brill, 2015.

Southwell, St. Robert. *The Collected Poems of Robert Southwell*. Edited by Peter Davidson and Anne Sweeney. Manchester: Fifield Books, 2007.

– *An Epistle of Comfort*. Ilkley, UK: Scholar Press, 1974.

– *The Poems of Robert Southwell, SJ*. Edited by James Harold McDonald and Nancy Pollard Brown. Oxford: Clarendon Press, 1967.

Spurr, Barry. *See the Virgin Blest: The Virgin Mary in English Poetry*. New York: Palgrave Macmillan, 2007.

Stanwood, Paul G. "Time and Liturgy in Donne, Crashaw, and T S. Eliot." *Mosaic* 12 (1979): 94–5.

Stapleton, Laurence, "Milton and the New Music." *University of Toronto Quarterly* 23 (1953–4): 217–26. Reprinted in *Milton: Modern Essays in Criticism*, edited by Arthur E. Barker, 31–42. New York: Oxford University Press, 1965.

Steinberg, Leo. *The Sexuality of Christ in Renaissance Art and in Modern Oblivion*. New York: Pantheon Books, 1983.

Steinmetz, David. "Calvin and the Absolute Power of God." *Journal of Medieval and Renaissance Studies* 18, no. 1 (Spring 1988): 65–79.

Strier, Richard. *Love Known: Theology and Experience in George Herbert's Poetry*. Chicago: University of Chicago Press, 1983.

– "'To All Angels and All Saints: Herbert's Puritan Poem.'" *Modern Philology* 77, no. 2 (1979): 132–45.

Summers, Claude J., and Ted-Larry Pebworth, eds. *"Too Rich to Clothe the Sunne": Essays on George Herbert*. Pittsburgh, PA: University of Pittsburgh Press, 1980.

Sweeney, Anne R. *Robert Southwell: Snow in Arcadia: Redrawing the English Lyric Landscape, 1586–95*. Manchester: Manchester University Press, 2006.

Sy, Belen. "Robert Southwell's Poetic Self-Fashioning." *Fu Jen Studies* 34 (2001): 41–74.

Tappert, Theodore G., trans. and ed. *The Book of Concord: The Confessions of the Evangelical Lutheran Church*. Philadelphia, PA: Mühlenberg Press, 1959.

Tarrago, Rafael Emilio. "Bloody Bess: The Persecution of Catholics in Elizabethan England." *Logos: A Journal of Catholic Thought and Culture* 7, no. 1 (Winter 2004): 117–33.

Tashiro, Tom T. "English Poets, Egyptian Onions, and the Protestant View of the Eucharist." *Journal of the History of Ideas* 30, no. 4 (October–December 1969): 563–78.

Tasioulas, Jacqueline. "'Heaven and Earth in Little Space': The Foetal Existence of Christ in Medieval Literature and Thought." *Medium Aevum* 76, no. 1 (2007): 24–48.

Tasso, Torquato. *Opere complete di Torquato Tasso in verso ed in prosa*. Vol. 1. Venice: Paolo Lampato, 1834.

– "Per il presepio di nostro signore nella cappella di sisto v in Santa Maria Maggiore." In *Opere*. Vo1. 2. Milan: Rizzoli Editore, 1963.

Tayler, Edward W. *Milton's Poetry: Its Development in Time*. Pittsburgh, PA: Duquesne University Press, 1979.

Teresa of Avila, St. *The Life of St. Teresa of Jesus of the Order of Our Lady of Carmel*. Edited by Benedict Zimmerman. New York: Benziger Brothers, 1918.

Teske, Roland J. "Augustine of Hippo on Seeing with the Eyes of the Mind." In *Ambiguity in the Western Mind*, edited by Craig J.N. de Paulo, Patrick Messina, and Marc Stier, 72–87. New York: Peter Lang, 2005.

Teskey, Gordon. *Delirious Milton: The Fate of the Poet in Modernity*. Cambridge, MA: Harvard University Press, 2006.

– *The Poetry of John Milton*. Cambridge, MA: Harvard University Press, 2015.

Theodore the Studite, St. "Sermon on the Precious and Life-Giving Cross." PG 99: 691–700.

Thompson, Bard. *Liturgies of the Western Church*. Cleveland: William Collins and World Publishing, 1961.

Thompson, Francis. *The Works of Francis Thompson*. Edited by Wilfred Meynell. London: Burns and Oates, 1913.

Thompson, Nicholas. "Martin Bucer." In *A Companion to the Eucharist in the Reformation*. Edited by Lee Palmer Wandel, 75–96. Leiden: Brill, 2014.

Todd, Richard. *The Opacity of Signs: Acts of Interpretation in George Herbert's* The Temple. Columbia: University of Missouri Press, 1986.

Toliver, Herbert. *George Herbert's Christian Narrative*. University Park, PA: Penn State Press, 1993.

Traherne, Thomas. "On Christmas-Day." In *Poems of Felicity*, edited by H.I. Bell, 48–52. Oxford: Oxford University Press, 1910.

Treip, Mindele Anne. *Allegorical Poetics and the Epic: The Renaissance Tradition to* Paradise Lost. Lexington: University Press of Kentucky, 1995.

Trompf, G.W. *The Idea of Historical Recurrence in Western Thought: From Antiquity to the Reformation*. Berkeley: University of California Press, 1979.

Trower, Katherine Bache. "Temporal Tensions in the *Visio of Piers Plowman*." *Medieval Studies* 35 (1973): 389–412.

Tuve, Rosamond. "George Herbert and Caritas." In *Essays by Rosemond Tuve*, edited Thomas P. Roche, 167–206. Princeton, NJ: Princeton University Press, 1970.

– *Images and Themes in Five Poems by Milton*. Cambridge, MA: Harvard University Press, 1957.

– *A Reading of George Herbert*. Chicago: University of Chicago Press, 1952.

Ulreich, John C., Jr. "Milton on the Eucharist: Some Second Thoughts about Sacramentalism." In *Milton and the Middle Ages*, edited by John Mulryan, 32–56. Lewisburg, PA: Bucknell University Press, 1982.

Umbach, Herbert H. "The Merit of Metaphysical Style in Donne's Easter Sermons." *English Literary History* 12, no. 2 (June 1945): 108–29.

Van Buren, Anne H. "The Canonical Office in Renaissance Painting: Raphael's Madonna at Nones." *The Art Bulletin* 57, no. 1 (1975): 41–52.

Van Den Berg, Sara. "Full Sight, Fancied Sight, and Touch: Milton's Sonnet 23 and Molyneux's Question." *Ben Jonson Journal* 16, nos. 1–2 (2009): 16–32.

Van den Broek, Roelof. *The Myth of the Phoenix According to Classical and Early Christian Traditions*. Leiden: Brill, 1971.

Van der Meulen, Jan. *De Picturis et Imaginibus Sacris, pro vero earum usu contra abusus* [*Treatise on Sacred Images*]. Leuven, 1570.

Vander Zee, Anton. "Milton's Mary: Suspending Song in the *Nativity Ode*." *Modern Philology* 108, no. 3 (2011): 375–99.

Vaughan, Henry. *Henry Vaughan: The Complete Poems*. Edited by Alan Rudrum. New Haven, CT: Yale University Press, 1976.

– *The Works of Henry Vaughan: Introduction and Texts 1646–1652; Texts 1654–1678, Letters, & Medical Marginalia; Commentaries and Bibliography*. Edited by Donald R. Dickson, Alan Rudrum, and Robert Wilcher. Oxford: Oxford University Press, 2018.

Veith, Gene Edward, Jr. *Reformation Spirituality: The Religion of George Herbert*. Lewisburg, PA: Bucknell University Press, 1985.

Vendler, Helen. *Invisible Listeners: Lyric Intimacy in Herbert, Whitman, and Ashbery*. Princeton, NJ: Princeton University Press, 2005.

– *The Poetry of George Herbert*. Cambridge, MA: Harvard University Press, 1975.

Vincent, Nicholas. *The Holy Blood: King Henry III and the Westminster Blood Relic*. Cambridge: Cambridge University Press, 2001.

Vitz, Evelyn Birge. "The Apocryphal and the Biblical, the Oral and the Written, in Medieval Legends of Christ's Childhood: The Old French *Évangile de l'Enfance*." In *Satura: Studies in Medieval Literature in Honour of Robert R. Raymo*, edited by Nancy M. Reale and Ruth E. Sternglantz, 124–49. Donington, UK: Shaun Tyas, 2001.

Von Balthasar, Hans Urs. *Light of the Word: Brief Reflections on the Sunday Readings*. San Francisco: Ignatius Press, 1993.

Walker, Alexander, trans. *The History of Joseph the Carpenter*. In *Ante-Nicene Fathers*, vol. 8, ed. Alexander Roberts, James Donaldson, and Arthur Cleveland Coxe. Buffalo, NY: Christian Literature Publishing, 1886. Revised and edited for New Advent by Kevin Knight, http://www.newadvent.org/fathers/0805.htm.

Walker, D.P. "The Cessation of Miracles." In *Hermeticism and the Renaissance: Intellectual History and the Occult in Early Modern Europe*, edited by Ingrid Merkel and Alan G. Debus, 111–24. Washington, DC: Folger Shakespeare Library, 1988.

Walker, Julia. "The Religious Lyric as a Genre." *English Language Notes* 25, no. 1 (September 1987): 39–45.

Wallace, Dewey D., Jr. "The Anglican Appeal to Lutheran Sources: Philipp Melanchthon's Reputation in Seventeenth-Century England." *Historical Magazine of the Protestant Episcopal Church* 52, no. 4 (December 1983): 355–67.

Wallerstein, Ruth. *Richard Crashaw: A Study in Style and Poetic Development*. University of Wisconsin Studies in Language and Literature 37. Madison: University of Wisconsin Press, 1935.

Walsh, Patrick Gerard, ed. *Cassiodorus: Explanation of the Psalms*. New York: The Newman Press, 1991.

Wandel, Lee Palmer, ed. *A Companion to the Eucharist in the Reformation*. Leiden: Brill, 2014.

Wardropper, Bruce. "The Religious Conversion of Profane Poetry." In *Studies in the Continental Background of Renaissance English Literature: Essays Presented to John L. Lievsay*, edited by Dale B.J. Randall and George Walton Williams, 203–21. Durham, NC: Duke University Press, 1977.

Warren, Austin. *Richard Crashaw: A Study in Baroque Sensibility*. Ann Arbor: University of Michigan Press, 1967. First published in 1939.

Watkins, Rowland. "Upon Christ's Nativity." In *Flamma sine fumo, or Poems without fictions*. London: William Leake, 1662.

Watson, Thomas Ramsey. "God's Geometry: Motion in the English Poetry of George Herbert." *George Herbert Journal* 9, no. 1 (1985): 17–25.

Werner, Martin. *The Formation of Christian Dogma*. Translated by S.G.F. Brandon. New York: A & C Black, 1957.

Werness, Hope B. *Continuum Encyclopedia of Animal Symbolism in World Art*. New York: A & C Black, 2006.

Whalen, Robert Hilliard. "George Herbert's Sacramental Puritanism." *Renaissance Quarterly* 54, no. 4, part 1 (Winter 2001): 1273–1307.

– *The Poetry of Immanence: Sacrament in Donne and Herbert*. Toronto: University of Toronto Press, 2002.

White, Helen C. *The Metaphysical Poets: A Study in Religious Experience*. New York: Macmillan, 1936.

White, James Boyd. *"This Book of Starres": Learning to Read George Herbert*. Ann Arbor: University of Michigan Press, 1994.

Wilder, Amos Niven. *Theopoetic: Theology and Religious Imagination*. Philadelphia, PA: Fortress Press, 1976.

Williams, George Huntston. "Stanislas Hosius." In *Shapers of Religious Traditions in Germany, Switzerland, and Poland, 1560–1600*, edited by Jill Raitt, 157–74. New Haven, CT: Yale University Press, 1981.

Williams, George Walton, ed. *The Complete Poetry of Richard Crashaw*. Translated by George Walton Williams and Phyllis S. Bowman. Garden City, NY: Doubleday, 1970.

Wilson, Adrian, and Joseph Lancaster Wilson, eds. *A Medieval Mirror: Speculum humanae salvationis, 1324–1500*. Berkeley: University of California Press, 2002.

Wollesen-Wisch, Barbara, ed. *Italian Renaissance Art: Selections from the Piero Corsini Gallery*. University Park: Penn State University Press, 1986.

Woolf, Rosemary. *The English Mystery Plays*. Berkeley: University of California Press, 1972.

Wright, T. *The Passions of the Minde in Generall* (1604). Edited by T.O. Sloane. Urbana: University of Illinois Press, 1971.

Wycliff, John. *De eucharistia tractatus maior*. London: Trübner, 1892.

Yates, Francis Amelia. *Giordano Bruno and the Hermetic Tradition*. London: Routledge, 1999.

– *The Occult Philosophy and the Elizabethan Age*. Vol. 7. London: Routledge & Kegan Paul, 1979.

Young, R.V. *Doctrine and Devotion in Seventeenth-Century Poetry: Studies in Donne, Herbert, Crashaw, and Vaughan*. Cambridge: D.S. Brewer, 2000.

– "Herbert and the Real Presence." *Renascence* 45, no. 3 (1993): 179–96.

– *Richard Crashaw and the Spanish Golden Age*. New Haven, CT: Yale University Press, 1982.

Zoozmann, Richard. *Laudate Dominum. Lobet den Herrn*. München, 1928.

Index

www.ingramcontent.com/pod-product-compliance
Lightning Source LLC
LaVergne TN
LVHW041113090826
844660LV00061B/849/J

* 9 7 8 1 4 8 7 5 0 9 0 6 4 *